THE SOUNDS AND HISTORY

OF THE

GERMAN LANGUAGE

BY

E. PROKOSCH

Professor of Germanic Languages in the University of Texas

NEW YORK

HENRY HOLT AND COMPANY

1916

PREFACE

No apology is needed for an attempt to write an introduction to the Phonetics and History of the German Language that is simple enough to be intelligible to students without linguistic erudition, and at the same time sufficiently comprehensive to meet to a reasonable degree the requirements of the teacher of German. Phonetics and historical grammar have at last come into their own as legitimate and indispensable elements of the training of foreign language teachers, but a text-book for these subjects adjusted to the complicated needs of our colleges has so far been a *desideratum*.

It goes without saying that in compiling this little manual I have made free use of the principal works on the subjects with which it deals. In fact, the phonetic part can hardly claim to be much more than an adaptation of the books of such phoneticians as Sievers, Viëtor, Jespersen, Sweet, etc. In the historical part, while consulting at every step the standard works by Wilmanns, Behaghel, Streitberg, and others, I have found myself compelled to follow a more independent course in characterizing the German tongue as a direct and nearly unbroken development of the Indo-European parent language, evolved by the continuous action of a homogeneous set of phonetic and psychological tendencies. Leaving aside the scientific aspect of my theory, this system, thru its consistent linking of phonetics and historical grammar, cannot fail to make the study of both more useful to the student than an independent treatment of these two

branches of linguistic science would be. May critics not
deal too harshly with me for having presumed to embody
in my booklet some new presentations of details (such as
the Germanic preterit and optative, the High German
sound shift, the derivation of the name *Germani*, the evolution of the German dialects and the German standard
language); I have rigidly suppressed such heresies wherever they did not seem unavoidable postulates of the
general pedagogical plan of my book; sometimes, I con-
fess, it was with some regret that I put them into the
background, as, for instance, when I professed to share
the present standard view of the Indo-European 'mediae
aspiratae,' which I described as 'middle stops,' while I
am strongly convinced that they really were voiceless
spirants; to introduce this theory seemed to me too bold
at this time, altho I realized the extent to which it would
have simplified the treatment of the Germanic sound
shift and Verner's Law.

The *Transcriptions-Misère* so frequently complained
of by philologists could not fail to give me considerable
trouble. I had to cut more than one Gordian knot in my
endeavor to reconcile the customary transcription of phonetics with that of historical grammar, chiefly so in the
use of the letters g and ɡ; in connection with the traditional use of Roman type for phonetic transcription and
Italics for philological examples, I have followed the ar-
bitrary principle of using with either type the regular
font sign for the common stop, thus reserving, in the
historical part, the type g for the labio-velar; this decision and the use of Greek χ and γ for the velar spirants
were dictated by practical rather than by scientific considerations. — During the typesetting my difficulties in
typographical matters were greatly alleviated by the un-
remitting care and sagacity of Mr. Adolph Linsenbarth,

of the University Press of Cambridge, Mass. My sincerest thanks are due to him and to several of my colleagues who have rendered me valuable assistance, especially to Dr. Max Diez and Dr. J. Lassen Boysen for their painstaking cooperation in revising the manuscript and proofs, and to Professor Francis A. Wood for a number of important suggestions, but most of all to Professor K. F. Muenzinger, with whom I have discussed many crucial questions during various phases of my work.

E. PROKOSCH.

AUSTIN, TEXAS, November, 1916.

CONTENTS

PART ONE — GERMAN PHONETICS

INTRODUCTION

CHAPTER I

The Organs of Speech

CHAPTER II

Analysis of German Sounds

I. THE LABIALS

A. Stops

B. Spirants

II. THE DENTALS (and ALVEOLARS)

A. Stops

B. Spirants

C. The Liquids

III. THE PALATALS

IV. THE VELARS

B. Spirants

V. UVULAR [R]

VI. GLOTTAL SOUNDS

VII. THE VOWELS

The German Vowel System

Note: English and German vowels.   PAGE

CHAPTER III

Synthesis of German Sounds

CHAPTER IV

Phonetic Transcriptions

APPENDIX

PART TWO — HISTORY OF THE GERMAN LANGUAGE

I. External History

II. Internal History

A. THE DEVELOPMENT OF SOUNDS

B. THE DEVELOPMENT OF FORMS

The Verb

The Adjective

PART ONE

GERMAN PHONETICS

INTRODUCTION

1. Phonetics is the science of the formation and combination of speech sounds. It is not statutory, but descriptive, that is, it does not state what speech sounds are to be used under certain circumstances, but it analyzes and defines the speech sounds actually occurring. The science that deals with 'correct pronunciation,' setting up regulations for the choice of speech sounds, is termed **Orthoepics;** a knowledge of phonetics is a necessary prerequisite for a rational study of orthoepics, while, on the other hand, the purposes of the modern language teacher require a connection of phonetics with orthoepics. — **Phonology** is the science of the historical development of speech sounds; without an intimate knowledge and constant use of phonetic principles, it deteriorates into a mechanical handling of formulas; phonetics, again, being the science of the actual character of sounds, is apt to receive a great deal of valuable assistance from phonology. In this way, phonetics, orthoepics and phonology, while distinctly differing from each other in aims, subject-matter and methods, are closely connected branches of linguistic science.

CHAPTER I

The Organs of Speech

2. **Speech Sounds** are produced by the breath, which is expelled by the lungs, is passed thru the windpipe (*trachea*), and is modified first in the larynx and then in the mouth, or mouth and nose.

In general, human speech is formed by *ex*halation exclusively; occasionally, however, sounds are formed by *in*halation. E.g., the word *ja* is sometimes pronounced that way by Germans, especially when in a mood of indifference or resignation. — The neighing of a horse is inhalation.

A. The Larynx

3. **The Larynx** (*der Kehlkopf*) is the upper part of the windpipe. It consists of a number of cartilages which are joined by muscle tissues and ligaments. The cartilages are:

(1) The **Ring Cartilage** (*cartilago cricoidea*, from Greek *krikos*, 'ring'). It has the shape and approximate size of a signet ring, the wider part being at the back. It can easily be felt with the finger tips, about three fourths of an inch below the so-called 'Adam's apple.'

(2) The **Shield Cartilage** (*cartilago thyreoidea*, from Gk. *thyreos*, 'door-shaped shield'). It resembles two shields that are joined in front, with an upper and a lower horn-like projection on each side. The lower, shorter 'horns' embrace the ring cartilage, while the upper, longer horns have attacht to them the horseshoe-shaped bony support of the tongue, the tongue bone. The two plates of

4

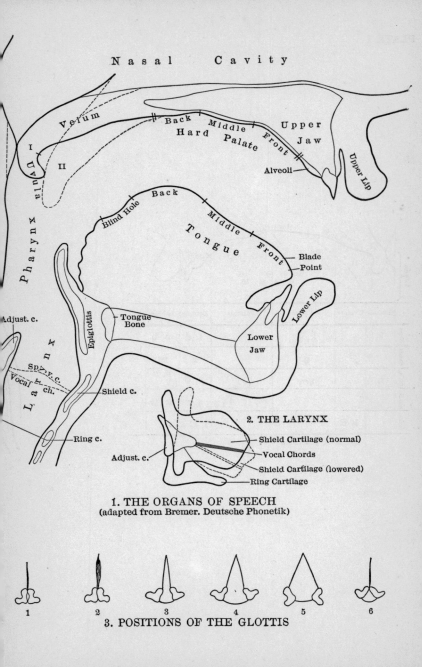

1. THE ORGANS OF SPEECH
(adapted from Bremer. Deutsche Phonetik)

2. THE LARYNX

3. POSITIONS OF THE GLOTTIS

PLATE I

	Glottals	Uvulars	Velars	Palatals	Dentals	Labials
Stops	ʔ		k, g		t, d	p, b
Nasals			ŋ		n	m
Slit Sp. Rill Sp.	h		x, γ	ç, j	þ, ð	F, v / f, v
				ʃ ʒ	s, z	w, ẘ
Sonor.		ʀ ʁ			l, r, ɹ	

Bold-face type = voiced

the shield cartilage form a curved edge in front, which is popularly termed the 'Adam's apple.'

(3) The two **Adjusting Cartilages** (*cartilagines arytae-noideae*, from Gk. *arytaina*, 'watering-can'). They have the shape of very irregular three-sided pyramids, and rest on the thick part of the ring cartilage. On this they can move in two ways: they can rotate on their axes (around their inner corners); and they can move sideways along the upper edge of the 'signet' part of the ring cartilage.

To the front corners of these cartilages are attacht two muscle cushions. These are joined to the front projection of the shield cartilage (the Adam's apple), thus being stretcht across the larynx. These muscle cushions are called the **Vocal Chords** (*ligamenta glottidis, chordae vocales*). They are not to be likened to strings or membranes, but rather resemble a pair of lips. Some German phoneticians (Klinghardt, for example) call them *Stimm-lippen* rather than *Stimmbänder*.

NOTE. The illustration (Plate I) shows a vertical section of the larynx, seen from behind. The vocal chords divide the larynx into an upper and lower half, the space between them being called *Glottis* (from Gk. *glotta*, 'tongue'; German *Stimmritze*). The projections above them are the spurious vocal chords (*Taschenbänder, falsche Stimmbänder*). The spaces behind these are the laryngeal ventricles (*ventriculi Morgagni*, named after the Italian physician Morgagni, who first described them). They secrete mucus, which lubricates the vocal chords, but have no function whatever in speaking.

(4) The **Epiglottis** (Gk. *epi*, 'upon,' and *glottis;* Ger. *Kehldeckel*). This is a pear-shaped, rather flexible plate, which is attacht to the shield cartilage above the vocal chords. It is raised in breathing and speaking, leaving the larynx open, but is lowered, covering and protecting the larynx, when food glides thru the œsophagus, directly behind the windpipe.

4. Positions of the Glottis. Thru varying positions of the adjusting cartilages, the vocal chords either touch one another, or draw apart more or less, so that the glottis may take different shapes, as shown in diagram 3 (Plate I). The most important positions are:

(1) The adjusting cartilages and, consequently, the vocal chords touch one another, and the latter are tightly stretcht. The glottis is closed; no air can pass from the lungs. This is the *Glottal Stop*, which is used quite frequently in German speech (see **36**), but occurs more or less in the speech of all nationalities. A sudden, spasmodic rupture of a glottal stop, combined with considerable friction of air passing between the vocal chords, is a *cough*. *Laughing* consists of a series of similar, but slighter explosions, usually without much friction, since the vocal chords are farther separated than in coughing.

(2) The adjusting cartilages and the vocal chords touch one another, but the latter are not stretcht so tightly as in the glottal stop. Breath passing between them causes them to vibrate more or less rapidly, according to the degree of tension. The tone produced by these vibrations of the vocal chords is called *Voice* (*Stimme*, *Stimmton*). Speech sounds are called *voiced* if the vocal chords vibrate during their production; e.g., *z, v, l, m, b, g*, and the vowels.

NOTE. There are several easy ways to determine whether a sound is voiced or not: Press the tips of two fingers tightly against the Adam's apple, and pronounce a given sound; if it is voiced, you will notice a distinct vibration of the Adam's apple, to which the vocal chords are attacht, while there is no such sensation if voiceless sounds (e.g., *s, f*) are pronounced; or press one hand firmly against your temples or the top of your head and pronounce voiced and voiceless sounds; you will feel the same presence or absence of vibration; or stop your ears with your hands and pronounce *v — f*, *z — s*: you will notice that voiced sounds are much louder, but voiceless sounds not so loud as otherwise; or try to combine some melody with the extended pronunciation of some sound; if the sound is voiced, you can 'sing a tune' during its pronunciation, while the pitch of a voiceless sound remains practically stationary.

(3) The adjusting cartilages separate slightly, so that their inner sides and the vocal chords form an isosceles triangle with a vertex angle of about fifteen degrees. The breath passes comparatively freely, but with some slight friction. This is the position in which *voiceless* (*unvoiced*) sounds are pronounced.

(4) The triangle between the vocal chords and the cartilages is wider, having a vertex angle of about twenty-five degrees. This is the position in normal *breathing*.

(5) The adjusting cartilages move apart as far as possible and rotate in an outward direction, so that the glottis becomes almond-shaped. The greatest possible amount of air can then pass thru the larynx; this is the position, therefore, in violent breathing (after running, etc.), or in energetic blowing.

The student should familiarize himself by frequent practise with these positions of the vocal chords, passing from the glottal stop to the widest opening, and *vice versa*. He will soon acquire a very definite feeling for each step. This is absolutely necessary in the study of phonetics. — Klinghardt's *Artikulations- und Hörübungen* is a book highly to be recommended for this practise.

NOTE. A sixth position, which usually occurs in whispering, is of less importance. The vocal chords are closed, but the adjusting cartilages, having rotated inwardly around their axes, form a small triangle, the so-called cartilage glottis. — If this cartilage glottis is very narrow, we get the sound of groaning.

The terms *chest-voice* and *head-voice* are misnomers. There is no kind of voice that is formed anywhere else but in the larynx. The so-called head-voice is merely voice with an unnaturally high pitch, due to the fact that the front one-third or front one-half of the vocal chords is closed, and only the back part vibrates. The voice of ventriloquists, also, is produced in the larynx, generally being 'head-voice,' at least to an extent.

B. The Velum

5. The Velum. From the larynx the breath passes thru a hollow space called the pharynx, and then either thru the oral cavity or thru the nasal cavity, or thru both, according to the position of the soft palate or velum. This is the back part (one third or more) of the roof of the mouth. The dividing line between the 'soft' and the 'hard' palate can easily be felt with the forefinger or the inverted tip of the tongue. — The soft palate passes over into the *Uvula* (diminutive of Lat. *uva*, 'grape'), which is not unlike a drop of some thick liquid or an icicle in formation. It can be seen distinctly by means of a mirror: Stand with your back against a window and hold the mirror at such an angle that it reflects the light into the mouth.

"It is surprising how few people have ever looked well into their mouths. The student of phonetics should always have a hand-glass by his side, and should use it constantly until he is quite familiar with the appearance of the 'oral' organs of speech. He will very soon find out the best angle at which to hold the mirror so that it will at once reflect light into the mouth and enable him to watch it." (Rippmann-Viëtor, *Elements of Phonetics*, 11.)

6. Positions of the Velum. The velum, with the uvula, acts like a trap-door, either closing or opening the passage from the pharynx into the nasal cavity. In position I (Plate I), it closes the nasal passage, its end being pressed against a projecting part of the back wall of the pharynx; the breath must pass thru the mouth. In position II, the natural position for breathing, the passage is open, and the breath passes thru the nose, or, if the mouth is open, thru mouth and nose. Speech sounds formed with the velum in position I are called *oral;* those formed with position II are **nasal,** if the breath passes thru the nose only; they are **nasalized** if it passes thru the mouth and nose. Thus, the common vowels and sounds like *p, b, s, z, l* are oral; *m, n, ng* are nasal; the French so-called 'nasal vowels' — *an, on, in, un* — are nasalized.

Note 1. Hold a narrow ruler with one edge against the upper lip, and with the other edge against a cold window-pane; pronounce [a]: the breath moistens the glass below the ruler; pronounce [m], and it will appear above the ruler; with the French 'nasal' (nasalized) vowels, it will show both below and above the ruler. — Or, you may place a cold polisht knife against the upper lip, and the breath will dim either its upper or its lower side, or both sides, according to the sound pronounced. — Observe, by means of a mirror, the action of the velum in the pronunciation of oral and nasal vowels, and in quiet breathing.

Note 2. Of persons suffering from a 'cold in the head' we are apt to say that their voice sounds 'nasal.' This is true to an extent only. The nasal passage usually being not entirely free, nasal sounds like [m] or [n] cannot be pronounced clearly; they sound like [b] and [d] (for instance, *Ebba* instead of *Emma, Hedde* instead of *Henne*). On the other hand, the edges of the velum and the uvula are usually more or less inflamed in such cases, and are unable to close the nasal cavity effectively; therefore, oral sounds, especially oral vowels, appear to have a more or less distinct nasal tinge.

C. The Mouth

7. The Roof of the Mouth consists of the soft palate or velum (5, 6), the hard palate, the upper gums or alveoles, and the upper teeth.

The *hard palate* is supported by the palate bone which is attacht to the upper jaw. It is, in general, concave in shape, but with very many people its middle third is slightly convex. It passes over into the *alveoles* without any definite line of demarcation; these consist in a more or less convex ridge above the upper teeth. In anatomy, the term '*alveoli*' does not denote the gums, as in phonetics, but (more properly, since Lat. *alveoli* means 'little hollows') the cavities in the upper jaw in which the teeth are fastened. — The *upper teeth* usually project somewhat over the lower teeth.

8. The Lips are capable of assuming various shapes. They may be protruded (as in the pronunciation of [u]), or withdrawn (as with [i]); they may be nearly parallel, as in the case of [i, e], or rounded, forming more or less of an ellipsis, e.g., with English [w], or with [u, o].

9. The Tongue when at rest has a rather spherical shape, somewhat resembling a clincht fist, the joint of the middle finger representing the tip of the tongue. It consists of a complicated set of very elastic muscles which enable it to change its shape even more than the lips. In the pronunciation of [u] it is withdrawn, in the pronunciation of [i] rather pusht forward. Its tip is inverted toward the hard palate with American *r*, vibrates with German *r*, and forms a distinct rill or groove in the pronunciation of *s*. (In accurate phonetic terminology, the term 'tip' or 'point' refers *only* to the front rim of the tongue; the elastic muscular part immediately behind it — 1 cm. or less — is the *blade*. The surface behind the blade is called the back of the tongue or *dorsum*.)

NOTE. The outline of the palate and alveoli as well as the shape of the teeth, lips and tongue differ very considerably with different people. A dentist can easily make a plaster cast of the roof of your mouth, such as is used in shaping an artificial palate, but you can get a sufficiently accurate sectional outline in this way: Fold a piece of heavy tin-foil several times so as to make a pliable, but firm, strip about a quarter of an inch in width and two inches in length. Bend one end of the strip over the edge of the upper teeth and press the strip firmly against alveoli and palate (up to the end of the hard palate); then transfer this outline on paper, carefully tracing the outline of the heavy tin-foil with a pencil. With the help of a long toothpick you can determine with fair accuracy the points of articulation, i.e., the points where the tongue comes into contact with the roof of the mouth. These points should be marked on your outline for every consonant studied.

D. Articulation

10. Place of Articulation. In the oral cavity, i.e., in the space extending from the uvula to the lips, the speech sounds are modified by the various positions of lips, tongue, etc. This adjustment is called articulation. According to the place where the adjustment is made, we distinguish: *Labials*, or sounds formed thru the action of the lips, e.g., [b, m, w]; *Dentals*, which are articulated by the tongue touching the upper teeth, e.g., [t, n, s] in Romance languages; *Alveolars*, formed at the alveoli, e.g., [t, n, s] in European English; *Palatals*, formed at the front palate, like *sh*; *Velars*, formed at the velum, e.g., [k, g]; *Uvulars*, formed by means of the uvula; lastly, *glottal* sounds, which are not modified in the mouth at all, but formed in the glottis exclusively, e.g., the glottal stop (4, 1).

11. Kinds of Articulation. Thru the adjustment of the tongue and the lips, the breath is either checked in the mouth, or it is allowed to pass freely. If it passes freely, without any obstacle in the mouth, we speak of *Vowels:* [a — i — u], etc. Otherwise, we have *Consonants*.

If the interception is complete, the breath being stopt altogether, we have a *Stop* (explosive, occlusive, *Verschlußlaut*), e.g., [p, b, m]; if it is incomplete, the breath being forced thru a more or less narrow passage, as with [f, s, v, z], we have a *Spirant* (fricative, continuant, open consonant, *Reibelaut*).

12. Intensity of Articulation. All consonants, but especially the voiceless stops ([p, t, k]), differ according to the intensity with which the breath is expelled. It is expelled with great intensity, e.g., in the case of initial [p, t, k] both in English and German, while the corresponding French consonants are pronounced with much less force of expiration. To the ear, German and English initial [p, t, k] are similar to [p+h, t+h, k+h]. Such sounds are called *aspirated*.

Besides, the muscles of the lips or tongue are either tense or relaxt (loose) in the pronunciation of a consonant; in general, it can be said that they are relatively tense with voiceless consonants, as [p, f], and relatively relaxt with voiced consonants, like [b, v]; consonants pronounced with tense muscles are called *Fortes* (singular *fortis*, 'strong'), the others are called *Lenes* (singular *lenis*, 'mild,' 'soft'). While in most cases this distinction coincides with that between voiced and voiceless, a voiced sound *can* be (relatively) fortis (e.g., *bb*, *gg* in German *Ebbe*, *Flagge*); while a voiceless consonant is sometimes lenis; this is the case in the South German pronunciation of *b*, *d*, *g*; they are voiceless, but pronounced with relaxt muscles, as the German term 'weiches *b*' indicates.

13. Requirements of Phonetic Analysis. In determining the phonetic character of any sound, we must answer the following questions:

(1) Are the vocal chords in vibration or not? This classifies a sound as *voiced* or *voiceless* (4, 3).

(2) Is the velum closed (raised) or open (lowered)? In the first case, the sound is *oral*, in the second case it is *nasal* (6).

(3) Is the passage thru the mouth open — partly closed — entirely closed? Thus we distinguish *vowels*, *spirants*, *stops* (11).

(4) In the case of consonants, is the expiration intense or normal? In the first case, the sound is *aspirated*. — Are the muscles tense or relaxt, i.e., is the sound *fortis* or *lenis?* (12).

(5) What is the place of articulation? (10).

CHAPTER II

Analysis of German Sounds

I. THE LABIALS

A. Stops

14. Bilabial Stops, [p, b]. The lips are closed, and the velum, with the uvula, closes the nasal passage (position I, Plate I). Thus bilabial (Lat. *bi–*, 'both,' and *labium*, 'lip') oral stops are formed. The vocal chords are either open, forming an isosceles triangle with a vertex angle of fifteen degrees, or they vibrate. In the first case we have a voiceless stop, e.g., *p*, *pp* in *Pein*, *Rappe*, or *b* in final position (see below): *ab*, *hübsch* = [ʔap, hypʃ]. In the latter case, we pronounce a voiced stop, e.g., *b* in *bei*, *Liebe* = [bai, liːbə].

In German and English we have aspiration (**12**) in the pronunciation of initial *p* and of *pp*: *Paar*, *Pein*, *Rappe*, *Lippe* = [pˤaɪr, pˤain, rapˤə, lipˤə]. — Simple *p* in the middle of a word is not a frequent sound in German; most speakers do not aspirate it, *p* in *Kneipe*, *Oper*, *Lampe* being weaker than in English *griping*, *hoping*, *rampart*. — Final *b*, i.e., *b* at the end of words or syllables and before voiceless sounds is voiceless, but not aspirated: *ab*, *liebreich*, *gibt* = [ʔap, liːpraiç, gi(ɪ)pt] (= [liːb̥raiç, giːb̥t], see below).

The lips are either tense or relaxt (**12**). They are tense in the pronunciation of all aspirated sounds, of *b* at the end of a short syllable, and of *bb*: *Paar*, *ab*, *Ebbe* = [pˤaɪr, ʔap, ʔɛbə]. They are relaxt for voiced *b*,

14

and for *b* in voiceless pronunciation (final *b*) after long vowels: *Beere, Liebe, geliebt*=[beɪrə, liːbə, gəliːb̥t]: we have lenes in the latter, fortes in the former case. ([b̥, d̥, g̊] are the accurate signs for the voiceless lenes, but in most cases [p, t, k] is sufficiently exact.)

NOTE. The difference between the aspirated voiceless stops of German and English, and the unaspirated (but fortes) stops in Romance and Slavic languages can be shown by a simple experiment: Hold a burning match close to your lips while pronouncing English *pain*, or German *Pein;* the flame will be extinguished, while it flickers but slightly when French *pain* is pronounced correctly.

Generally speaking, Middle and South German do not possess any voiced stops, but [b] is replaced by the voiceless lenis [b̥], *bei* = [b̥ai]; between vowels, the bilabial spirant [v] (17) is substituted: *aber* = [ʔaːvər].

15. The Bilabial Nasal, [m, m̥].

The lips are closed, and the velum takes position II° (Plate I), thus opening the nasal passage; the vocal chords vibrate. This is the sound of *m* in *mir, am, Mutter*, equivalent to English *m*. — Voiceless [m̥] occurs in such interjections as '*hm*,' in phonetic transcription [m̥m]: the lips are closed, the velum is open, the vocal chords are at first open, then they begin to vibrate. In [m'mm] (sign of approval) they vibrate — are opened — and vibrate again. — Occasionally [m] is at least partly voiceless in words like *Schmerz, Lampe* = [ʃm̥mɛrts, lamm̥pə].

It is important to pronounce final *m* short, not long, as in English after short vowels. Compare German *Lamm* with English *lamb*. *German has no long consonants.*

NOTE. Such groups of labials as occur in *Amtmann, nebenbei* when carelessly pronounced [ʔampman, neːbmbai], are characteristic of the real nature of a stop: in *Amtmann* the lips are closed before the first *m*, and opened after the second *m*; consequently, *p* is formed neither by the closing nor by the opening of the lips — they are closed both before and after it — but merely by the position of the velum. From this it appears that the characteristic element of a stop is neither the formation nor the release of the obstruction, but the obstruction as such. — Cf. Jespersen, *Lehrbuch der Phonetik*, p. 12.

B. Spirants

16. Slit and Rill. The passage thru which the breath is expelled in the formation of a spirant can be of different shapes: It can be a narrow slit with approximately parallel lines, or a more or less round channel for which we use the term 'rill.' We, therefore, following the Danish phonetician Jespersen, speak of *slit-sounds* and *rill-sounds* (slit-spirants and rill-spirants). English *th*, for instance, is a slit-spirant: The front of the tongue is convex and nearly parallel to the inner surface of the upper teeth. With *s*, on the other hand, the breath is forced thru a narrow channel ('rill') along the blade of the tongue, as we can observe in a mirror.

17. Bilabial Slit-Spirants, [ꜰ, *v*]. The two lips are nearly parallel, leaving a very narrow passage nearly along their whole length. This is the articulation of the Middle and South German voiced bilabial spirant [*v*] which is used for the letter *w* (*wer, wo, Löwe*) and for *b* between vowels (*aber* = [ʔaɪʋər]). In the combinations *qu, schw, zw* the North Germans also use this sound very frequently: [kveɪr, ʃveɪr, tsvaɪr]. — [ꜰ] is the voiceless sound caused by blowing, but is sometimes used instead of [*v*] after voiceless sounds, e.g., [kꜰeɪr].

18. Bilabial Rill-Spirants, [w, ʍ]. The lips are closed at the sides, a round opening of pea-size, or a little larger, being left in the center. At the same time the back of the tongue is raised, as in the pronunciation of [u]: this is English *w*, which is generally voiced, but which is voiceless after voiceless consonants and in the usual American pronunciation of *wh*: *wine, witch, whine, which, queen* = [waɪn. wɪtʃ, hʍaɪn, hʍɪtʃ, kʍiːn]. In German this sound does not exist.

19. **Labio-dental Spirants,** [f, v], are formed by the lower lip and the upper teeth. They are necessarily slit-sounds for obvious reasons: The upper teeth being rigid, and the lower lip being much less flexible than the tongue, no channel (rill) can be formed. — German [f, v] have much less distinct friction than have the corresponding English sounds. This is due to the fact that in the latter the teeth touch the central line of the lower lip, while in German the lower lip slightly projects over the edge of the upper teeth, so that the friction takes place on the inner, softer skin of the lip. Besides, German [v] is less distinctly voiced than English [v]. Compare English *fine, father, vine, vile,* with German *fein, Vater, Wein, weil.*

NOTE 1. Especial care should be used in the pronunciation of the groups *qu, schw, zw.* For pedagogical reasons, the bilabial pronunciation described in **17** is not advisable, English [w] being substituted for it too easily. The labio-dental pronunciation [kvelə, ʃveːr, tsvaːr] is quite as correct, and is preferable in the classroom.

NOTE 2. The letter *v* in foreign words is usually pronounced [v], but in a few foreign words quite commonly used [f] is substituted: *Vers* (also pronounced [vers], especially in South Germany), *Veilchen, Vogt,* usually also in *brave* (always in *brav*), *Sklave, Pulver.*

The following German words are spelled with *v* (pronounced [f]): *Vater, Vetter, Vieh, Vogel, Vließ, Vläme, Volk, vier, viel, von, vor, vorn, vorder-, ver-;* names (mostly Low German) like *Havel, Bremerhaven, Voß, Virchow (-ow =* [oː]). Be careful not to pronounce any of these names with [v] instead of [f].

The teacher should lay stress on the correct pronunciation of *pf =* [p+f]: *Pfund, Pflaume.*

II. THE DENTALS (AND ALVEOLARS)

20. **Dentals**[1] are sounds which are formed with the tip or blade of the tongue against or near the upper teeth.

[1] As a matter of convenience, the term 'dentals' is used here in a wider sense than its literal meaning; it includes alveolars and even cacuminals.

If formed against the teeth, they are *Dentals proper; inter-dentals* if the tip (point) of the tongue is between the upper and lower teeth; *post-dentals* if the tip or the blade of the tongue touches the inner surface of the upper teeth; *supra-dentals* or *Alveolars* if it touches the upper gums. An articulation that takes place still farther back, the tip of the tongue being inverted and touching the front palate, is called *cacuminal* (from Lat. *cacumen*, 'top').

A. Stops

21. Dental Stops, [t, d], are formed much farther back in English than in German. The American 'dentals' are articulated by the tip of the tongue behind the alveoli; they are 'point-inverted' or 'cacuminal.' Grandgent, *G.E.S.*, p. 7, says: "The point of the tongue is turned up to the roots of the teeth." British dentals are formed somewhat farther forward, viz., at the back of the alveoli (they are post-alveolar). German [t, d] are, in general, pre-alveolar, i.e., the tip, and often the blade, of the tongue is pressed against the front edge of the upper gums. It is very important that the teacher insist on this 'fronting' of the dentals. It is advisable even to exaggerate slightly by making the pupils pronounce post-dental [t, d], the tip of the tongue being pressed against the upper teeth — which usage, by the way, is by no means uncommon in German pronunciation. Few mispronunciations are so detrimental as an English (especially American English) articulation of the dentals in German.

When practising the German dentals, the pupils should first press the tip of the tongue against the front alveoli (or the teeth); *then* they should pronounce words like *die, dich, tief, Tisch*, etc.

Voice and voicelessness, aspiration, and the distribution of fortis and lenis pronunciation follow the same principles as with the labials: Initial *t* and medial *tt* are aspirated fortes: *Tier, Teil, Tor; Ritter, Ratte, Futter;* medial *t*, final *t* and *tt*, unvoiced *d* after a short vowel, and *dd* (voiced, of course) are fortes, but unaspirated: *rieten, Rat, hat, Schritt; Land; Kladde, Edda.* — Voiced *d* and unvoiced *d* after a long vowel are lenes: *du, reden, leiden, Rad*=[duː, reːdən, laidən, raɪd̦].

NOTE 1. It is not necessary — indeed, it is hardly advisable — that the teacher insist on the distinction between lenis and fortis for final unvoiced [d̦] after a long vowel (lenis) and final *t* (fortis) as in *Rad* and *Rat*. Many Germans, especially in the North, do not distinguish these sounds. It is better to insist on an intensive (fortis) pronunciation for all final stops.

NOTE 2. South and Middle Germans substitute their voiceless lenis [d̦] for voiced [d], as in the case of the labials, so that the same sound is used in *dein* as in *Neid* — [d̦ain, naid̦]. In teaching, of course, this is strictly to be avoided.

22. The Dental Nasal, [n], is formed at the same place as the oral dental stops. We have pre-alveolar or post-dental articulation in German, post-alveolar or cacuminal articulation in English. — The sound [n] is preferable to [ŋ] (**33**) in words like *Knabe, Gnade*. [n] must be carefully pronounced before and after labials where in careless pronunciation [m] is frequently substituted: *fünf, leben, anbieten*=[fynf, leːbən, ʔanbiːtən], not [fymf, leːbm̩, ʔambiːtən].

B. Spirants

23. Dental Slit-Spirants do not exist in German. We find them in the English *th*-sounds: voiceless [þ] in *thin*, voiced [ð] in *then;* the blade of the tongue is pressed against the inner surface of the upper teeth, the tip frequently slightly projecting over the edge of the lower teeth.

24. Dental Rill-Spirants, [s, z]. The blade touches the front alveoli, while the tip frequently, tho not necessarily, touches the lower teeth. The breath is expelled in a narrow current thru a sharp rill along the median line of the blade. Observe this by means of the hand-glass and compare the sharpness of the air current with the comparatively weak and broad current in the pronunciation of *th*. The upper and lower teeth leave only a narrow passage so that the breath is directed against the edge of the lower incisors, where it is frequently divided into an inner and outer current. This is the cause of the sharp, hissing sound of [s] and [z].

So-called 'lisping' may be due to different causes. Most commonly, the tip of the tongue covers the edges of the lower teeth; frequently, the blade does not form a rill; and sometimes the upper and lower teeth are too far apart. In each of these three cases, lisping can rapidly be cured by self-observation, with the help of a mirror and steady practise.

German [s, z] are more distinctly 'hissed' than the corresponding English sounds. — [s] and [z], and frequently also [ʃ] and [ʒ] (**30**), are often called *sibilants*.

In standard German, we pronounce initial *s* before vowels and medial *s* when a vowel follows and a vowel, nasal or liquid, precedes, voiced: *See, Rose, Linse, Ferse, Felsen*. In initial position in the second parts of compounds, [s] is pronounced after voiceless, [z] after voiced sounds: *vorsichtig, versichern, Entsatz, Absicht* = [foːr|ziçtiç, fər|ziçərn, ʔɛnt|sats, ʔap|siçt]. — In all other positions, except initial *sp* and *st* (see **30**, Note 1), [s] is used: — *s* after consonants other than liquids and nasals: *Ochse, Erbse* = [ʔɔksə, ʔɛrpsə]; final *s: das, las; ß: fließen, Fluß; ss: rissen, Flüsse*. — Southern and Middle Germany do not possess any [z], but use [s] in lenis pronunciation ([s̬]) instead; in teaching, however, the voiced pronunciation, in accordance with Northern and stage usage, is preferable.

NOTE 1. It is to be admitted, however, that even in Northern Germany initial s is not entirely voiced; it begins voiceless, and ends voiced: See = [sze:]. Similarly, English inflectional –s is only half voiced: is = [izs].

NOTE 2. As to spelling, remember that ss stands only between vowels if the preceding vowel is short; otherwise, ß is used: Flüsse, but fließen, Fluß. — The letter ſ usually denotes the sound [z], while all other spellings — ß, ſſ, ß — denote voiceless [s].

German z is pronounced [ts]. To substitute the sound [z] is one of the most frequent and most irritating mistakes. If phonetic transcription is used at the outset, it will be largely obviated. No pupil is apt to pronounce [zvaɪr] or [zwaɪr] if the phonetic spelling [tsvaɪr] is used. If phonetic transcription is not resorted to, frequent reference to such English words as cats and rats will gradually remedy the defect.

x, ks, gs, and chs have the same pronunciation, viz., [ks]: Axt, des Werks, des Tags, des Rocks, Ochse. However, where ch belongs to the stem, and s is an ending, the ch-sound must be used: des Lochs = [lɔχs].

C. The Liquids

25. Sonorous Sounds. According to the definition given in section 11, the [l] and [r] sounds must be classed as spirants, since in producing them the breath is partly checkt in the mouth. But in their acoustic impression they resemble vowels more than do other spirants. As a matter of fact, they frequently have the function of vowels, e.g., l in German handeln = [handḷn], English middleman = [midḷmæn], or r in Bohemian words like prst, čtvrtku. This is due to the fact that in their pronunciation a comparatively large resonance room is left in the mouth, while with other spirants the tongue fills most of the oral cavity (cf. vowel palatograms on page 45). Therefore a much larger body of air vibrates in the pronunciation of [r] and [l] than in that of [v] or [z], and it is this factor that lends to these sounds their peculiar 'sonorous' resonance. — With the nasals, conditions are somewhat similar, the air in the nasal cavity being caused to vibrate by the action of the vocal chords, so that these sounds too may be said to occupy a position between consonants and vowels, and can be used in syllabic (vocalic) function: *rechnete* = [reçntə]. — For that reason, [l, r, m, n, ŋ] are called **sonorous sounds**. Compare section **53**.

[l] and [r] are frequently called 'liquids.' While this designation has no phonetic meaning whatever, being merely a metaphorical description of their acoustic character (their resonant quality), it may be used as a familiar, practical technical term.

26. Lingual *r* is either a pure spirant (of sonorous quality) or a trilled sound. Spirant lingual *r* (written [ɹ] in phonetics) is the usual *r*-sound of American and British pronunciation. The tongue is in a position similar to that for [d], — in British, against the back alveoli; in American, the tip of the tongue is turned back against the front palate, behind the alveoli, so that it is very decidedly a 'point-inverted sound.' In German, spirantic [ɹ] is used by many speakers, and at least in beginning instruction it may be tolerated as a substitute for trilled [r]; but the teacher must absolutely insist that it be formed at the front alveoli, or even at the teeth (by way of pedagogical exaggeration).

American [ɹ] in German pronunciation is the most typical, and the worst of all mistakes. It greatly influences the pronunciation of the preceding vowel; the vowels in words like *werden, wird, worden, wurde, würde,* or *Berg, birgt, borgen, Burg, Bürge,* lose their distinctive qualities if this mistake is tolerated.

The normal *r*-sound of German standard pronunciation is trilled lingual [r]: The tip of the tongue, very thin and very elastic, touches the front alveoli; a strong current of air is forced thru between it and the alveoli. Frequently, the tip of the tongue does not touch them exactly in the center, but articulates slightly to the left or right.

To learn trilled lingual *r* it is best to pronounce a strongly voiced ('buzzed') *z*; then pronounce the combinations *zr — zzrr*, trying to attain some vibration. To strengthen this slight vibration, change the pronunciation to *zdrrr*. Having practised this sufficiently, pronounce *tritt, Triller, Drill, irren, irrt, irden, Herren, Herz, Herd, Zorn, fort, Orden, surren, surrt, Kurde, harren, harrt, Garde*. *r* must be pronounced distinctly in all positions, also in the suffix *-er*, as in *Lehrer, Bänder*.

The number of vibrations differ. In general, there are about two vibrations in initial *r* and in medial *r* after a long vowel, two or three after a short vowel, and one in final *r*. In British English a trilled *r* with one vibration is frequently used between vowels (as in *very*), and sometimes initially.

Standard German *r* is always voiced. English spirantic *r* becomes unvoiced or semi-voiced after voiceless sounds, as in *pray, try, cry* = [pɹ̥ei, tɹ̥ai, kɹ̥ai].

27. Lateral Sounds. [l] is a spirant, but the air does not pass along the median line of the mouth: the tip of the tongue forms a complete occlusion with the teeth, alveoli or front palate (according to the language), and the breath passes on one or both sides of the mouth thru a narrow opening between the molars and the sides of the tongue. According as there are one or two lateral openings we may speak of uni-lateral and bilateral [l], but this distinction is without any practical importance.

English [l] differs materially from German [l] in regard

to the point of articulation and the shape of the tongue. In English [l] the tip of the tongue touches the back alveoli or even the front palate (in American pronunciation). The tongue is 'hollow' — spoon-shaped, as it were. Its front third is depressed, but the back is raised towards the soft palate, without touching it, however. In German, the articulation takes place at the same place as with [t, d, n, r], i.e., at the front alveoli, or even at the upper teeth. The body of the tongue is flat, or slightly convex, but not concave, as in English.

It is advisable first to practise words like *Lilie*, *Iltis*, *Filz*, *gilt*, emphasizing the 'fronting' of the [l]; then proceed to words like *Atlas*, *Taler*, *Kultus*. Often a comparison of the German and the English pronunciation of names like *Willy*, *Tilly*, *Lilly* is very effective.

NOTE. Semi-voiced *l* is frequent in English after voiceless sounds: *play*, *clay*. Welsh *ll* is an intensive (fortis) voiceless *l*: *Lloyd*, *Llewellyn*. The sound is easily learned by pronouncing such pairs of voiced and voiceless sounds as [v — f, z — s, l — ll] (observing the principle that voiceless spirants are much more intensive than voiced spirants).

III. THE PALATALS

28. Palatals, in the literal sense of the word, are sounds formed by the tongue being in contact with the hard or soft palate, but in phonetics the use of the term is practically always restricted to those sounds that are formed at the front part (one-half, or less) of the hard palate. More accurately, they are often called prepalatals. It should be observed that the hard palate is distinctly concave (verify this by means of your palate outline, according to 7 and 9, Note). Hence, the tongue cannot easily touch a 'point' of the front palate, but is compelled to articulate over a larger surface. This fact lends a peculiar spirantic quality to palatal stops, since the tongue does not cover or release the whole surface at one moment, but gradually. In German and English, palatal stops hardly exist, except perhaps in certain North German pronunciations of the word *ja*, sounding like [tɕaʔ], but they are very frequent in Slavic languages. — French *gn*, as in *montagne*, is not a dental nasal stop with a *j*-sound attacht, as *ni* in English *onion*, *union*, but strictly 'palatal *n*,' spelled [ɲ] in phonetic transcription. The front part of the tongue articulates against the hard palate, while the tip is at rest, usually touching the lower teeth or the lower gums.

29. Prepalatal Slit-Spirants, [ç, j]. In German, [ç] is expressed by the spelling *ch* after front vowels (*i, e, ä, ö, ü, ei, ai, eu, äu*) and after consonants. The suffix *–chen* is always pronounced with the prepalatal or *ich*-sound, never with the velar or *ach*-sound: *dich, recht, Nächte, Löcher, gleich, aichen, euch, räuchern, Märchen, durch, Häuschen, Frauchen* (but *pfauchen* = [pfauxən], cf. **34**, Note). — The front of the tongue touches the front palate, the tip is neutral (it may or may not touch the lower teeth or lower gums).

In certain parts of Germany, especially the vicinity of Frankfort on the Main and parts of the province of Posen, the prepalatal spirant [ç] is frequently articulated with a slight rill in the front and blade of the tongue, which makes it somewhat similar in sound to [ʃ] (**30**). The statement is sometimes heard that this so-called *isch*-sound is customary on the stage and in singing, and perhaps even preferable to the '*ich*-sound' on account of its 'carrying power.' This belief is entirely erroneous. In the pronunciation of [ç] the tongue must be pressed firmly against the front palate, thus making a rill impossible.

In teaching this sound it is well to start with pairs of voiced and voiceless sounds as mentioned for voiceless [ʃ]: [v — f, z — s, ð — þ, j — ç]. The students should pronounce the spirantic sound of [j] very energetically, exaggerating the spirantic sound of *y* in *yes, year*, and noting the presence of voice in the first kind of spirants, and its absence in the second kind. In this way, a correct pronunciation of [ç] cannot fail to be attained even by the most 'heavy-tongued' students. — Sometimes it may be helpful to compare this sound with the spirantic sound, greatly intensified, in English *hue, human* = [çjuː, çjuːmən], or with strongly whispered *h* in English *he, heal.* — It is sometimes stated that the *ich*-sound can be learned by whispering words like *key*; such statements are misleading: However mildly or intensively *key* may be whispered, it will always begin with a stop, tho it may end in a voiceless spirant; therefore, this suggestion is apt to cause the students to acquire that well-known mispronunciation [ikç]. — Reference to words like *cure, cube* is nearly as bad.

⟋ The *ich*-sound is voiceless. The corresponding voiced sound [j] is much sharper, i.e., has more friction, in German (at least in the North and in stage pronunciation) than in English. The tongue touches the palate in the same way (only with less pressure) as in the pronunciation of [ç]. In English and South German the tongue is slightly concave (shows a slight rill, or groove): *yes, year, young; tube, human, literature* (see **30**, Note 2); German *ja, Jahr, jung.*

NOTE 1. For French palatal *lle*, [lç] should not be substituted: *Versaille* = [vɛrzaj], not [vɛrzalç].

NOTE 2. In many parts of Germany the *ich*-sound is also used for the letter *g* after front vowels in 'final' position, while [j] is used for *g* after front vowels when a voiced sound follows (except before suffixes, where the voiceless sound [ç] is used). Stage pronunciation permits (and requires) the substitution of [ç] only in the suffix *-ig: liegen, liegt, Sieg, König, Könige* are pronounced [liːgən, liːkt, ziːk, køːmiç, køːnigə] in stage usage, but [liːjən, liːçt, ziːç, køːmiç, køːnijə] in many of the German dialects, chiefly in the North.

30. The Prepalatal Rill-Spirants, [ʃ, ʒ], differ from the corresponding slit-spirants (see above) in two respects: (1) the front and blade of the tongue show a rather flat groove (rill), being here concave, while the front of the tongue is convex in the pronunciation of [ç, j]; (2) the tongue articulates differently: It is either raised and retracted, so that the blade touches the back alveoli; or it is lowered and protracted, so that the tip of the tongue rests very low in the mouth (frequently touching the ligament below the tongue), and a part of the tongue, which is considerably farther back than the blade, touches the front palate. In other words, the tongue does not articulate up and down in a vertical direction, but moves diagonally, either backward and upward, or forward and downward. In English, and frequently in German, especially in North German, the first mode of articulation is the usual one; the second kind prevails to a great extent in South German, French, and, partly, the Slavic languages. Tho it is quite unnecessary to mention this difference to your pupils, it is advisable to insist upon another peculiarity of German [ʃ]: the lips are somewhat rounded and protruded, so that German [ʃ] has a distinctly lower pitch than English [ʃ]. Compare German *Schein, Schuh, schon,* and English *shine, shoe, shone.*

Voiced [ʒ] is found in English words like *measure, azure;* it should be pronounced in German in such foreign words as *Loge, Journal,* but [ʃ] is substituted very frequently.

NOTE 1. The *s* of the combinations *st-* and *sp-* in the beginning of words is to be pronounced [ʃ] but the lips are usually not rounded: *Stein, Speer* = [ʃtain, ʃpeːr]. In middle and final position *st* and *sp* are to be pronounced with [s], not with [ʃ]: *Ast, Äste, Wespe, erst* = [ʔast, ʔɛstə, vɛspə, ʔɛrst]. In foreign words, the usage is not entirely fixt. Words in very common use are usually pronounced with [ʃ], those that are less common, with [s], e.g., [ʃpatsiːrən, reʃpɛkt], but [spɔnzor, ʔaspɛkt]. Stage pronunciation (Siebs, p. 56) requires [sp, st] in all foreign words, but in school and daily life the authority of Viëtor's *Aussprachewörterbuch* is preferable on this point, and it should be consulted in doubtful cases. Foreign words, in which initial *s* is followed by any consonant other than *p* or *t* must, of course, be pronounced with [s], not [ʃ], e.g., [sklaːvə, skelɛt, skaːt].

NOTE 2. Carefully avoid pronunciations like [daʃjaːr, hatʃaː] for [das jaːr, hat jaː]. In English, British as well as American, the 'palatalization' of *s* and *t* before [j] is customary and defensible — in words like *nature, literature, don't you,* [tʃ] is by all means preferable to an artificial, affected [tj], — but in German such assimilations are not admissible.

IV. THE VELARS

31. **Velars** are sounds that are articulated at or near the dividing line between the hard and soft palate. In looseness of application, the term 'velar' is similar to the term 'dental' (see **20**).

NOTE. Instead of 'velar' (sometimes including 'palatal'), grammarians commonly use the term 'guttural,' and for technical reasons this may be tolerated in grammatical works. In phonetics, however, this misnomer must be avoided. Latin *'guttur'* means *throat*, and if the term were used at all, it would apply to sounds produced in the larynx, which, however, are generally designated as *'glottal'* or *'laryngeal.'* — The application of the term 'guttural' to the general character of languages that possess velar spirants, like German, is silly.

A. Stops

32. **Velar Stops,** [k, g]. The articulation varies somewhat according to the neighboring sounds, but in German this variation is but slight ('ein paar Millimeter'; Viëtor, *El. d. Phon.*, p. 238), decidedly less than in English. [ka, kn, kr, kl, ga, gn, gr, gl] are pronounced at the dividing line between hard and soft palate, [ki, ke, gi, ge] slightly in front, [ko, ku, go, gu] slightly back of it. Hence, there is much less difference between the [k]-sounds of German *Kind, kalt, Kuh,* than of English *king, calf, cool.* — [k] is the sound of *k, ck,* and of *g, gg* in final position, [g] is used for initial and medial *g, gg; kalt, Rock, Tag, sagt, eggt, Brigg; Gasse, legen, Tage, Roggen.* The distribution of voiced and voiceless, fortis and lenis, aspirated and unaspirated pronunciation is the same as in the case of labial and dental stops: *Kind, kalt, Kuh, Röcke* have aspirated fortes; *Dank, Rock, flugs, weg, Augsburg* have unaspirated fortes; *Tag, Bug,* voiceless lenes; *Gasse, Tage,* voiced lenes. — The suffix *–ig* has the *ich*-sound; see **29**, Note 2.

NOTE 1. These statements are in accordance with stage usage and Viëtor's *Aussprachewörterbuch*. In many parts of Germany, however, spirants are pronounced for *g* in medial and final position. South and Middle Germany have voiceless lenis for the voiced sound, as in the case of *b* and *d*, and do not aspirate initial *k* before consonants: *Kram* is nearly like *Gram*, the former, perhaps, leaning slightly more towards fortis pronunciation. In Saxony, and to an extent in Thuringia, voiceless lenis is generally used for *k* in all positions: *Kaffee* = [ĝafeː].

NOTE 2. The pronunciation of initial *ch* is very uncertain, but in general it may be said that in familiar German names and in familiar foreign words, especially before consonants, it is pronounced [k], while in other cases [ç] is used: [k] in *Chemnitz*, *Chur*, *Christ*, *Chor*, but [ç] in *Chirurg*, *Choreographie*. In doubtful cases, consult Viëtor's *Aussprachewörterbuch*.

33. The Velar Nasal, [ŋ].

The middle part of the tongue articulates against the middle palate (at the dividing line between hard and soft palates or slightly farther back); the velum is lowered. [ŋ] is spelled *ng*, or *n* before *k*: *lang*, *länger*, *Dank*. Note especially that *ng* is always pronounced [ŋ] in strictly German words; only in foreign words it should be pronounced [ŋg] (as in English *finger*): *Ungarn*, *Alba Longa*, *Singular* = [ʔuŋgarn, ʔalbaɪ lɔŋgaɪ, ziŋgulaːr]. — Final *ng* is pronounced [ŋ], not [ŋk] (the latter is a dialect pronunciation in many parts of Germany, especially in the Northwest): [laŋ, juŋ], not [laŋk, juŋk].

German [ŋ] varies much less according to the neighboring sounds than does English [ŋ], there being decidedly less difference in this respect between German *singen*, *sang*, *gesungen*, than between English *sing*, *sang*, *sung*.

NOTE. French nasal vowels in adopted words should not be pronounced [aŋ, ɔŋ, ɛŋ, øŋ], as is very common, especially in the North, but the French pronunciation must be retained: [departˈmã, baˈl5].

B. Spirants

34. The Velar Spirants, [χ, γ], are of necessity slit-spirants because the back of the tongue is much less flexible than the front, especially the blade, and so is unable to form a distinct rill. [χ] (the so-called *ach*-sound) and [γ] are generally formed at the dividing line between hard and soft palate, or somewhat farther back. It is doubtful whether there is any habitual difference in the articulations of [aχ, oχ, uχ]; if so, it is scarcely perceptible. — [χ] is expressed by the spelling *ch* after back vowels (*a, o, u, au*): *Bach, doch, Tuch, auch.*

NOTE. Observe that the suffix *–chen* is always pronounced [çən] (29): [rauxən, pfauxən] are verbs, but [frauçən, pfauçən] are diminutives.

[γ] is voiced [χ] (lenis); it is used in North Germany for *g* in medial position if a back vowel precedes, as in [taːɣə, boːɣən, truːɣən], but in standard pronunciation it does not occur. Similarly, [χ] is used for final *g* (in some parts of Germany also for medial *g*) instead of [k (g)] which is required by the stage: [ta(ː)χ, tsoːχ, truːχ, ʔauɣə (ʔauχə)] for [taːk, tsoːk, truːk, ʔauɡə].

To teach [χ], it is best to start from [ç]: The students should notice that [ç] is articulated in the same place as [i], and should plainly feel the difference in the articulation of [i] and [u]; then they should pronounce [ʔiç — ʔux; buːχ, dɔχ], thus proceeding from the palatal to the velar spirant. It is better to avoid any comparison with the velar stop [k]; this would only be apt to lead to such mispronunciations as [akχ, ukχ].

V. UVULAR [R]

35. The Uvula (for description, see 5) is used by many Germans and Frenchmen in the pronunciation of so-called 'uvular *r*' ([R] in phonetic transcription). Hempl, *German Orthography and Phonology*, p. 146, says:

"During its formation the front of the tongue lies down while the part farther back assumes the form of a trough in which the uvula lies and, as the breath strikes it from behind, vibrates up and down like a little tongue. But the trough is very generally not well formed; the breath gets around the uvula without putting it into vigorous vibration; then the sound produced approaches very closely that of [γ] (compare *Waren* and *Wagen*) and, before voiceless consonants, that of [χ] (compare *Art* and *Acht*).

Remark: A uvular *r* with falsetto voice is often made by boys in this country in imitating a crow."

The stage pronunciation and the majority of phonetic authorities unconditionally require dental *r*. As to the origin and spread of uvular *r* in German, compare Trautmann, *Kleine Lautlehre*, p. 97 ff.:

„Das zäpfchen-r ist kein ursprünglich deutscher laut, sondern ist vor wenig mehr als 150 jahren aus Frankreich eingeschleppt worden. Dies wird am meisten durch die tatsache bewiesen, dass die zäpfchen-r-laute hauptsächlich bei den gebildeten und in den städten zu hause sind. Es wird oft gesagt, in dieser oder jener gegend werde zäpfchen-r gesprochen. Ellis, E.E.P. 198, schreibt gar, zäpfchen-r gelte 'in a great part of Germany.' Grundfalsch; es gibt keine ‚gegend' und keinen ‚teil' Deutschlands, wo dies der fall ist. Die verbreitung und verteilung von zungen- und zäpfchen-r war bis vor kurzem und ist in der hauptsache noch heute keine örtliche, sondern wesentlich eine gesellschaftliche. Und hierin liegt der beweis, dass das zäpfchen-r aus Frankreich zu uns gekommen ist. In diesem lande ward bald nach 1650 das zäpfchen-r-sprechen aufgebracht, und es kam im laufe der zeit in der feinen französischen gesellschaft immer mehr in aufnahme. Um 1650 und noch hundert jahre länger schlief das selbstgefühl des deutschen volkes einen totähnlichen schlummer; der gebildete deutsche kannte kein höheres ziel als zu denken und zu tun wie der Franzose und keinen schöneren ruhm als dessen sprache so vollkommen wie möglich zu lernen. Das französische war die sprache der vornehmen deutschen gesellschaft. Dass diese gesellschaft mit der französischen sprache auch die ‚gebildete' französische aussprache übernommen hat, war eine naturnotwendigkeit; wie jede französische mode getreulich von ihr nachgeahmt wurde, so musste auch geschnarrt werden, wie man in Paris schnarrte. Liessen sich nun jene trefflichen deutschen herbei, ihre muttersprache zu reden, so übertrugen sie natürlich die ‚feinen' französischen laute auch in diese, und so kam das deutsche zum zäpfchen-r. Diese tatsache hat nicht viel schmeichelhaftes für uns, aber sie lässt sich nicht leugnen. Nur wer die geschichte des 17. und 18. jahrhunderts nur oberflächlich kennt, wer nicht weiss, in welch erbärmlicher abhängigkeit in sittlicher und geistiger hinsicht deutschland damals von Frankreich stand, kann an der einführung des zäpfchen-r von dorther zweifeln. Da dieser laut, ehe er in Deutschland nachgeahmt wurde, in Frankreich eine gewisse verbreitung gefunden haben musste, so werden wir sein erstes auftreten bei uns um das jahr 1700 setzen dürfen. Zuerst ward, nach dem Pariser vorbilde, von einigen wenigen ‚eine annehmlichkeit ins schnarren gesetzt.‘ Nachdem unsre höchsten kreise vorangegangen waren, fing auch der bürgerstand an zu schnarren, der in der feinen sitte nicht zurückbleiben wollte, und nach und nach verfielen ganze städte dem schnarren. In Berlin, Hannover, Dresden, Leipzig und vielen anderen grösseren städten ist zäpfchen-r heute alleinherrschend. Wer zungen-r spricht, ist kein einheimischer. Und nicht nur in den städten, auch auf dem lande dringt zäpfchen-r beständig vor, namentlich in gegenden, die sich durch regen verkehr und fabrikbetrieb auszeichnen, und in denen ländliche und städtische bevölkerung sich fortwährend enge berühren und mischen. Den meisten boden gewonnen hat das zäpfchen-r im königreiche Sachsen. Zwar gibt es dort kaum ein dorf, in dem nicht wenigstens die älteren leute noch zungen-r sprechen, aber es gibt nur noch sehr wenige, in denen zungen-r allein gilt. In der gleichen notlage befindet sich das zungen-r fast im ganzen königreiche, und in vielen gegenden Thüringens, Hannovers, der provinz Sachsen steht es nicht viel besser mit ihm. Kann man auch heute noch nicht von ‚gegenden‘ und ‚teilen‘ Deutschlands sprechen, in denen nur zäpfchen-r gilt, so wird man es doch in wenigen jahrzehnten können. Es ist wahr, selbst einzelne grosse städte, wie Wien, München, Breslau, Lübeck, und viele mittlere, wie Darmstadt, Giessen, Erlangen, Hof, sind an das zäpfchen-r noch nicht ganz verfallen, und man kann auch von kindern noch zungen-r hören. Eine grosse zahl kleiner städte und weite ländliche gebiete sind noch so gut wie unberührt von der zäpfchen-r-seuche, und es sprechen noch mindestens ⅔ der bevölkerung des deutschen bodens zungen-r. Dennoch scheint der endliche sieg des fremdlings unabwendbar. Mägde, lehrlinge, schüler gewöhnen sich, sobald sie in die stadt übersiedelt sind, in unzähligen fällen ihr gutes zungen-r ab, um zu schnarren;¹ zäpfchen-r gilt für feiner. So lange diese meinung besteht, muss die zahl der zäpfchen-r-sprechenden mit jedem jahre zunehmen. Eine andere mächtige förderung findet das schnarren in der tatsache, dass das zäpfchen sich leichter in schwirrende bewegung setzen lässt als die zungenspitze. Dieser umstand gewinnt besonders die kinder. Man bringe ein kind, das eben anfängt zu sprechen, unter den einfluss einer anzahl personen, von denen die eine hälfte zungen-r, die andere zäpfchen-r spricht, und das kind wird sich unfehlbar auf die seite der zäpfchen-r-sprecher schlagen. — Aus dem vorhergehenden ergibt sich, dass der guten deutschen aussprache nur zungen-r gemäss sein kann."

Passy, *Petite Phonétique Comparée*, p. 79, says:

«Au point de vue de l'enseignment, il est indifférent de faire prononcer [r] ou [ʀ] en parlant français, et le mieux est de laisser les élèves adopter le son qui leur est le plus facile. Il y a des professeurs — surtout des Anglais et des Américains — qui se donnent beaucoup de mal pour prononcer eux-mêmes et inculquer à leurs élèves le 'r parisien'; c'est une enfantillage, car lors qu'on réussirait, le résultat ne vaudrait pas tant d'efforts; et le plus souvent on réussit très mal. (Je pourrais citer tel professeur anglais, dont la prononciation, excellente d'ailleurs, est gâtée par un effort maladroit pour prononcer le r parisien.)»

In English, uvular *r* is known as the 'Northhumbrian Burr.' The passages quoted contain convincing arguments that it has no place in German (or French) instruction in American schools.

VI. GLOTTAL SOUNDS

36. The Glottal Stop (Glottal Catch), [ʔ] (as to its formation, see 4, 1), precedes in German all initial accented vowels, even in the second parts of compounds: [ʔaus, ʔiç, ʔapʔirən, fərʔainiçt, himəlsʔau]. In certain compounds, however, that are not clearly felt as such, it is not used, especially in adverbial compounds with *dar-, wor-, war-, her-, hin-, vor-*: *daran, woran, warum, herein, hinaus, vorüber;* also in *Obacht, beobachten, selbander, einander, allein, vollenden* it is omitted. Hard and fast rules for the use or omission of the glottal stop cannot be stated, but it may be said that in general it is used much less in South Germany than in North Germany; even in the North it is frequently omitted in words of slight emphasis, like *er*, *es*, *ich*, *und*, etc. Compare the phonetic texts.

The teacher ought to insist continually on the proper use of the glottal stop. To a German, its omission seems like 'running words together' and will often render words or sentences entirely unintelligible to him: 'Der Igel,' without glottal stop, sounds like 'der Riegel,' 'dein Eid' cannot be clearly distinguisht from 'dein Neid,' and the poetic 'Himmelsau,' without the glottal stop, becomes a vulgar word.

The glottal stop is a real consonantal stop, like any other. In many languages it plays a much more important part than in German. In Danish, for instance, its use or omission frequently marks a distinction between words otherwise alike: [ma°lər] 'he paints,' [malər] 'painter.' In Semitic languages it is recognized as a regular consonant having its proper alphabetic sign. It is generally supposed that the existence of the glottal stop was the cause of so-called vocalic alliteration in Old Germanic poetry: All accented initial vowels alliterate with each other, while only like consonants alliterate, e.g., *f* only with *f*, *r* only with *r*, etc. This is explained by assuming that in a verse like '*Her was Otachre Unmett Irri*' (from the Old High German 'Hildebrandslied') the initial vowels were preceded by the glottal stop. — Jespersen, however, and others adduce strong reasons against this theory.

37. The Glottal Spirant, [h]. When the glottis is slightly open, but less so than in the pronunciation of other voiceless consonants (see **4**, 3), the breath passes thru with a slightly audible friction. This is the usual pronunciation of *h* both in German and American English. The tongue and lip position is generally the same as with the following vowel, so that [h] is hardly much more than a voiceless vowel (or other sonant): *ha* = [ḁa], *hu* = [u̥u], [hw] (*wh*) = [w̥w], *hm* = [m̥m] (**15**). — The greater intensity of voiceless spirants is, in part, caused by a narrower passage and a greater tension of the muscles of the tongue or the lips; in the case of [h], it is due to the narrowing of the glottis.

In German, [h] exists only before stressed vowels, including those with secondary stress: *Hof, Vorhof, Schönheit, Uhu, Ahorn.* Before unaccented *e, h* is always silent, serving merely as a sign of length: *sehen, gehen, drohen.*

VII. THE VOWELS

38. Vowel Resonance. The 'voice' produced by the vibrations of the vocal chords has a definite pitch, depending on the degree of tension of the vocal chords. This pitch is modified by the proportion between the size of the air-space in the mouth and the width of the opening between tongue and palate. The smaller the air-space in comparison to the opening, the higher is the 'resonance' of a vowel. This can be demonstrated by means of a wide-mouthed bottle partly filled with water. The bottle represents the oral cavity, its mouth the place of articulation (i.e., the place where the tongue is closest to the palate), and its bottom the teeth and lips. Blow into the bottle, and you will notice that the sound reaches a higher pitch when you add water, thus decreasing the size of the air-space; if you make the opening smaller, the pitch will be lower.

The vowel of highest resonance is [i], while [u] has the lowest pitch. According to their resonance ('Eigenton') the vowels may be arranged as follows: [i, e, a, o, u].

39. Positions of the Tongue. The size of the oral cavity depends on the position of the tongue (which, in turn, is in correlation to the angle between upper and lower jaw). It may be raised in front; in this case, we have 'front vowels.' If it is raised in back, towards the velum, while the tip of the tongue is withdrawn, we have 'back vowels.' If the middle part of the tongue is raised toward,

or near, the dividing line between hard and soft palate,
we pronounce a 'mixed vowel.'

NOTE. The term 'mixed vowel' was originally due to the misconception that in the production of these vowels both the front
and the back of the tongue are raised, but it has been retained for
the practical reason that it avoids a confusing duplication of the
term 'mid' (see below).

According to the height to which the tongue is raised,
we distinguish high, mid, and low vowels; e.g., [i] is a
'high front vowel,' [æ] (in *hat*) a 'low front vowel,' [u] a
'high back vowel,' etc.

40. Muscle Tension. With consonants, we distinguish
between fortes and lenes according to the degree of
muscle tension (12); in a similar way, vowel sounds differ
according to the degree to which the muscles of the
tongue, and to an extent of the cheeks and lips, are tense
or lax. If they are tense, the tongue is distinctly archt
(its surface being convex), as in the formation of slit-
spirants, [þ, ç, χ]. If they are relaxt, the tongue is comparatively concave or, at least, rather flat. Accordingly,
we distinguish 'narrow' (tense — *gespannt*) and 'wide'
(relaxt — *weit, ungespannt*) vowels. German *ie* in *sie* is
narrow, *i* in *mit* is wide. In German, long vowels are
practically always narrow, short vowels, wide. In English, the tendency is similar, but not so uniform.

Phoneticians do not agree concerning the distinction between
narrow and wide vowels. Some, e.g., Viëtor, lay stress chiefly on
the fact that with wide vowels the median line of the tongue is lower
than with narrow vowels, and accordingly prefer to speak of 'close'
and 'open' vowels. Others, who might be classed as the 'English
School,' represented chiefly by Henry Sweet, emphasize only the
mere fact of muscle tension, without paying any attention to the
fact that relaxation of the muscles results in a lowering of the median line. Jespersen combines the two factors approximately in
the method followed above; however, he considers the narrow

vowels as related to rill sounds rather than slit sounds. While it is true that the stream of air that passes in the pronunciation of a 'narrow' vowel is narrower than in the case of a wide vowel (see the palatograms on pp. 44, 45) it seems more systematic to distinguish according to the shape of the tongue rather than according to the width of the opening; the latter naturally increases both when the muscles of the tongue are relaxt, and when the whole body of the tongue is lowered; the former is the case when we pass from narrow [i] to wide [ɪ], the latter when we pass from [i] to [e]. — The concave shape of the tongue in the pronunciation of wide vowels can easily be felt with a toothpick, especially in the case of [ɛ] and [ɔ] when compared with [e] and [o].

This explanation of the difference between narrow and wide vowels accounts for the fact that with a very narrow [e] the median line of the tongue is higher than with wide [ɪ]: in passing from [ɪ] to [e], the body of the tongue is lowered, but the surface remains convex; in passing from narrow [i] to wide [ɪ], the tongue becomes concave, so that its body remains nearly at the same height, but its median line is lowered a considerable distance.

41. Positions of the Lips. In the formation of vowels the lips must be far enough apart to let the air pass without any friction. Still, their shape modifies the character of a vowel considerably. If they are drawn tight, being nearly parallel and leaving a comparatively narrow opening, as in [i, e], the vowel has the highest pitch compatible with its tongue position. If they are rounded and protruded, as with [u, o], the resonance space is increased, and the vowel pitch lowered correspondingly.

Theoretically, any position of the lips, rounded or unrounded, wide or narrow opening, can be combined with any tongue position. Normally, however, the degree of tongue elevation is accompanied by a proportionate width of the angle of the jaws, and, accordingly, by a proportionate lip-opening. The lip-opening is smallest with high vowels, largest with low vowels. Aside from this, lip-rounding is found chiefly in connection with low-pitch vowels, that is, the high-back and mid-back vowels, [u] and [o]; it may be said to be used as a supplementary means of lowering the pitch and thus increasing the contrasts between vowels. However, under certain circumstances, vowels of high pitch (front vowels) are rounded, and vowels of low pitch (back vowels) are unrounded.

The following combinations of tongue and lip positions are to be considered the normal ones:

> High vowels — narrow opening
> Mid vowels — middle opening
> Low vowels — large opening
> Front vowels — lips drawn
> Mixed vowels — lips neutral
> Back vowels — lips rounded

NOTE. Neither these lip positions, nor the normal tongue positions are absolute necessities within certain vowel ranges. They are merely the average, normal articulations. E.g., with some men the angle of the jaws hardly varies at all because they are in the habit of speaking with a pipe or a cigar between their teeth. Many people pronounce [o] farther back than [u] (compare palatograms, page 45), and some pronounce [e] with greater tongue elevation than [i]; in such cases various auxiliary tongue movements counterbalance these peculiarities. The following table represents the average articulation in German:

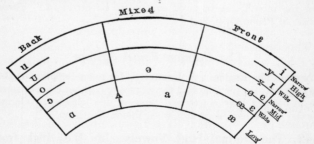

EXPLANATION. The place of the phonetic signs indicates the place of articulation, i.e., the point of the highest tongue elevation in the pronunciation of each vowel. The vowel diagrams on pp. 44, 45 will serve to elucidate further the varying shapes of the tongue. — In the diagram on p. 38, corresponding narrow and wide vowels are separated by short lines, thus indicating a lower articulation for the latter. But it should be remembered that in reality the actual tongue elevation for each set of vowels, e.g., for [u] and [ʊ], is practically the same, and only the median line of the tongue is depressed with wide vowels.

The following abbreviations are in common use:

h = high	f = front	n = narrow
m = mid	x = mixed	w = wide
l = low	b = back	r = round

These abbreviations, and the system on which they are based, were originated by the English phonetician Alexander Melville Bell. Notwithstanding severe criticism, the system is recognized as the most practical one by most of the leading phoneticians, e.g., Sievers and Sweet.

"It is absolutely indispensable that the student should familiarize himself entirely with these vowel articulations. 'Whispering' the vowels is a great help in analyzing their formation. After a time the student will be able to recognize each vowel solely by the muscular sensations associated with its formation: he will be able to say to himself, 'now my tongue is in the position for [u], now I have changed it into the [o] position,'[1] etc., while not uttering the slightest sound, confident that if whispered or voiced breath is allowed to pass thru the mouth, the required sound will be produced." (Sweet, *Primer of Phonetics*, p. 23.)

The German Vowel System

NOTE. The English vowel system is far more complicated than the German. In the following paragraphs only those English vowels are mentioned that correspond more or less closely to German vowels. For others, compare Sweet, Viëtor, Jespersen.

42. The Normal High Vowels hfn (i.e., high front narrow, unrounded) [i] and hbnr [u] are the German long

---

[1] Instances in quotation differ from original.

i and *u* vowels, as in *wie, nie, mir, ihn, du, Uhr, Huhn* = [viɪ, niɪ, miɪr, ʔiɪn, duɪ, ʔuɪr, huɪn].

The British vowels in *fee, too*, especially in London, are decided diphthongs, gliding from the wide vowels [ɪ] and [ʊ] to a very close, practically consonantal [i, j] and [u, w] — [fɪj, tʊw]. In the average American pronunciation, the diphthongal glide is much less marked, and the first element is narrower than in British: [fiɪ̆, tuŭ].

hfw [ɪ] and hbw [ʊ] are the sounds of short *i* and *u* in German, as in *bis, mit, muß, Mutter. (ie* is pronounced short — wide — in *vierzehn, vierzig*, often in *siebzehn, siebzig*, usually in *Viertel*, sometimes in *vielleicht.)* — English *i, u* in *pit, put* are the same sounds, perhaps slightly wider.

NOTE. In foreign words, unaccented *i* and *u* are rather short ('half-long'), but narrower than [ɪ, ʊ]: *Miliz, Brutus* = [miliɪts, bruɪtus].

43. The Normal Mid Vowels.

mfn [e] and mbnr [o] are the sounds of German long *e* and *o: See, legen, geht, so, logen, Moos* = [zeɪ, leɪgən, geɪt, zoɪ, loɪgən, moɪs]. The corresponding English vowels are still more diphthongal than the narrow high vowels, the glide being more marked in British than in American: British [seɪ, sɔu], American [seĭ, soŭ]. In teaching German, diphthongization of [eɪ] and [oɪ] must vigilantly be guarded against.

Long *ä, äh (gäbe, nähme)* is generally pronounced opener than [eɪ], nearly lfn, as in English *care*. Still, there is also good authority for using the same sound in *gäbe* and *gebe, nähme* and *nehme, Säle* and *Seele*, namely, mfn [eɪ]. In teaching German, this is decidedly to be recommended since it simplifies the treatment of the *e*-sounds to the one principle: regardless of the spellings *e* and *ä*, use the narrow pronunciation [eɪ] for the long vowel, the wide pronunciation [ɛ] for the short vowel.

Viëtor, *Aussprachewörterbuch*, p. ix, says: „Wer der ziemlich sicheren Entwicklung der Dinge vorauseilen will, mag für dieses auch in meinem Wörterbuche durchgeführte [eː] überall den geschlossenen Laut [eː] sprechen."

mfw [ɛ] and mbwr [ɔ] are the sounds of German short *e* (*ä*) and short *o* in *Bett, nett, stecken, behende, Hände, Nächte, Rock, Gott* [bɛt, nɛt, ʃtɛkən, bəhɛndə, hɛndə, nɛçtə, rɔk, gɔt]. — The teacher must constantly oppose the American tendency of pronouncing a low-back vowel (practically [ɑ]) instead of [ɔ].

NOTE. Many German dialects, especially in the South, are retaining more or less of the historical distinction between original (Germanic) *e*, which was wide, and the narrow 'Umlaut-*e*'; they distinguish [bet — nɛt], transitive [ʃtekŋ] from intransitive [ʃtɛkŋ], etc. Standard pronounciation does not accept this difference. Cf. II, 38.

44. The Low Vowels.

The mouth is wide open, while the tongue lies nearly flat, with a slight elevation not too far from the center: this is 'pure *a*' in German *da, Vater* — lx, according to Viëtor; Sievers, Bell, Sweet, Storm consider the normal German *a* a back vowel: lbn for the long sound, lbw for the short sound. — If the articulation takes place considerably farther back than the center, the sound resembles a very open *o* [ɔː], as in English *all* (this is slightly rounded, however: lbnr), and in Bavarian *Vater*. — If the tongue is slightly raised in front, we have 'clear *a*,' approaching in sound the vowel of *past, half* (Eastern American pronunciation); if the elevation takes place still more in front, we come to the short sound [æ] in English *hat*, lfw, and the long sound [æː] in the occasional (Austrian) pronunciation of *spät*. — The phonetic signs are: [ᴀ] for 'pure' or 'middle' *a*, [ɑ] or [a] for 'back' *a*, [a] for 'front' *a*, but in general practise the letter '*a*' is sufficient for all three varieties, at least in German.

Generally speaking, the South of Germany inclines more toward back articulation, the North toward front articulation (especially Hanover and Brunswick). Short *a* is usually slightly farther front than long *a* (according to Jespersen): South German [mʌn, vɑɪn], North German [man, vʌɪn].

NOTE. The vowel in English *father, art* is [ʌ]: [fʌːðə, ʌːt]; French makes a definite distinction between front *a* and back *a: madame, art* have [a], *pas, âme* have [ɑ].

45. The Rounded Front Vowels, hfnr [y], hfwr [ʏ], mfnr [ø], mfwr [œ] are the sounds of German long and short *ü*, long and short *ö: kühl, hübsch, Töne, können* = [kyːl, hʏɪpʃ, tøːnə, kœnən]. They can roughly be said to combine the tongue position of [i, ɪ, e, ɛ] with the lip positions of [u, ʊ, o, ɔ], but this statement describes rather the French vowels in *pur,* [y], *peu,* [ø], than the corresponding German sounds. With the latter, the tongue articulation is considerably lower, so that German *ü* approaches rounded [e], and German *ö* is nearly rounded [æ]. This is due to the fact that the energetic lip rounding that is necessary for the formation of [y, ʏ, ø, œ], under German habits of articulation, requires a wider jaw angle than the slit-shaped opening of the lips that is used with [i, ɪ, e, ɛ]. It is easy to convince oneself of this tendency by observing the lower teeth in a mirror when changing the lip-opening from slit to rounding.

In teaching these sounds to American pupils, it is better to treat [y, ʏ, ø, œ] strictly as rounded [i, ɪ, e, ɛ]. The tendencies of articulation in this respect being nearly identical in both languages, the necessary widening of the jaw angle will unconsciously accompany the rounding of the lips. — Have the pupils round their lips *first,* and *then* they should pronounce such words as *Kiel (kühl), Kissen (küssen), heben (höben), kennen (können).* — The teacher should strictly insist on energetic rounding of the lips.

46. **The Slurred Vowel,** mxw [ə], is used for German *e* in unaccented position: *Gerede* = [gəreːdə]. The tongue is slightly raised (nearly to middle position) towards the end of the hard palate; the muscles of the tongue, the lips, and the velum are relaxt; not infrequently, the slurred vowel has a nasal tinge on this account. The vocal chords, too, are not so tightly stretcht as with other voiced sounds, so that their vibrations are comparatively weak and indistinct ('Murmelstimme'). The tongue position varies in different parts of Germany; it is highest in Austria, lowest in and near Berlin, so that the sound approaches an [ɪ] in Vienna, but an [ʌ] in Berlin. In English, [ə] is, in general, pronounced farther back than in German; it is used not only for unaccented *e*, but also for unaccented *a, o, u,* etc.

The teacher should constantly insist on a clear pronunciation of unaccented [a, o, u] in German, in words like *Drama, Cato, Brutus;* American pupils are inclined to substitute [ə].

In the unaccented suffixes –*el* and –*en* (more rarely in –*er*) most Germans drop the [ə], pronouncing [handl̩, reːdn̩] instead of [handəl, reːdən]. It is of pedagogical value to insist on a distinct pronunciation, retaining the [ə], of these and all other unaccented syllables.

47. **The Nasal Vowels.** As to articulation, see **6.** Standard German possesses nasal vowels only in words borrowed from French: *Ballon, Comment, Teint, Verdun* should be pronounced with [õ, ã, ɛ̃, œ̃], as in French, not with the velar nasal stop; see **33,** Note. — In very familar words of old adoption, oral vowels are used: *Leutnant, Kapitän, Balkon* = [lɔytnant, kapiteːn, balkoːn]. — In many German dialects, nasal vowels are very common.

48. **The Diphthongs.** Diphthongs are combinations of two or more vowels in one syllable. German possesses only three diphthongs: *ai* = *ei, au,* and *äu* = *eu.* The first element of [ai] and [au] is generally back *a* ([ɑ]); their second elements are lower than the spelling indicates; in

TONGUE POSITIONS. Full lines indicate narrow vowels, dotted lines (except for [ʌ, a]), wide vowels.

PALATOGRAMS. Light shaded areas show the tongue contact of narrow, dark shaded areas, of wide vowels.

[ə], like [a], has no tongue contact.

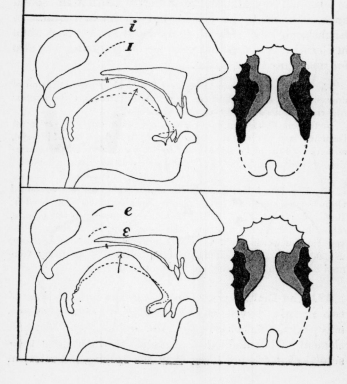

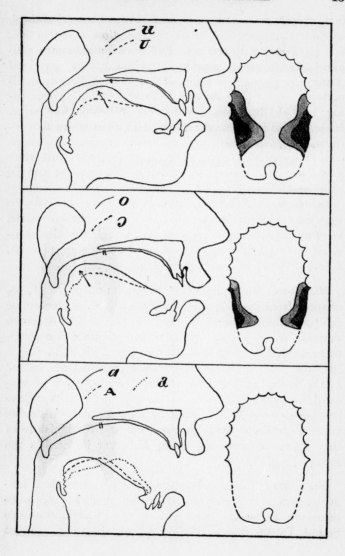

fact, they approach the articulation of a loose [e] and [o], so that an accurate phonetic transcription would be [ae, ao]; [kaezər, maen, haos]. — *äu = eu* varies greatly in pronunciation in different parts in Germany, but in general it may be defined as rounded [ɑi] or [ae], i.e., approximately, [ɔy] or [əø]: [hɔyzər, həøzər]. — The corresponding English diphthongs, occurring in words like *mine, house, oil*, differ from the German diphthongs in two respects: their first elements are longer (at least in American pronunciation) and articulated farther front; they may best be described as standing between [ʌ] and [ə] or [ɔ] and [ə]: [mʌ⅘· en, hʌ⅘· os, ⅘· el].

In practical phonetic spelling it is hardly necessary to take into account the fact that the second element of the German diphthongs is really a mid vowel; practical considerations speak rather in favor of the spellings [ai, au, ɔy] than the more exact spellings [ae, ao, əø].

49. Vowel Diagrams. The diagrams on pages 44, 45, adapted from Bremer, *Deutsche Phonetik*, show the tongue positions in the pronunciation of the typical German vowels. In each case, the left-hand diagram is a longitudinal section thru the mouth, the right-hand one a 'palatogram.' Palatograms (palate pictures) are gained in the following way: An artificial palate, made of vulcanite or metal, is adjusted in the mouth, after its surface has been covered with chalk or some similar substance; then, a certain vowel is pronounced, and the moisture of the tongue removes the chalk wherever it touches the artificial palate.

50. Sound Tables. For the purposes of modern language teaching, the most convenient sound tables published are those by Viëtor (Marburg, Elwert); Rausch's Sound Tables possess certain advantages, but are not well adapted for American schools because they represent strictly European English pronunciation. — For the teacher of German, the following sound table (from which [γ, ʀ, ʒ, ꜰ, *v*] and the signs for wide vowels have been omitted) may be found practical:

TABLE OF GERMAN SOUNDS

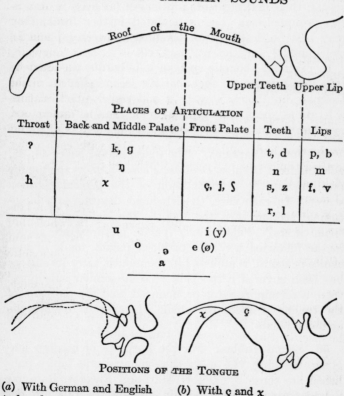

Roof of the Mouth

Upper Teeth   Upper Lip

PLACES OF ARTICULATION

Throat	Back and Middle Palate	Front Palate	Teeth	Lips
ʔ	k, g		t, d	p, b
	ŋ		n	m
ɦ	x	ç, j, ʃ	s, z	f, ᴠ
			r, l	

u   i (y)

o   ə   e (ø)

a

POSITIONS OF THE TONGUE

(a) With German and English
t, d, n, l, r (. . . . . . English)

(b) With ç and x
(= 'ich' and 'ach'-sounds)

CHAPTER III

Synthesis of German Sounds

51. Phonetic Basis and Phonetic Tendency. The habitual ways of producing and combining speech sounds constitute a group of habits for each language which is generally called its basis of articulation, or its organic or phonetic basis. Even by people without any phonetic training, it is felt as the dominant note of a language, impressing upon it its peculiar stamp: the clean-cut delicacy of French, the ever-youthful strength of German, the self-restrained calmness of English, the 'insinuating charm'[1] (Jespersen) of Russian. This can be understood only when we realize that the individual habits of sound production and combination harmonize with each other in their typical characteristics to such an extent that they yield, as it were, an acoustic unit — one chord composed of many single elements.

Within certain limits, this acoustic dominant of a language is a permanent quality pervading its whole life and governing its historical changes. As such, the sum of these habits of articulation may be called the phonetic tendency of a language. The phonetic basis is the static, descriptive aspect of the acoustic character of a language, the phonetic tendency its dynamic, historical aspect.

The phonetic tendency (or, tendencies) of German will be discussed in the historical part of this book.

52. The Phonetic Basis of the German Language is characterized by an inclination towards extremes in re-

[1] Jespersen, *Growth and Structure of the English Language*, p. 3.

gard to expiration, muscle tension and, in a measure, the place of articulation. The great contrasts in the strength of expiration and the tension of the vocal chords (see **56**) cause sharp distinctions between accented and unaccented syllables — somewhat more so than in English, and much more so than in the Romance and Slavic languages. For related reasons, the difference between long and short vowels is greater than in most other languages. The tongue and the lips articulate much more energetically than in English. The muscles of the tongue are, in general, inclined to be tense, a fact which largely prevents the rill formation so common in Romance and Slavic tongues (cf. Lat. *natio* > French *nation* = [nɑːtjoː > nasjɔ̃ː]). The energetic expiration makes the language rather averse to a distinct voicing of consonants.

Similar contrasts, although to a minor extent, appear in regard to the places of articulation. While the dentals are formed far in front (tho they are not as strictly 'dentals' as in French), [χ, γ] are formed far back in the mouth. The vowels differ from each other more distinctly than in English, the distances being greater both between high and low vowels (wider jaw angle) and between front and back vowels.

The practical needs of German instruction necessitate an insistence on the following elements of the German phonetic basis:

(1) The fronting of dentals, (2) great contrasts between vowels in regard to quantity, quality and accent, (3) tenseness of the tongue, especially in the pronunciation of [ç] and [χ], (4) energetic lip-rounding in the production of the sounds [u, y, o, ø].

At least during the first year of the German course, each recitation should begin with a 'gymnastic drill' in phonetics in order to produce the German phonetic basis.

This drill — lasting not more than one or two minutes — should be suggested by such commands as 'Zunge an die Zähne,' 'Vokal-Dreieck,' 'ich und ach,' 'Lippen rund' and practised by a small number of suitable instances.

53. Assimilation is the influence that neighboring sounds exert upon each other. It is common in all languages, but apparently less so in German than in most others.

Lip articulations have little, if any, influence on surrounding vowels in German. Possibly, they sometimes cause a rounding of front vowels in words like *schwören*, *zwölf*, for older *sweren*, *zwelf*, but it is more likely that this vowel change is primarily due to the tongue position (see below). As to the change of *n* to *m*, see velum articulations, below.

Tongue articulations seldom cause vowel assimilations except in the case of *r*: the necessity of considerable free space for the trilling of the tongue tip is apt to lower high and mid vowels: *mir, wer, Ohr* = [mɪɪr, vɛɪr, ʔɔɪr]. — It is not necessary to indicate this assimilation in phonetic spelling. — Consonants, too, are but little influenced by the tongue articulation of surrounding sounds; the most noteworthy case is the difference between [ç] and [x], [ç] being the historical development, by assimilation, of [x] after front vowels (see **29**); the same assimilation, of course, is found in the pronunciation of the corresponding voiced spirants [j, γ] in words like [liːjən, laːγən], while the stops [k, g] are much less subject to assimilation (**32**).

The rounded front vowels in such words as *Löffel*, *schwören, zwölf, lügen*, where the older language had unrounded vowels (**II, 39,** 3), are probably due in the first place to the elevation of the back of the tongue in the (older) pronunciation of *l, w*, which brought about the rounding of the lips habitually connected with that articulation (41).

[s] before [ʃ] is generally assimilated, at least in colloquial pronunciation: *ausschließen*, *'rausschmeißen*, *Hausschlüssel* = [ʔauʃliːsn̩, rauʃmɑesn̩, hauʃlysl̩].

Lowering of the velum is frequently, in colloquial speech even regularly, transferred to the preceding (in English also to the following) vowel, 'nasalizing' it (6): *hin, kann, ohne, gähnen* = [hĩːn, kãn, ʔõːnə, gɛ̃ːnən] (but *gehen*, with elision of the unaccented *e* appearing in NHG. spelling, usually = [geːn], without nasalization). The stage pronunciation forbids such nasalization, but this standard can hardly be observed consistently, although it is certainly worth while for the teacher to counteract the tendency towards nasalization, which is especially strong with American students.

Nasalization is due to an inaccurate synchronizing of the articulations of the velum and the tongue, the lowering of the velum usually lasting longer than an exact articulation of the individual sounds would require. On the other hand, the nasal consonants are especially apt to adopt the tongue or lip articulations of surrounding consonants. Therefore, [g] after and before [n] becomes [ŋ], as in [laŋ] (standardized pronunciation) and [leiŋ] (colloquial pronunciation), and [b] after and before [m] is changed to [m], as in [lam], from older [lamb], and colloquial [leim, siːm] as the final result of a transition from [leibən, siːbən] to [leibm̩, siːbm̩]. The change of the place of articulation in the case of nasals is shown by the latter instances, and by words like *legen, merken, Ankunft* = [leiŋ, mɛrkn̩, ʔaŋkumft]; in many words we find mutual assimilation, as in [leim, laŋ], where the oral sound is nasalized, while the nasal sound changes its place of articulation. — Explain [ʔampman, neibm̩bai, ʔɛmpfaŋən].

Assimilation of the *Glottis position* appears in the change
from [s] to [z], between vowels, as in [roːzə]. — Voiced
stops become voiceless before voiceless consonants: [gaːpst,
gaːpt] ([gaːb̥st, gaːb̥t]) (14). — Usually, initial voiced stops
are voiceless, when a closely connected preceding word
or syllable (especially an article or prefix) ends with a
voiceless consonant: [dər baχ — das b̥uːχ, bədɛŋkən,
ʔausd̥ɛŋkən, ʔɛntɛkən].

54. Syllables. Speech sounds are grouped in words
and syllables. The term 'word' has no meaning in
phonetics — a word is a grammatical, logical and psychological structure. The phonetic unit is the *syllable*.
An entirely adequate definition of this term has not been
given as yet; the following description covers it approximately: A syllable is a phonetic unit which is determined
by a relative maximum of sonorousness, and separated
from each surrounding unit by a relative minimum of
sonorousness. — The term 'sonorous' has been explained
in section **25**; a voiced sound is sonorous in direct proportion to the free space in the mouth cavity in which
the air vibrates. Therefore, the sonorousness of voiced
sounds shows the following gradation: low vowels (greatest), mid vowels, high vowels, 'sonorous sounds' proper,
nasals, voiced spirants, voiced stops (least); voiceless
sounds, strictly speaking, do not possess any sonority at
all, but the element of time makes spirants more force-
ful, as far as their position in a syllable is concerned,
than stops. The most natural and frequent element of
highest sonority in a syllable is a vowel; choosing, arbitrarily, the figures 9 to 1 for the nine classes of sounds
arranged above according to their sonority, we could accept the following equations: [ta, tan, tanə] = 1:9, 1:9:5,
1:9:5:(8). The figure 5, in the last of these expressions,

represents a relative minimum, and, therefore, the beginning of a new syllable. Jespersen uses the following
diagram to indicate the differences of sonority (the arrangement of figures differs slightly in detail but not in
principle):

„Ich mache hier den Versuch, die Sonoritätsverhältnisse bei einer
Reihe von Lautverbindungen, den Worten: *sprengst, Tante, Atten-
tat,*[1] *keine,* graphisch darzustellen:

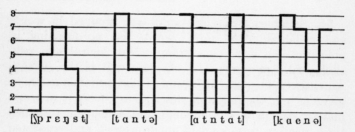

[Spreŋst]　　[tantə]　　[atntat]　　[kaenə]

¹ Ohne Vokal zwischen *t* und *n,* die Zunge in derselben Stellung
vom ersten *t* durch *n* zu *t.*" (*Elementarbuch,* S. 146.)

We see from these instances that [n] assumes a different position in different words. In [kaenə] — 1:9:8:5:
(8), — it is a relative minimum, beginning a new syllable;
in [ʔatntaɪt] — 1:9:1:5:1:9:1, — it is a relative maximum, of the same syllabic value as a vowel; and in [tantə]
— 1:9:5:1: (8), — it marks the transition from the maximum to the minimum of sonority in the same way as
does [e] in [kaenə] — 1:9:8:5:(8). Its function in the
word [ʔatntaɪt] is often called 'vocalic,' but should rather
be called 'syllabic.' The liquids and nasals are frequently
found in syllabic function — compare words like German
[handl̩tə], English [midl̩mæn], Czech *čtvrtku* = [tʃvr̩tku].
Even a voiceless spirant may now and then have syllabic
function, e.g., in interjections like [pst].

NOTE. Where it is necessary to indicate syllabic function — which is rarely the case — this book does so by a dot below the letter, as above. Philological works generally use a small circle, but in a book combining phonetics and historical grammar, this would be confusing since the same diacritic mark indicates the voiceless pronunciation of sounds that are usually voiced (see 14, 15, 18, etc.).

If we call [e] in [kɑenə] a 'diphthongal element' — namely, an element of transition from a sonorous maximum to a sonorous minimum, the same term must be admissible, and, as a matter of fact, is used in philology, for [n] in [tantə], [r] in [vɛrfən], [l] in [hɛlfən]. Compare II, 17.

55. Quantity. German consonants are practically always short, at least in comparison with English consonants. This must be observed especially strictly in the case of final *m, n, ng, l, r*, which in English are long after short vowels. The teacher must insist on short final consonants (and short vowels) in words like *Kamm, kann, lang, soll, Herr*.

The quantity of German vowels underwent a radical change at the end of the Middle High German period (II, 41), and is, to a certain extent, still changing. It is not yet possible to formulate definite rules, but the general tendency is this, that vowels are long if they are accented, and followed by not more than one consonant. The details are of a strictly orthoepic character (see 1), and Viëtor's *Aussprachewörterbuch* should be referred to in all doubtful cases.

56. Stress. The linguistic factor generally termed 'accent' can be of a twofold character: we distinguish *musical accent* or pitch, and *dynamic accent* or stress. Stress and pitch are not diametrically opposed to each other, but merely indicate a predominance of one of two elements, namely, of an increased tension of the vocal chords, and of an increased force of expiration. An 'accented' syllable is, generally speaking, not only higher in pitch — on account of the tension of the vocal chords, — but also stronger in force, on account of a greater activity of the lungs. In the Romance and most of the Slavic languages, the prevailing element is pitch, in the Germanic languages, in general, stress — in German decidedly so.

German stress is considerably stronger than English stress and must be practised as such. American students are frequently inclined to use a rather strong secondary stress in the third syllables of such words as *wanderte*, *Lehrerin*, *Lehrerinnen*. This must be counteracted by suitable imitative exercises.

The place of accent in German, and in those English words that are of Saxon origin, is fixed according to logical principles, i.e., the most important syllable of the word, from the standpoint of meaning, is strest. In general, this is the first syllable. The apparent exception concerning inseparable prefixes is well-known (*vernehmen : aufnehmen*).

57. Pitch. In standard German, the syllable of greatest stress in a word is almost always also marked by the highest pitch. Dialects show considerable variation from this principle. — The physiological cause of higher or lower pitch is the greater or lesser tension of the vocal chords, and this difference appears not only in single words, but in the 'intonation' of the whole sentence as well. While, on the whole, American English and German intonation do not differ very materially, the difference is considerable enough to deserve special attention on the part of the teacher of German. Rules of any kind are of little avail in this respect, but expressive reading on the part of the teacher, and conscious, careful repetition, sentence by sentence, by the pupil, will soon bear fruit.

The best information concerning orthoepic details of stress and pitch is found in Hempl's *German Orthography and Phonology*, a book which is strongly recommended to all teachers of German.

CHAPTER IV

Phonetic Transcriptions

58. Standard German. Energetic efforts towards the adoption of a uniform standard of German pronunciation — supplanting, in a measure, the various dialect forms used even by the educated classes — are of comparatively recent date. A final result has not been reached as yet by any means, but the principle which has found the most general recognition is the one stated by Wilhelm Viëtor, that the 'best' pronunciation should betray as little local coloring as possible. There is no part or region of Germany where 'the best German' is spoken. — The historical basis of what may be called standard German is described in the second part of this book. Aside from the historical moments discussed there, an apparently unessential, external element has lately exerted considerable influence, namely, the uniformity of spelling. Especially Wilhelm Braune (*Über die Einigung der deutschen Aussprache*, Heidelberg, 1904) maintains that the existence of uniform orthography thruout the territory of the German language is recognized by many speakers as a determining factor in doubtful questions of pronunciation — *so schreibt man's, also spricht man's so aus.* This has been true, for instance, with regard to the recent development of the pronunciation of medial and final *g*, as characterized by Braune in the article mentioned.

An agreement of great importance was reached in 1898 by the *Deutsche Bühnenkonferenz* in Berlin, where representatives of German linguistic science and of the German stage establisht a preliminary standard of pronunciation for the needs of the stage. This agreement was publisht by Siebs, *Deutsche Bühnenaussprache* (with a phonetic introduction by Sievers). — Of equal importance was the publication of Viëtor's *Deutsches Aussprachewörterbuch*, which, on the authority of best usage, states the present standard of German pronunciation in a conservative and careful manner. No teacher should be without this reliable guide.

59. The Alphabet of the International Phonetic Association. It is clear beyond any argument that, due to the gross imperfection of the common spelling of nearly all languages, a phonetic transcription is an unavoidable necessity for the student of phonetics, and an invaluable advantage for the learner of a foreign language. A phonetic transcription is, generally speaking, such a graphic representation of the sounds of a language, in which every sound is always expressed by the same sign, and every sign always denotes the same sound. — Among the great number of transcriptions devised for this purpose, the alphabet of the *Association Phonétique Internationale des enseigneurs des langues modernes*[1] easily deserves the first place. It is represented chiefly by the *Maître phonétique*, a monthly publication printed in different languages, but entirely in phonetic transcription.

This system (with a few very slight modifications[2]) has been used in the preceding paragraphs of this book. The following connected text is taken from Viëtor's *Lesebuch in Lautschrift:*

[1] Progressive language teachers are advised to become members of this organization; they can do so by applying to M. Paul Passy, Bourg-la-Reine, France. Annual dues, including subscription for the Maître Phonétique, $1.

[2] Chiefly in the use of [g:g] and [x].

dərnrøːsçən.

foːr ˈtsaitən | vaːr ain ˈkøːnɪ⁽ᵏ⁾/ç | (ˀ)ʊnt ainə ˈkøːnɪɡ/ᵢm, ‖diː ˈʃpraːxən | ˈjeːdən | ˈtaː ᵏ/ₓː ‖ „ˀax, | vɛn viːr dɔx ain ˈkɪnt hɛtən!“ ‖ ˀʊnt ˈkriːᵏ/çtən | ˀɪmər kains. ‖ da truːᵏ/ₓ zɪç ˈtsuː, ‖ ˀals di ˈkøːnɪɡ/ᵢm | (ˀ)ainmaːl ɪm ˈbaːdə zaːs, ‖ das ain ˈfrɔʃ | (ˀ)aus dəm ˈvasər | (ˀ)ans ˈlant krɔx | (ˀ)ʊnt tsu iːr ˈʃpraːx: ‖ „dain ˈvʊnʃ | vɪrt ɛrˈfʏlt veːrdən; ‖ ˀeːə ain ˈjaːr fɛrgeːt, | vɪrst du ainə ˈtɔxtər tsʊr vɛlt brɪŋən.“ ‖ vas dər frɔʃ gəˈzaː ᵏ/ₓt hatə, | das gəˈʃaː, ‖ ˀʊnt di ˈkøːnɪɡ/ᵢm | gəbaːr ain ˈmɛːtçən, ‖ das vaːr zo ˈʃøːn, | das dər ˈkøːnɪ⁽ᵏ⁾/ç | foːr ˈfrɔydə | zɪç nɪçt tsu ˈlasən vʊstə | (ˀ)ʊnt ain ˈgroːsəs | ˈfɛst ˀanʃtɛltə. ‖ ˀɛr ˈlaːdətə | ˈnɪçt bloːs | zainə fɛrˈvantə, | ˈfrɔyndə | (ˀ)ʊnt bəˈkantə, | zɔndərn ˀaux di ˈvaizən | ˈfrauən datsu ˀain, ‖ damɪt zi dəm ˈkɪnt | ˈhɔlt | (ˀ)ʊnt gəˈvoː ɡ/gən vɛːrən. ‖ ˀɛs ˈvaːrən | iːrər ˈdraitseːn | (ˀ)m zainəm ˈraiçə; ‖ vail ɛr ˀaːbər nuːr ˈtsvølf | ˈgɔldənə | ˈtɛlər hatə, | fɔn vɛlçən zi ˈˀɛsən zɔltən, ‖ zo mʊstə ˈˀainə fɔn iːnən | daˈhaim blaibən.

The needs of the teacher of German in American schools permit certain simplifications of this system, and make certain minor changes advisable. The simplifications consist chiefly in a lessened emphasis on those points where the phonetic tendencies of German and American English are nearly, or quite, identical; the indication of stress and pitch may be reduced to the traditional minimum of common punctuation, and the use of the accent sign only in apparently (from the learner's standpoint) anomalous cases; the difference between narrow and wide vowels need not be indicated, since it is, as far as the needs of the classroom are concerned, coincident with the difference between long and short vowels. — The following changes are recommended: to replace the sign [x] by

Greek χ, in order to avoid confusion with [ks]; the distinction between narrow and wide vowels[1] and between [g, g] is to be abolisht, the common lower-case sign being used in either case; the accent is to be indicated by the use of heavy type for the accented vowel where necessary. (The Phonetic Association indicates it by placing the accent mark *in front* of the stressed syllable; while this is, theoretically, entirely correct, it is confusing for students who, unfortunately, are used to the illogical principle followed in most dictionaries, of placing it *behind* the accented vowel). Accordingly, the text given above, would read as follows in "simplified phonetic spelling":

dornrøɪsçən

foɪr tsaitən vaɪr ain køːniç/k ˀunt ainə køːnigin, diɪ ʃpraːχən jeːdən taːk: „ˀaχ, ven viːr doχ ain kint hetən!" ˀunt kriːktən ˀimər kains. da truːk ziç tsuɪ, ˀals di køː-nigin ˀainmaːl im baːdə zaːs, das ain froʃ ˀaus dəm vasər ˀans lant kroχ ˀunt tsu iːr ʃpraːχ: „dain vunʃ virt erfylt veɪrdən; ˀeɪə ain jaɪr fərgeɪt, virst du ainə toχtər tsur velt briŋən." vas dər froʃ gəzaːkt hatə, das gəʃaɪ, ˀunt di køːnigin gəbaɪr ˀain meɪtçən, das vaɪr zo ʃøːn, das dər køːniç foɪr froydə ziç niçt tsu lasən vustə ˀunt ain groɪsəs fest ˀanʃteltə. ˀer laːdətə niçt bloɪs zainə fərvantə, froyn-də ˀunt bəkantə, zondərn ˀauχ di vaizən frauən datsu ˀain, damit zi dəm kint holt ˀunt gəvoɪgən veɪrən. ˀes vaɪrən ˀiɪrər draitseːn ˀin zainəm raiçə; vail er ˀaɪbər nuɪr tsvølf goldənə telər hatə, fon velçən zi ˀesən zoltən, zo mustə ˀainə fon ˀiːnən dahaim blaibən.

The following (taken from Meyer's *Deutsche Gesprä-che*, Leipzig, Reisland, 1906) is a sample of educated North-German pronunciation, with the retention of all those North-German peculiarities which are rejected by

[1] [ɑ, ʌ, a] are not distinguished by Viëtor either.

the stage pronunciation. While some teachers are still inclined to give it the preference over the standard set up in that agreement and in Viëtor's *Aussprachewörterbuch*, it is the author's firm conviction that it has no place in American schools.

fo·rijəs 'jɑːr hat zi miɪ das lɛtstə‾,maːl jə,ʃriˑbm. — 'næːçstə vɔxə fɑˑɾn zi nax ,pɔtsdam, nɪçt 'diːzə. — ʔalzo ,næˑçstn 'zɔn- ɑːbmt ['zamstax], abɪ 'kɔmm zi 'jɑː !

den ,tax foɪ'heːɪ vɑr eɪ nɔx ,gants jə'zunt. — vas man 'glaeç tuˑn kan, ,zɔl man nɪçt ɑof d(ə)n næˑçstn 'tax fɪʃiˑbm. — eɪ kɔmt den 'tax foɪ ,ʔoːstɪn [am ʃtɪln 'zɔnɑˑbmt, ,ʔoːstɪn haeljən 'ʔɑːbmt] 'ʔan unt raest am 'tsvaetn ʔoˑstɪ- tax [,ʔoˑstɪn tsvaet 'faeɪtax] vidɪ 'ʔap.

viɪ bəkɔmm unzrə ,tsaetuŋ alə 'tɑːgə [— jeˑdn ,tsvaetn 'tax]. — deɪ 'briˑftræˑjɪ kɔmt (tæˑçlɪç) tsvae'maːl, fryˑ 'mɔrjns unt nax'mɪtaxs tsvɪʃn ,tsvae unt 'drae.

vɛn jeˑmant 'tsuː miɪ kɔmm zɔltə, dan 'zɑːgn ziˑ im nuˑɪ, ɪç væˑɪ m ˶aenɪ halbm 'ʃtundə vidɪ 'dɑː. — ,hɔɪt ybɪ axt 'tɑːgə bɪn ɪç ,hɔfntlɪç mɪt maenɪ ʔarbaet 'fɛrtɪç. — eɪ ɪst zaet ,fɪrtseˑn tɑˑgn 'fɔrt. — foɪ tsvae 'ʃtundn ɪst eɪ 'ʔaosjəgaŋŋ. —,'zɑːg mɑˑl ,karl, voˑ'vɑˑrst du foɪ axt ,tɑˑgn um diˑzə‾,tsaet?

60. Jespersen's Analphabetic System. The system of the Phonetic Association is 'alphabetic' in so far as it sets up a definite, conventional 'letter' for each sound, i.e., a symbolic sign, the shape of which, however, has no connection with the production or the acoustic impression of the sound it symbolizes. The ingenious system called 'Visible Speech' (invented by Alexander Melville Bell, and brought to perfection by Henry Sweet — compare especially his *Primer of Phonetics*) — is also 'alphabetic,' but each sign is cleverly made up of single elements symbolizing the phonetic character of the sound it represents. — Technical difficulties are in the way of reproducing this interesting system in these pages.

The Danish phonetician Jespersen has devised a strictly 'analphabetic' system of phonetic transcription, which every student of phonetics should master since it furnishes an admirable test of his ability to analyze both familiar and new speech sounds. It is called analphabetic because the individual sounds are not expressed by conventional letters, but by formulas minutely representing nearly every detail of their production. The articulating organs are expressed by the first six letters of the Greek alphabet: α lips, β tip of the tongue, γ surface of the tongue, δ velum, ϵ vocal chords, (ζ expiratory organs). Arabic figures denote the shape and size of the opening thru which the air is expelled: 0 stop, 1 rill, 2 slit, (ϵ1 stands for voice, ϵ2 for narrowed, ϵ3 for wide glottis), and the higher figures larger openings, 3, 5, 7 denoting rounding of the lips, or tenseness of the tongue,[1] while 4, 6, 8 indicate slit-shaped (neutral) lip-opening or relaxation of the tongue surface; intermediate positions are expressed by 1 2, 2 3, etc. (read one—two, two—three, etc., not twelve, twenty-three). Latin letters denote the place of articulation, in the way indicated in the diagram on page 63.

The letters are to suggest 'meridian lines,' as it were, so that 'a' indicates protruded, 'b' neutral, and 'c' drawn

[1] As stated in the note to 40, the author differs with Jespersen on this point; he uses the figures 4, 6, 8 for the narrow vowels, and 5, 7, 9 for the wide vowels, reserving 3 for intermediate sounds like English [j]; e.g., he designates [i] by γ 4, while J. uses γ 3.

lips. 'ab' means: between a and b, but nearer to **a**; 'ba': between a and b, but nearer to b; 'a.b': in the exact center between a and b. — I stands for lateral opening, R for trilling, V for the resonance chamber characteristic of [ʃ, ʒ]; ,, denotes relative inactivity; . . means: articulation of preceding sound continues.

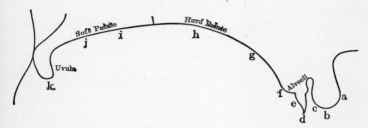

For instance: [b] = α0a, b, c — β,, — γ,, — δ0 — ε1 means: [b] is a sound of the following description: the lips are closed, and are either protruded, neutral, or withdrawn, according to the character of the following sound; the point and back of the tongue are at rest; the velum is raised; the vocal chords vibrate. (The index letters, a, b, c, etc., are usually placed above the line, but this is hardly necessary.)

The system is, of course, not intended for the transcription of whole texts, but single words may advantageously be transcribed in the following way:

	d	iː	d	ə	ɣ	t	ʃ	ə	ʃ	p	r	aː	χ	ə
α	,,	4c	57ba	..	5a	..	..	,,	57ba	0ba	,,	8b	,,	,,
β	0ef	e	0ef	fg	e	0ef	1fg	fe	1fg	,,	Rf	fe	..	..
γ	,,	4g	,,	7ji	75gh	,,	V	56h	V	,,	,,	8hi	2i	56h
δ	0	..	..	..	..	..	..	01	0	..	..	..	..	01
ε	1	..	..	..	..	3	3	13	3	..	1	1	3	13

APPENDIX

A. BIBLIOGRAPHY

The General Principles of the formation of sounds can best be understood with the help of

KLINGHARDT, *Artikulations- und Hörübungen*, Cöthen 1897.

Further training in the same direction, but on a more technical, scientific basis, is to be gained thru

BREMER, *Deutsche Phonetik*, Leipzig 1893.

A broader scope of the whole field of sound physiology is offered in the foremost standard book on phonetics,

SIEVERS, *Grundzüge der Phonetik* [5], Leipzig 1901.

Similar principles on a smaller scale are carried out in

PASSY, *Petite Phonétique comparée des langues européennes*, Leipzig 1906;

TRAUTMANN, *Kleine Lautlehre des Deutschen, Französischen und Englischen*, Bonn 1903, and

SWEET, *Primer of Phonetics* [3], Oxford 1906.

(This booklet is especially noteworthy on account of its introduction to "Visible Speech.")

A clear, concise survey of general phonetics is contained in the phonetic part of

BLOOMFIELD, *The Study of Language*, New York 1914.

Mooted questions are discussed mainly in

STORM, *Englische Philologie*, I, Leipzig 1892;

JESPERSEN, *Phonetische Grundfragen*, Leipzig 1904, and

VIËTOR, *Elemente der Phonetik* [5], Leipzig 1904 (containing, at the same time, an abundance of orthoepic material and the greatest number of examples offered in any book on phonetics).

SÜTTERLIN, *Lautbildung*, Leipzig 1908, is especially valuable as a first introduction to the elements of experimental phonetics.

GRANDGENT, *German and English Sounds*, Boston 1892, characterizes in a clear and reliable way the most essential differences between American English and German articulation.

The Teacher of modern languages will find the following books especially well adapted to his purposes:

JESPERSEN, *Lehrbuch der Phonetik*, Leipzig 1904, on the whole, the best pedagogical presentation of modern language phonetics. An abbreviated edition of this book is:

JESPERSEN, *Elementarbuch der Phonetik*, Leipzig 1912.

RIPPMANN-VIËTOR, *Elements of Phonetics*, London 1906, is far more than it modestly professes to be, namely, a translation of Viëtor's Kleine Phonetik. It is an exceedingly clever adaptation of Viëtor's book to the needs of modern language teachers — in certain points even superior to Jespersen's Lehrbuch.

HEMPL, *German Orthography and Phonology*, Boston 1891, is indispensable for the understanding of the development of German print, script and orthography, and very helpful on many points of orthoepics.

For the orthoepic side of phonetics, the following books deserve recommendation:

VIËTOR, *Deutsches Aussprachewörterbuch*, Leipzig 1912 — absolutely indispensable to the teacher of German, as indispensable as a German-English dictionary, or a German grammar.

VIËTOR, *Deutsches Lesebuch in Lautschrift* — extremely valuable for those teachers who feel the need of improving their own pronunciation of German.

SIEBS, *Deutsche Bühnenaussprache* [10], Bonn 1912. This book states briefly the results of the Bühnenkonferenz of 1898, has an excellent phonetic introduction by Sievers, and a fairly complete index of words.

LUICK, *Deutsche Lautlehre*, Wien 1904, is a splendid book on phonetics in every respect, but its most characteristic feature is the presentation of the South-German attitude towards the stage pronunciation.

Braune, *Über die Einigung der deutschen Aussprache*, Halle 1905, is an interesting discussion of the basis and the probable future of a uniform German pronunciation.

The most important **journals** are:

Maître Phonétique, Organe de l'association phonétique des professeurs de langues vivantes, Bourg-la-Reine 1886 ff.

Die Neueren Sprachen, Marburg 1894 ff, continuation of Phonetische Studien, Marburg 1887–93 (the most important publication for general questions of modern language teaching).

B. EXERCISES

The following kinds of exercises are recommended:

Reading — with practise of different kinds of pronunciation, e.g., bilabial and labio-dental v, voiced stops and voiceless lenes, stop and spirant for the letter g.

Phonetic script, in transcription and dictation.

Phonetic analysis of spoken sounds and words, both in sentences and by means of Jespersen's system.

Sketches of articulation thru self-observation and measurements, compare pages 6, 8, 9, 10, 11, 15, 37, 46.

Material for Practise

Labials. Ein paar Bauern blieben dort und bewachten den Dieb. — Die Abgaben waren wirklich schwer. — Es schmerzt mich, daß wir viel Liebe an unwürdige Wesen verschwenden. — Die Quelle ist zwar im Walde, aber der Bach läuft quer über die Wiese. — Glaubt mir, euer Lob ist mir nicht lieb; laßt lieber ab! — Der Knappe schwang sich auf den schweren Rappen und sprengte im Galopp davon. — Wir Wiener Waschweiber würden wohl weiße Wäsche waschen, wenn wir wüßten, wo weiches, warmes Wasser wäre. — (*French;* Poisson sans boisson est poison.)

Dentals. Dieser Turm steht seit dreihundert Jahren. — Niemand errät es; das Rätsel ist unlösbar. — Lesen Sie gleich den Zettel, sonst könnten Sie die Sache vielleicht vergessen. — Er bat den Arzt um ein kaltes Bad. — Sei treu und grad in Rat und Tat. — Hoffen und Harren macht manchen zum Narren. — Die Herren werden sich wahrlich nicht daran kehren. — Es irrt der Mensch, so lang er strebt. — Meßwechsel, Wachsmaske. — (*French:* Ton thé t'a-t-il ôté ta toux?)

[ʃ], [ç] *and* [χ]. Das Rauschen des Baches machte mich jede Nacht wach. — Die Rache des Rechts wird dich doch noch erreichen. — Jetzt verstehe ich erst, daß ihr sicher recht habt. — Was nützt euch all die Macht und Pracht! — Rechts vom Rande des Fuchslochs erhaschten die Jäger den Dachs. — Der Kottbuser Postkutscher putzt den Kottbuser Postkutschkasten.

Velars. Tag für Tag ging das gute Kind in den Garten, um Gemüse zu jäten. — Ein solches Ding mag vierzig bis fünfzig Pfennig kosten. — Er ist ein Mann in den Dreißigern — kann sein, daß er nahe an vierzig ist. — Wer nicht wagt, der siegt nicht. — Ohne Wagen kein Siegen.

PART TWO

HISTORY OF THE GERMAN LANGUAGE

I. EXTERNAL HISTORY

1. The Indo-European Languages. German belongs to the Germanic or Teutonic group of the Indo-European languages. The term 'Indo-European' is generally used by English, French, and Scandinavian philologists; in German works, the term *indogermanisch* prevails. The term *Aryan*, which is still found to some extent in historical, archeological, and anthropological works, applies in linguistics only to the Indo-Iranian branch of the Indo-European languages.

NOTE. None of these terms is wholly satisfactory. 'Indo-European' is an illogical compound, combining the name of an individual language and the name of a continent, which does not even entirely belong to this group of languages. 'Indo-Germanic' is intended to refer to the most Eastern and the most Western branch of the group, but fails to take Celtic into account, which is farther west than Germanic (aside from Iceland). The term 'Indo-Celtic' has been suggested, but has not found favor. The application of the term 'Aryan' to the whole group is due to the misconception that the original home of the Indo-Europeans had to be sought somewhere in India or Persia.

The following languages, or groups of languages, belong to the Indo-European family:

A. In Asia: (1) *Indo-Iranian,* i.e., Indic and Iranian; the most important branch of Indic is Sanscrit, the sacred language of Brahmanism; in its oldest form, Vedic, it dates back to the beginning of the second millennium B.C. — The chief representatives of Iranian are Old Persian (preserved in inscriptions relating to the deeds of Persian kings) and Avestan, the language in which religious works connected with the name of the prophet Zoroaster (Zarathushtra) are written.

(2) *Armenian*, the language of the mountainous regions to the northwest of Persia.

B. In Europe: (3) *Balto-Slavic*, i.e., the Baltic languages (Lithuanian, Lettish, Old Prussian, along the southeastern coast of the Baltic Sea) and the Slavic languages (Russian, Polish, Bohemian, Servian, Bulgarian, etc.).

(4) *Albanian*, spoken in the middle western part of the Balkan peninsula.

(5) *Greek*, with its numerous dialects, of which Doric, Attic, Ionic and Aeolic are the most important.

(6) *Italic;* aside from Latin, which is continued in the Romance languages (Italian, French, Spanish, Portuguese, Rumanian, etc.), the most important Italic languages were Umbrian (spoken by the Volsci, etc.) and Oscan (spoken, among others, by the Samnites and the inhabitants of Pompeii).

(7) *Keltic (Celtic)*, which formerly occupied most of Western Europe (France, parts of Spain, Western and Northern Germany, and the British Isles), but is now extinct with the exception of (Gaelic-)Irish, Welsh, Breton, and Manx.

(8) *Germanic*.

NOTE. The most important non-Indo-European languages of Europe are: Finnish and Magyar (Hungarian), both belonging to the Finno-Ugrian group; Turkish, one of the languages of the Ural-Altaic family, to which also the Finno-Ugrian group belongs; Bask and the extinct language of the Etruscans, both of which are of unknown origin.

2. The Home of the Indo-Europeans. It is probable, indeed almost certain, that in a remote time the Indo-Europeans formed a more or less homogeneous race. The home of this race was formerly sought in Asia (India, Pamir Plateau, etc.), but at present an overwhelming majority of the scholars who are attempting to solve the problem consider Asia as out of the question. Strong arguments have been advanced (especially by Much, *Die Urheimat der Indogermanen*, Jena 1901, and Hirt, *Die Indogermanen*, Strassburg 1904–5) for the assumption that the Indo-European home was in the 'Baltic Basin,' i.e., the countries adjacent to the western part of the Baltic Sea: Northeastern Germany, Denmark, and Southern Scandinavia. Aside from a great number of archeological and historical facts, the evidence of the linguistic development is so decidedly in favor of this theory, that its acceptance as a 'working hypothesis' is amply justified.

3. The Germanic Languages. For thousands of years before the beginning of our era, an expansion of Indo-European tribes over the greater part of Europe and over Western Asia had been in progress. These tribes mingled with the native populations of their new homes, and in consequence of this changed their racial and linguistic characteristics to a greater or lesser extent. The Indo-Iranian group was undoubtedly the first to emigrate, the Celtic group the last but one. The Germanic group consists of those Indo-Europeans who had not left the countries of the Baltic Basin up to a few centuries before Christ. For this reason, the Germanic people and the Germanic language must be considered the most direct representatives of the Indo-European peoples and languages.

Up to the time of the Germanic migrations (about 200–568 A.D.), we distinguish the following Germanic groups: *West-Germanic*, in Northern Germany, extending as far east as the river Oder; *North-Germanic*, in Denmark and the southern part of the Scandinavian peninsula;

East-Germanic, in Northern Germany, east of the river Oder.

NOTE. '**Germanic**' and '**Teutonic**.' In German works, the collective name for the Germanic group is 'Germanen, germanisch'; in English, the adjective 'Germanic' is frequently used to denote the languages, while the people are generally denoted as 'Teutons.' This seems to be a misnomer, since the 'Teutons,' who invaded the Roman Empire about 100 B.C., were probably of Celtic, not of Germanic origin.

The name 'Germani' is generally explained as a Celtic word meaning 'neighbors,' but it is more probably of purely Germanic origin and meant something like 'ready men, armed men, gerüstete, waffenfähige Mannschaft' (*gēr-, *gār-, related with German gar =fertig, OHG. garwen 'make ready,' etc.). This hypothesis is supported by the fact that the Romans originally applied the name 'Germani' not to the whole nation, but only to small tribes — scarcely more than troops — that invaded Roman (Gallic) territory west of the Rhine. Apparently, in times of overpopulation, expeditionary forces — *Jungmannschaft* — were sent out to find new homes, in the same way as was the custom with other Indo-European peoples (compare Ihering, Die Indo-Germanen, p. 128 ff.). Those raiders — if the term be applicable to such home-seekers — called themselves 'Germani,' not unlike the Roman *ver sacrum*,[1] but referred with pride to the Suebi-Semnones, as to the original representatives of their nationality — '*quibus ne di quidem immortales pares esse possint.*' (Compare, e.g., Caesar, Bellum Gallicum, IV, 8, and Tacitus, Germania, cap. 2). — The *Suevi=Suebi* (the Germanic form must have been *Swēvjōz) were a tribal league, or, rather, the general federation of the West-Germanic group, inhabiting present Brandenburg and the adjacent territory, and were generally regarded as their political, national and religious center. Their name — if we should call it a name — merely denotes 'the people themselves' (*se-, *swe-, reflexive pronominal stem, compare Latin se, suus, and *bhe(u)-, 'be'). — The name 'Semnones,' altho they are referred to by Roman authors as the principal tribe of the Suevi,

---

[1] 'the sacred spring'; in ancient Rome, it was customary in times of overpopulation to send a certain part of the young men away to find new homes; these expeditions, which always took place in spring, were consecrated to Mars.

has the same meaning; also 'Swede' (=*Swí-thíód* — *thíód* =people) is a synonymous appellation.

The historical interpretation of these names, borne out by the testimony of the Roman historians, is undoubtedly this: smaller groups of home-seekers from the West-Germanic, i.e., Suevian, center, were collectively termed as 'Germani' — *Jungmannschaft*, but after a successful settlement adopted some name that suggested their political superiority over the conquered Celts (see **5**, Note); emigration on a larger scale, however, gave rise to such names as that of the 'Suevi' of Ariovistus, and the later 'Suebi' =*Schwaben*, the *Marcomanni-Bajuvarii* (see below), and others. The 'Germani,' in general, were the pioneers of Germanization, but in most cases doomed to destruction or absorption.

The most important document of Old Norse (the older language of the North-Germanic group) is the *Elder Edda*, a collection of mythical poems from the tenth century; East-Germanic is known to us chiefly thru the Bible translation of the West-Gothic (Visi-Gothic) bishop *Wulfila (Ulfilas)*, who lived in the fourth century.

For Germanic ethnology, compare Zeuss, *Die Deutschen und ihre Nachbarstämme*, München 1837; Bremer, *Ethnographie der germanischen Stämme;* Paul's *Grundriss der germanischen Philologie* [2], III, 735; Much, *Deutsche Stammeskunde*, Leipzig 1900.

Old Norse: Kahle-Heusler, *Altisländisches Elementarbuch*, Heidelberg 1912; Noreen, *Abriss der altnordischen Grammatik*, Halle 1896; Ranisch, *Eddalieder*, Leipzig 1898.

Gothic: Braune, *Gotische Grammatik* [5], Halle 1900; Streitberg, *Gotisches Elementarbuch* [3], Heidelberg 1912; von der Leyen, *Einführung in das Studium der gotischen Sprache*, Strassburg 1905; Kluge, *Die Elemente des Gotischen*, Strassburg 1911.

4. The West-Germanic Group. The expansion of the North-Germanic group was comparatively slight: it extended chiefly over the greater part of Scandinavia, Iceland, and a part of the British Isles. About 200 A.D., the East-Germanic people began to migrate South and East, founded kingdoms in Northern Africa (*Vandals*), Italy (*Ostrogoths*), and Spain (*Visigoths*), and were ultimately exterminated, or absorbed by the native population.

The West-Germanic tribes gradually spread over the whole area of present Germany, France, and England. About 400, perhaps nearly as late as 300 B.C., they occupied only the territory between the rivers Elbe and Oder (or, possibly, Vistula); like the opening of a fan, with the old Indo-European home as its 'pivot,' this colonization spread first over the Northwest, then the middle, and last, the South of Germany. Giving the approximate dates of final, permanent colonization, this expansion may be outlined as follows: Between 400 and 200 B.C. the coast of the North Sea was Germanized as far as the Zuyder Sea (Holland); the ethnic mixture of these Germans with the native Celtic population gave rise to the *Anglo-Frisian* group — just as centuries before the Celts had resulted from the settling of Indo-Europeans among a prehistoric, aboriginal population of Northwestern Europe. Between 200 and the beginning of our era, a wide belt south of the Frisian territory was settled and became the home of the later *Saxons*. The country north and south of the Main became German — *Franconian* — during the first two centuries A.D. Southwestern Germany, while frequently invaded in former centuries, was permanently Germanized about 250 A.D. by Suevians (see preceding paragraph); these were the nucleus of the *Alemannians*. Meanwhile (during the last decades B.C.) other parts of the Suevian center had migrated south, had occupied the home of the Celtic Boii, which they called Boiohaemum, i.e., 'home of the Boians, Bohemia,' and had stayed there, under the name of *Marcomanni* = frontier men, until, in the fifth century A.D., the Romans withdrew their garrisons from Southern Germany. Then they migrated southwest and occupied, under the name of *Bajuvarii*, i.e., Boian warriors, most of present 'Bavaria,' mingling with Ostrogoths in the Alpine districts of the South. — Thus, the Anglo-Frisians, Saxons, Franconians, Alemannians, and Bavarians (to which the *Thuringians*, a comparatively late combination of various tribes, are to be added) represent the most important divisions of the West-Germanic group; their migrations had been very gradual, and each group originally consisted of a large number of entirely detacht tribes; during and after the 'Germanic migration,' they formed those tribal alliances — *Stammesverbände* — which in history and linguistics are known under the names given above.

During the fourth and fifth centuries, parts of the Anglo-Frisian, Saxon, and Frankish groups migrated to the Northwest and West and founded the Anglo-Saxon kingdoms in England and the Frankish kingdoms in France.

5. The German Language is the continental branch of the West-Germanic group. As has been stated above, it originated in Central and Northeastern Germany — east of the Elbe river. By the end of the Germanic migrations (during the fifth century A.D.) most of the old home had been abandoned and was settled by Slavs. Meanwhile, however, the western and southern parts of present Germany had been Germanized. It is self-evident that the German settlers in every case transferred to their new homes their language in that stage of development in which it was spoken in their homes at the time of their emigration. Every language has certain inherent tendencies of development, as will, in the case of the German language, be shown in the second part. These tendencies continued consistently in the old territory; but in the new settlements they ceased soon after the immigration and were, in part, replaced by the linguistic tendencies of the old (chiefly Celtic) populations (see **3**). This was the most important factor in the rise of the dialect differences within the German language. In general it can be said that the northern dialects represent an older form of the language, the southern dialects a newer form. To this day, the linguistic characteristics of the German dialects preserve to a considerable extent the historical order of the German colonization, similar to the arrangement of geological strata: in certain important respects, especially in the development of the consonants, each German dialect is, so to speak, a petrified preservation of a former state of the general German language.

NOTE. The progress of the Germanization of Western and Southern Germany is in part reflected in the names of the historical dialect groups — the *Stammesverbände*. The Saxons had their name from their characteristic weapon, the (stone) knife, *sahs* = Lat. *saxum* 'rock,' probably because the German conquerors formed a kind of a patriarchal aristocracy which alone had the right to bear arms (similarly, the Greek Dorians had their name from *doru* 'spear'). The Franks = 'freemen' also represent the free, ruling class, in a territory settled by right of conquest. These two groups are apparently the later development of those older invasions that had been characterized by the name *Germani*. But the name of the Alemannians seems to point to one or several of those more general movements that history connects with the name of the 'Germanic migrations'; most probably, it means 'the whole people' as differing from mere raiders, the 'Germani'; this would be in keeping with the fact that 'Alemanni' is used more or less synonymously with 'Suevi' (= *Schwaben*), 'the people themselves.' Another, less probable, explanation of the name, as 'temple men, guardians of the shrine,' would point to the same direction, since the religious and political center of the West-Germanic group had been situated east of the Elbe river, in old Suevian (Semnonic) territory. — The name of the Bavarians has been explained above; at the time when they took possession of Bohemia, their name was *Marcomanni* or 'frontier men', i.e., essentially 'Germani.' — The name *Thuringi* (Duringi) is probably an abbreviation of the name *Hermunduri*, the leading tribe among them, but this name itself has not been explained in a satisfactory way.

The name *deutsch* (from Germanic **theoda*, 'people,' and suffix *–isk–*=NHG. *–isch*) means 'popular,' *völkisch, volkstümlich*. It is first found in Latin sources of the eighth century in the form *theotiscus, theodiscus*. The Germanic word **theoda*, OHG. *diot*, also appears in the name of the East-Gothic king Theodoric (Gothic *Thiudareiks*, NHG. *Dietrich*) = 'ruler of the people.' — For bibliography, see Behaghel, *Geschichte der deutschen Sprache*, p. 3.

6. Geographical Boundaries.

At the end of the Germanic migrations, the eastern boundary of the German language is formed approximately by the rivers Elbe and Saale, and the Bohemian forest (see line of colonial expansion in the map). France, Italy, Spain, and a part of Northern Africa were in the hands of Germanic tribes at that time; these were annihilated or absorbed by the Roman or Romanized population of those countries. But in long and bloody wars of colonization during the later Middle Ages and the Modern Period, most of the old Indo-European (Germanic) home east of the Elbe and Saale was recovered; at present, it forms the larger part of the kingdom of Prussia. After many fluctuations, the following approximate boundaries of the German linguistic territory have become fairly stationary:[1]

A. German-Danish Boundary: From the bay of Flensburg on the Baltic to a point south of Hoyer, on the North Sea.

B. German-French Boundary: From a point between Gravelines and Dunkirk (Gravelingen, Dünkirchen) south to St. Omer, east nearly as far as Aachen (leaving Brussels and Maastricht north, Lille and Liége south of

---

[1] More accurate details will be found in Behaghel's *Geschichte der deutschen Sprache*, third chapter.

it), approximately south to Thionville (Diedenhofen), southeast to a point west of Strassburg (Metz is in French territory), then south, to a point east of Lake Geneva, southeast to Gressoney in Italy (south of Brieg); at this point the Italian territory begins.

C. German-Italian Boundary: Around the northern slopes of Monte Rosa and St. Gotthard, then approximately east as far as Martinsbruck on the Inn, around the Ortler to Salurn on the Etsch, slightly northeast, then east as far as Villach where it joins the German-Slovenian frontier.

D. German-Slovenian Boundary: From Villach to Radkersburg on the Mur, then northeast to St. Gotthard on the Raab.

The eastern boundary cannot be stated quite definitely because it is still fluctuating to an extent, in general moving rather east than west; a great number of isolated German settlements (*Sprachinseln*) are situated in Magyar and Slav territory.

E. German-Magyar Boundary: From St. Gotthard to the mouth of the Raab, thence northeast to the mouth of the Thaya.

F. German-Czech Boundary: From Nikolsburg on the Thaya east to the Moldau, then following, in a concentric curve, the Austro-German boundary as far as (approximately) the source of the Oder.

G. German-Polish Boundary: From the source of the Oder northwest to Birnbaum on the Warthe, then, in a right angle, northeast to the Masurian Lakes, where the Lithuanian territory begins.

A glance at the map will show the following discrepancies between the German linguistic boundary and the political boundary of the German Empire: Holland, Northern Belgium, the greater part of Switzerland, and a considerable portion of Austria are German linguistically, but not politically; on the other hand, the German Empire includes some French territory in Lorraine, and a very narrow French strip in Alsace, some Danish territory in Northern Schleswig, and some Polish and Lithuanian territory in the East and Northeast. On the whole, the linguistic boundaries are much wider than the political ones.

The German linguistic territory is subdivided into a great number of dialects which form the general groups stated in section 5, Note. According to the stage to which the consonant development had progressed at the time of the emigration, we distinguish two large divisions which we call *Low German*, i.e., the German language of the Lowlands, in the North, and *High German*, i.e., the German of the Highlands, in the South. Roughly speaking, the territories colonized before the Christian era are Low German, the later colonies High German. Centuries before the Christian era, Indo-European *d*, for instance, had changed to *t* in the general Germanic language (compare Latin *edo*, *duo*, English *eat*, *two*), and the Low German dialects have remained at this stage: LG. *eten*, *twe*. During the first centuries of our era, this *t* passed over into *ss* or *ts*: we have High German *essen*, *zwei*. — The boundary between the two divisions, the *niederdeutsche Sprachgrenze* or *Benrather Linie*,[1] begins south of Aachen, goes northeast and crosses the Rhine near Düsseldorf, goes slightly southeast to Siegen, northeast to Kassel and the mouth of the Saale, and thence, in an irregular line (leaving Berlin, as a sort of *Sprachinsel*, north of it) to Frankfort-on-the-Oder and Birnbaum on the Warthe. Aside from Berlin which has, in general, adopted the

[1] Benrath is a small town near Düsseldorf, where the boundary line crosses the Rhine.

High German standard on account of its metropolitan character (compare especially Jespersen, *Phonetische Grundfragen*, page 42), there are High German *Sprachinseln* in Low German territory near Kleve on the Rhine, in the Harz Mountains, and in East Prussia, south of Elbing; these were formed thru High German immigration in comparatively recent times.

Low German is divided into *Low Franconian* and *Saxon* (*Low Saxon*) by a line which begins at the southern end of the Zuyder See and ends west of Siegen — running, in general, parallel with the Rhine. The most characteristic difference is the ending of the first and third persons plural of the present indicative, which is *-en* in Low Franconian, but *-et* in Saxon. — Low Franconian is the dialect of Northern Belgium and Southern Holland and the adjacent districts of Germany, and forms the essential basis of *Dutch*, the literary language of Holland; in Belgium, it is called *Flemish*. Northwestern Holland contains a rather small remnant of *Frisian*. — *Low Saxon*, commonly called *Plattdeutsch* or *Niederdeutsch*, in the narrower sense of the word, was originally only the language of the West Elbian territory, but spread to the east, so that it is now the dialect of most of the kingdom of Prussia and the grand duchies of Oldenburg and Mecklenburg; the eastern part is often termed *East Elbian*.

Within the *High German* dialects we distinguish *Middle German* and *Upper German*. They are divided by a line that begins west of Strassburg, crosses the Rhine near Hagenau and runs east to a point just north of the mouth of the Lech, and thence northeast to the source of the Eger. The difference between the two was more sharply marked in the older periods of the German language than it is now; it was most clearly apparent in the change of *b* and *g* to *p* and *k* (fortis); see **32**, 8–10.

Middle German is divided into a *Franconian* part and an *East Middle German* part (colonial territory), separated by a line that runs north and south between the rivers Werra and Fulda. The dialects of the former group are *Middle Franconian* (subdivided into a northern half, *Ripuarian*, around Cologne, and a southern half, *Moselle Franconian*, around Trier), *Rhenish Franconian*, and *East Franconian*. The boundary lines between them run, roughly speaking, parallel to that diagonal line from the mouth of the Lech to the source of the Eger: A line from Saarbrücken to Siegen separates Middle Franconian from Rhenish Franconian, a line from Heilbronn to the source of the Fulda, Rhenish Franconian from East Franconian; a line from the source of the Fulda to the source of the Eger forms the northern boundary of East Franconian against East Middle German (Thuringian). — Upper German consists of *Alemannian* (in the wider sense) and *Bavarian* (including *Austrian*), separated by the river Lech; within the Alemannian group, a diagonal line from the northwest to the southeast separates *Swabian* from *Alemannian* in the narrower sense of the term, and the latter again is subdivided into *Low Alemannian* and Alsatian (northwest), and *High Alemannian*, chiefly Swiss (southwest).

NOTE. Some scholars, e.g., Behaghel, prefer to class East Franconian with Upper German rather than Middle German. While, from the viewpoint of modern dialects, there are strong arguments in favor of this, the needs of historical grammar make our arrangement — which is the more general one — appear better justified.

A convenient way to remember these boundaries is the following:

(1) The linguistic boundary of the German language: Draw a line west to east from Calais to Aachen, then south to the east end of Lake Geneva, east to the point where the Mur enters Hungary, north to the mouth of the Thaya, west to Budweis, in a concentric curve within the Bohemian and Moravian boundary to the source of the Oder, northwest to Birnbaum, northeast to the Mazurian Lakes.

(2) Boundary between Low German and High German: Düsseldorf to Frankfort-on-the-Oder.

(3) Boundary between Upper German and Franconian: Hagenau to the mouth of the Lech (east), thence to the source of the Eger (northeast).

(4) Boundaries between the Franconian dialects: Two diagonals parallel to the line Lech-Eger — one begins near Heilbronn and ends near Eisenach; the other crosses the Rhine near Coblenz.

(5) Boundary between Alemannian and Bavarian: the river Lech.

The relation between the political and linguistic geography of Germany is approximately the following:

Low Franconian comprises Southern Holland, Northern Belgium, and the northern part of the German Rhine Province; Aachen is south, Düsseldorf north of the dialect line.

To Low Saxon belong: Westphalia, Hanover, Oldenburg, Schleswig-Holstein, Brunswick, and the northern part of the Prussian province of Saxony; the rest of Prussia is East Elbian or East Middle German.

The East Middle German territory contains most of Thuringia, the southern part of the province of Saxony, the kingdom of Saxony, Silesia, Southern Brandenburg, and the German part of Posen.

The principal cities of Middle Franconia are Cologne (Ripuarian) and Trier (Moselle Franconian); therefore, Middle Franconian is essentially the dialect of the Rhine Province.

Rhenish Franconian is spoken in German Lorraine, the Bavarian Palatinate, Northern Baden, and Hessia; its principal cities are Mainz, Frankfort, Worms, Speier, Heidelberg.

East Franconian, with the cities of Würzburg and Bamberg, comprises chiefly the north of Wurttemberg and Bavaria.

Swabian is the dialect of most of Southern Wurttemberg,

together with the southeast of Bavaria (around Stuttgart, Ulm, Augsburg); Alemannian is spoken in Alsace, Southern Baden and the utmost south of Wurttemberg, in German Switzerland and the Austrian province of Vorarlberg.

Bavarian is spoken in the greater part of Bavaria (with Nuremberg, Regensburg, Munich), and in the German part of Austria with the exception of Northern Bohemia, Moravia, and Silesia, which are East Middle German.

While these delineations are by no means accurate, they may be helpful for the beginner in German linguistics.

7. The Periods of the German Language. Since the High German group of dialects became the literary standard from early times, it is customary to designate the general development of the German language according to the stages of High German. We distinguish:

Old High German, from about 750 to 1100;
Middle High German, from 1100 to 1500;
New High German, from 1500 to the present time.

The abbreviations used in this book are: OHG., MHG., NHG. — Of course, an Old Low German or Old Saxon, Middle Low German, and New Low German period can likewise be distinguished.

The most characteristic difference between OHG. and MHG. consists in the weakening of the vowels of unaccented syllables to [ə]; compare OHG. infinitives like *neman, salbōn, habēn,* with MHG. *nemen, salben, haben.* The transition from MHG. to NHG. is marked chiefly by the diphthongization of MHG. *ī, ū, iu* (=*ü*) and the monophthongization of MHG. *ie* (=[iə]), *uo, üe* to [iː], [uː], [yː]; compare MHG. *mīn, hūs, liute, biegen, guot, güete:* NHG. *mein, Haus, Leute, biegen, gut, Güte.*

8. The Old High German Period. It is certain that before their Christianization the Germans possessed a considerable literature, chiefly of epic character, which, however, was transmitted by word of mouth only. The Germanic alphabet, the *Runes*, was not used for literary purposes. For this reason, very few remnants of the literature of that time have come down to us; the most important poetical work which is based on national sources is the *Hildebrandslied*, probably a fragment of some larger epic, composed in a mixt dialect containing both Low German and High German forms (see Specimen Text II). — Charlemagne had caused a collection of German epic poems to be made, but his son, Louis the Pious, is said to have destroyed them on account of their pagan character. — Most of the Old High German literature that is preserved consists of translations or paraphrases of the New Testament and other religious works; the Gospel Harmony (*Evangelienharmonie*) of the monk *Otfrid of Weissenburg* (South Rhenish Franconian), dating from the ninth century, and the numerous philosophical and religious prose works of the monk *Notker*, who lived in the monastery of St. Gaul (in High Alemannian territory) in the eleventh century, are the most important works of this class. Of secular works, aside from the Hildebrandslied, the *Ludwigslied* (Rhenish Franconian) is to be mentioned, which celebrates the victory of the West Franconian king Louis III. over the Normans, at Saucourt, in 881.

Low German (Saxon) contributes in this period a Gospel Harmony in the Old Germanic alliterating verse (*Stabreim*), in which also the Hildebrandslied is composed: the *Heliand* ('Saviour').

The Old High German literature does not represent a uniform language. Every literary document is written in

the specific dialect of its author. Still, the language of
the Carolingian court, the Rhenish Franconian, began to
exert a standardizing influence. In the ninth century,
the name *Franciscus* (Franconian) is used more or less
synonymously with *Theodiscus* (= *deutsch*) — see **5**, Note,
— 'Germania' is translated by *Francōno lant* (Otfrid),
and not until the year 1000 does *lingua Francisca* denote
French in contrast to German, the *lingua Theodisca*. —
For the purposes of historical grammar, however, OHG.
words are usually quoted in their East Franconian form
which is represented chiefly by the so-called *Tatian*, a
gospel harmony in prose that was written in the monastery of Fulda in the ninth century; the reason for this is
the fact that East Franconian which is preeminently the
language of the East Middle German colonization, can
be considered the principal source of the NHG. language.

9. The Middle High German Period. Two forces contributed to a rejuvenation of German literature at the
beginning of the MHG. period: the influence of French and
Provençal, to a minor extent also Italian literature, due,
to an extent, to the close contact between German and
French chivalry during the crusades; and an awakening
of German national feeling, fostered especially by the
rule of the brilliant Hohenstaufen dynasty (1137–1252).
Most of 'court epic' and the 'court lyric' of this first
classical period of German literature stands under French
influence at least in regard to its sources and motifs, but
to an extent also in its form and spirit. *Heinrich von
Veldeke* in his *Eneit*, *Hartman von Aue* in his *Erec*, *Iwein*,
Gregorius and *Arme Heinrich*, *Gottfried von Straßburg*
in his *Tristan und Isolde* follow French models, and
lyric poets like *Dietmar von Aist*, *Friedrich von Hausen*,
Reinmar von Hagenau show strong Romance influence.

Wolfram von Eschenbach's Parzival, and *Walther von der Vogelweide's* lyric poetry are independent at least in spirit; and the great 'national Epics' — *Nibelungenlied, Gudrun,* etc. — grow out of German tradition in contents, spirit and form.

During the greater part of the nineteenth century it was an ardently discussed question among philologists, whether there existed, during the MHG. period, anything like a 'standard language' — a *mittelhochdeutsche Schriftsprache.* At present, the following facts are more or less generally agreed upon: A real 'standard' of MHG. did not exist; but several factors were favorable to the avoidance of the most striking dialect peculiarities in the works of the best MHG. poets: their wayfaring from court to court; the literary enthusiasm of the Hohenstaufen in Swabia, the Babenberger in Austria, and the Landgraves of Thuringia, which caused literary centers of equal importance to develop in those parts of Germany; and, finally, the mutual influence of the poets upon each other. So it occurred that Swabian poets avoided long vowels in endings (e.g., *tagā* 'days'), which their dialects had retained to a certain extent; Bavarians avoided the dual forms *ös, enk,* which their dialect uses instead of the plural forms of the pronoun of the second person; the Austrian dialect diphthongized *ī, ū, iu* since the twelfth century (7), but Austrian poets like Walther von der Vogelweide use the older forms *mīn, hūs, liute* (instead of *haus, mein, leute*) in their poems.

10. The New High German Period is characterized by the rise of a well-defined standard language which, in its beginnings, goes back to the last centuries of the MHG. period. At the end of the Germanic migrations, the old territory of the West- and East-Germanic tribes, between

Elbe and Vistula, had been vacated and had gradually been settled by Slavic tribes (5). Since the rule of the Saxon dynasty (919–1024), large portions had been recovered by conquest and colonization. In these colonial districts dialects of settlers from different parts of Germany mingled; this led to a certain leveling of the language, altho the principal characteristics of each colonial district corresponded in the main to the adjacent dialects. Therefore, the East German colonies (Bohemia, new Saxony, etc.) were especially favorable to the development of a standard language.

Another factor which tended towards uniformity was found in the administrative activities of government offices, especially the Imperial Chancellery. Under Charlemagne, imperial documents had been issued in German, but under his successors in Germany Latin was used exclusively, until Louis the Bavarian, in 1329, reintroduced the use of German. His successor, Charles IV., of the house of Luxemburg, establisht his court at Prague, the capital of Bohemia, and in 1348, the year after he had ascended the throne, founded the first German university in that city. These facts are characteristic: A tradition of German imperial documents, started by Charles' predecessor; a Middle Franconian ruler; a chancellery in colonial territory, with a chiefly Franco-Bavarian population; and a university that attracted teachers and students from all parts of Germany. The large correspondence of the Imperial Chancellery with government offices thruout the empire, especially with the courts of Meissen (in new Saxony) and Vienna — the son-in-law of Charles IV., Rudolph, of the house of Habsburg, resided in Vienna, where he founded the second German university in 1365 — created a considerable uniformity of official writings, resulting in a compromise between Upper

German and Middle German peculiarities. For instance, it is characteristic for this beginning standardization of the language that the Imperial Chancellery in Prague uses the diphthongs *ei, au, eu,* which are of southeastern (Austrian) origin, instead of the Middle German monophthongs *ī, ū, iu,* but the Middle German monophthongs *ū, ü* instead of the South German dipthongs *uo, üe* (compare 7 and 37).

The invention of printing — the first book was printed at Mainz around 1450 — was exceedingly favorable to the standardization of the language, since the great printing establishments in the different parts of Germany (chiefly, however, in South Germany) endeavored to attain a certain degree of uniformity.

But the greatest influence for the development of standard German lay in the appearance of Luther and the Reformation. Luther did not create the New High German language; he says himself (see Specimen Text IV) that he is using the language of the Saxon Electorate, i.e., the product of the combination of the colonial dialects of Saxony, German Bohemia and Austria, as it appeared in the official language of the Saxon Chancellery. But he greatly enriched this language, which followed, on general lines, the standards that had been set by the Imperial Chancelleries of Prague (1347–1437) and Vienna (since 1438). He describes how he and his friend Melanchthon would often search for weeks to find one single word; especially the translation of the book of Job caused him great difficulties on account of the large number of expressions from daily life contained in it. He states that he sometimes could not translate more than one line in a whole day. — Luther was not the first to translate the Bible into German. Not less than nineteen High German and five Low German translations had appeared before him; his great merit, from the linguistic point of view, lies in the fact that he introduced the common people into church administration and induced them to read the Bible in German. Another potent factor in the spread of this standard language were his church hymns, his letters, and his polemic writings. The immense increase in the number of German books, as an immediate consequence of the Reformation, may be seen from the following figures: From the invention of printing, about 1450, to 1518, from 50 to 100 books were printed annually; in 1519, the number amounted to 250; 1524, to nearly one thousand; between 1524 and 1584, the printer Hans Luft in Wittenberg alone sold more than one hundred thousand Bibles.

The language of Luther spread very rapidly parallel with the Reformation, so that it was adopted first in the Protestant parts of Germany, chiefly in the north, while Catholic Southern Germany and Calvinic Switzerland resisted its spread much longer. During the seventeenth century, German grammarians contributed greatly to the general recognition of the new standard, and the classical literature of the eighteenth century completed the work of the artistic perfection of the New High German language.

German differs in a characteristic way from all other European languages. English, for instance, is essentially the dialect of London; French, the dialect of Paris; Italian, that of Toscany; Spanish, the dialect of Madrid. German, however, is not a continuation and development of any single German dialect, but a compromise between a large number of them, based on the administrative centralization of newly recovered colonial soil, extended by the spiritual awakening of the Reformation, and crowned by the rise of a great literature. It is a peculiar turn in the destinies of the German nation that its political and cultural misery began with the abandonment of the old Germanic home, east of the Elbe, and south of the Baltic, and ended with its partial recovery thru the dukes of Saxony and the rulers of the house of Hohenzollern: in the same way, German linguistic unity had been lost after the migration period, was reestablisht thru East-German colonization and the spiritual and cultural reawakening of the German nation, and is being completed in our days, at a time when the political center of the Germans has returned to the place where Roman historians had found it at the beginning of the Christian era — to Old Semnonic soil, in present Brandenburg.

II. INTERNAL HISTORY

A. THE DEVELOPMENT OF SOUNDS[1]

11. Phonetic Law and Analogy. Languages never are at a standstill; they develop continually, either thru certain changes going on with certain sounds, or thru the mutual influence of grammatical forms or whole words upon each other. In the first case, we speak of phonetic changes brought about by *phonetic laws*. In the second case, we speak of *analogy*.

For instance: An Indo-European *p*, preserved as such in most Indo-European languages, is represented by *f* in Germanic words: Lat. *pater*, Gk. *pater*, Sanscrit *pitar* — but Gothic *fadar*, English *father*, German *Vater* = [faɪtər]. Such a correspondence of sounds establishes a 'phonetic law' (*Lautgesetz*), which is expressed like this: Indo-European *p* becomes *f* in Germanic, or, as a formula: IE. *p* > Gc. *f*. A phonetic law is the scientific statement of the fact that, at a certain time, and in a certain language, a given sound underwent a definite change in all words in which it occurred under like conditions. In this sense, we are entitled to say that phonetic laws do not admit of any exceptions. IE. *p* MUST become *f* in Germanic wherever it is found, unless this law is counteracted by some other law. A phonetic law is either *spontaneous*, or it is caused by *assimilation*. In the first case, the transition is caused by some inherent tendency of the language (see **12** and **I, 51**), in the second case it is due to the influence of the surrounding sounds (**I, 53**). IE. *g*,

[1] or *Phonology* — see **I, 1.**

as preserved in Lat. *gelidus*, changes to Gc. *k*, as is seen
in Eng. *cold*, Ger. *kalt* — this is spontaneous transition,
caused by intensive expiration (**13**, 2). But when we
find that the past participle of the Lat. verb *rego* 'rule'
is *rectus*, instead of *regtus (an asterisk before a word
indicates that it is not actually found in this form, but
theoretically reconstructed), we know that this change
was merely due to the fact that *g* in this form was
followed by voiceless *t*.

An instance of analogy is the following: In older German,
the preterit of the verb *singen* was *sang* in the singular,
but *sungen* in the plural (compare: *Wie die Alten sungen, so
zwitschern die Jungen*). When in Modern German the
form *sangen* was substituted, the reason was not any
phonetic law that establisht a change of *u* to *a*, but a
tendency to level the singular and plural forms of verbs, as
far as the stems are concerned. This is *internal analogy:*
the influence came from some other form of the same
word. On the other hand, we speak of *external analogy*
when a word is influenced by the form of other words.
E.g., in OHG. the word *hand* had the plural *hendi*, which
developt into NHG. *Hände;* but the plural of *naht*
'night' was *naht;* the NHG. plural *Nächte* did not arise
thru any phonetic law, but thru an imitation of the
plural *Hände* (compare **61**, *B*).

12. Phonetic Tendencies. Phonetic laws are not ar-
bitrary products of chance. The change from *p* to *f*, or
from *g* to *k*, mentioned above, was caused by an inherent
disposition of the language, that is, by certain habits of
articulation on the part of the speakers. We call these
habits *phonetic tendencies* (**I**, 51). — At a time when the
Indo-Europeans had not yet separated into widely different tribes, i.e., before the emigration from their original

home had assumed considerable dimensions, their phonetic tendencies were, generally speaking, uniform. But whenever Indo-European tribes emigrated, they mingled with people speaking different languages, whose phonetic tendencies differed from their own. The old habits ceased in part, and in part they continued; but under the influence of the non-Indo-European elements of the new homes, new habits develop, and the result was an unconscious compromise between the Indo-European and the aboriginal population of the new home. The new habits of speech created new phonetic laws, and in this way the different Indo-European languages gradually diverged to such an extent, that at present, without philological training, their relationship can hardly be recognized (compare 1 and 3).

With those Indo-Europeans who remained in the old home, namely, the Germanic peoples, the old phonetic tendencies continued and led to a remarkably uniform development along definite lines.

13. Strengthening and Weakening of Articulation. Theoretically, the number of phonetic tendencies is unlimited. But in practise they can roughly be classed under two heads: Strengthening and weakening of articulation. The fundamental difference between these two directions of phonetic changes is indubitable. Nevertheless, it is not always possible to class a given sound change under either principle with absolute certainty. The chief reason for this is, that with most articulations there are two opposing factors counteracting and balancing each other, namely, the force of expiration and the tension of the articulation muscles (lips, tongue, and, under certain circumstances, the vocal chords). Instances will make this clear:

(1) Conditions are simplest in the case of *voiceless stops* (*p, t, k*).

(*a*) If the force of expiration is *increased*, the muscle tension, too, will increase to a certain degree, and aspirated stops (**I, 11**) will ensue. But the force of expiration may [reach a degree at which the muscles of the lips or tongue can no longer resist it: the occlusion is forced open, and the result will be an affricate[1] (*pf, ts, kχ*), or a voiceless spirant (*f, þ, χ*); this is the case, e.g., when IE. *p, t, k* become *f, þ, χ* in the Germanic languages (see **22, 1**).

NOTE. In theory, but not in fact — at least, not in the case of the Germanic languages — this change could also be explained as a weakening of the resistance of the muscles against a normal air-pressure; but the fact that we find with it other contemporaneous linguistic conditions which definitely show an increasing energy of articulation precludes this interpretation. For it is by no means to be assumed that the same language, at the same time and under similar conditions, might show both weakened and strengthened articulation. — In general, it may be said that of the two factors the intensity of expiration is the primary, the muscle tension the secondary one.

(*b*) If the force of expiration *decreases*, the vocal chords close, and the sounds become voiced: *b, d, g* — pronounced with relatively relaxt muscles, as is always the case with voiced stops; compare the change from Lat. *amatum* 'loved' to *amado* — *amaðo*, and even *amao* in Spanish (at first, the decrease of expiration permits the change from *t* to *d*; then, relaxation of the muscles of the tongue causes the change from *d* to *ð*, and, at last, the complete dropping of the consonant).

(2) In the case of *voiced stops*, the force of expiration is much smaller to begin with, and therefore it is obvious

---

[1] Affricates are combinations of a stop and a spirant of the same place of articulation.

that the articulating muscles can withstand the air-pressure as long as the glottis remains nearly closed, i.e., as long as the sounds are voiced. An *increasing* air-pressure will force the glottis open, thus changing the voiced stops to voiceless lenes (**I, 11**); these, in turn, may become fortes — aspirates — voiceless spirants (or affricates) if the force of expiration and the corresponding muscle tension continue to increase. — But if the muscle tension *decreases* while the expiration remains normal, voiced spirants [*v*, ð, γ] will result, as is seen in the development from *amado* to *amaðo*, mentioned above.

(3) *Voiceless spirants* present a difficult problem. Obviously, *increased* articulation need not necessarily have any effect at all, since the breath can escape without considerable obstruction. In fact, in many cases they remain unchanged, as is seen in Germanic *f*, χ, *s* under certain conditions. That part of the articulating muscles which is most inert, namely, the muscles of the back of the tongue, is apt to give way to the pressure of expiration, so that χ may change to *h*, or even disappear (compare German *hoch — der höchste: höher*). — The change from þ to *t* in Scandinavian (Eng. *think:* Swed. *tänka*) is due to a slight *decrease* of the expiration. — In a number of cases, voiceless spirants become voiced. This development of [f, þ, χ, s] to [*v*, ð, γ, z] *may* be due to an unusual tension of the vocal chords (especially in the neighborhood of voiced sounds), strong enough to overcome even a high degree of expiratory force. But in general it is safer to interpret this change as a weakening of articulation — a lessened force of expiration permitting the closure of the glottis; this is all the more probable since this sound transition occurs very frequently in languages of little energy of articulation — especially the change of *s*

to *z.* — In certain cases, conditions are so complicated that, at this time, a definite answer seems hardly possible.

(4) While *voiced spirants*, too, may show a twofold development, the explanation is simple in either case. Increased expiration leads to voiceless spirants, the glottis being forced open, as in (2), while increased muscle tension, under normal conditions of expiration, changes them to voiced stops. Different conditions lead to different results, but the interpretation presents no difficulties.

(5) *Liquids* and *Nasals* are not subject to any changes of great importance, except that weakened articulation is apt to increase their vocalic (sonorous) quality — in some cases to such an extent that they become real vowels (compare especially the treatment of *r* in English: in a word like *sir*, it is either decidely vocalic, or even a vowel proper).

(6) *Vowels* are open sounds, and, therefore, the muscle tension is the only factor to be considered (the expiration being unhindered in the oral cavity, increased expiration will not materially affect the articulation); generally, the position of the tongue is the primary, the activity of the lips and the angle of the jaws the secondary factor.

(*a*) *Increased* articulation either causes the tongue to be raised (thru greater muscle tension), or the lips to be widened or rounded and the jaw to be lowered. Special conditions may decide for one or the other of these alternatives. In this way, [ɑː] may change to [oː, uː] in consequence of a gradual rising of the tongue (connected with the habitual lip-rounding); open [ɛː] might either become close [eː], the tongue being raised, or, thru a widening of the jaw angle and a more and more energetic opening of the lips, it may change to [æː — aː — ʌː].

Thus, the probable direction of vowel changes thru increased articulation is this:

(b) *Decreased* articulation must obviously lead to the opposite results, as far as it entails any change at all: [o] changes to [ɑ], [u] to [o], and in extreme cases all vowels may result in the most decided relaxation, namely, the habitual position of the tongue when at rest ('basis of articulation,' in the narrower sense of the word), the slurred vowel [ə].

Merely as a mnemotechnic help, it may be noted that in the great majority of cases of actual occurrence, increased articulation leads to a vowel of lower pitch, decreased articulation to a vowel of higher pitch; thus the direction of change thru strengthening is: e — æ — a — o — u, while changes thru weakening show the series u — o — a.

NOTE. Since the basic principle of vowel change is muscle tension, while the primary cause of consonant changes is increase or decrease of the expiration, it is not surprising that languages frequently show a tendency towards weakening of consonants, but strengthening of vowels. This does not in any way contradict the principle stated in (1) Note, that contemporaneous strengthening and weakening in the same language is not to be assumed.

First Cycle

The Indo-Germanic Period

BRUGMANN, *Kurze vergleichende Grammatik der idg. Sprachen,* **1904.**
OERTEL, *Lectures on the Science of Language,* 1901.
DELBRÜCK, *Einleitung in das Studium der idg. Sprachen,* ⁵, 1908.
BLOOMFIELD, *The Study of Language,* 1914.

14. The Indo-European Language. Since the art of writing was not known to the Indo-Europeans before their separation, their common language has not been preserved to us in any documents whatsoever. Still, thru a systematic comparison of the individual Indo-European languages, comparative philology has succeeded in reconstructing to a considerable extent, and with a reasonable degree of certainty the original sounds and forms of the parent tongue. Strictly speaking, a 'reconstructed' language form like *$\hat{k}mt\acute{o}m$ 'one hundred' means neither more nor less than a formula denoting some undefined sound combination that resulted in Lat. *centum,* Gk. *(he)katón,* Ger. *hund(ert),* etc., but as a matter of fact, in most cases such words are certainly not far from the actual forms used by the ancient Indo-Europeans. — The sign of an asterisk before the word is used to indicate that we are dealing with a reconstructed form.

Unfortunately, there exists a great deal of confusion in the way of transcription; undoubtedly, it would be best to agree on some such system as that of the International Phonetic Association, but as long as philologists as yet have not come to such an agreement, it is better to use it only as a subsidiary means of explanation in certain cases, and in general to accept, tho in a slightly simplified form, the system in use in the majority of standard works, especially in Brugmann's *Grundriss der vergleichenden Grammatik der indogermanischen Sprachen.*

15. The Indo-European Consonants. According to the results of philological reconstruction, the Indo-European language before its breaking up into dialects possessed very few spirants (probably only *s* and *z*, and possibly *j* and *w*), the nasals *m*, *n*, *ŋ*, the liquids *l*, *r*, and a comparatively large number of stops.

According to the *place of articulation*, the STOPS were front, middle and back stops, i.e., labials, dentals, and velars (palato-velars); compare diagram on page 102.

According to the *kinds of articulation*, they were strong (voiceless fortes — either aspirated or unaspirated), middle (voiced aspirates: a glottal spirant followed the explosive), or weak (voiced lenes). — The strong stops, *p*, *t*, *k*, are generally termed *tenues*, the middle stops, *bh*, *dh*, *gh*, *mediae aspiratae*, the weak stops, *b*, *d*, *g*, *mediae*.

NOTE. "Velars are sounds that are articulated at or near the dividing line between hard and soft palate" (I, **31**). — For the term gutturals, see I, **31**, Note.

The difference between *ki-*, *ka-*, *ku-*sounds (I, **31**) seems to have existed to a marked degree in primitive Indo-European; originally, it was almost certainly due to the influence of the following sound (especially vowel), but in historical times analogy and other circumstances have frequently changed conditions to such an extent that a *ki-*sound, for instance, may also be found before an *a*, a *ku-*sound before an *i*, etc. Therefore, comparative philology recognizes three subdivisions of 'gutturals': *palatals* — pronounced at the front palate, and transcribed by *k̂*, *ĝh*, *ĝ*; *velars*, pronounced at the dividing line of the hard and the soft palate, and transcribed by *q*, *gh*, *g*; the *ku-*sounds had the peculiarity that their articulation was apt to be accompanied by a simultaneous lip-rounding, so common with articulations of the back of the tongue (compare I, **41**). They resembled Engl. *qu*, Ital. *gu*, but the tongue and lip articulation took place at the same time. They are called *labio-velars* and transcribed by q^u, g^uh, g^u. — The standard transcription of Brugmann's *Grundriss* reserves the signs *k*, *gh*, *g* for those numerous cases where it is not certain to which of the three groups a 'guttural' belongs. However, on account of the special conditions

explained in the following paragraph, it is more advisable for the
purposes of an elementary introduction into Germanic phonology
to use *k*, *gh*, *g* for palatals and velars indiscriminately, and *q*, *gh*, *g*
for labio-velars; only where special conditions require it, palatal
pronunciation may be indicated by the signs used in the diagram.

Using Brugmann's symbols, the IE. stops can be arranged as
follows:

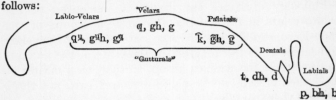

16. Centum and Satem Languages. In the different IE.
languages, the three groups of 'gutturals' show a different
development.   In the eastern branches — Indo-Iranian,
Armenian, Albanian, and Balto-Slavic — the assimilation to the following vowel seems to have been especially
marked; in prehistoric times, a decrease in muscle tension caused rill formation, and sibilants [ʃ, ʒ, s, z] resulted:
the IE. word for '100,' *ḱmtóm (with 'palatal' *k*), develop t
to ʃatám in Sanscrit, satəm in Avestan, səto in Slavic, ʃimtas
in Lithuanian, etc.; but it is *centum* (= *kentum*) in Latin,
(*he*)*katón* in Greek, *kēt* in Irish.   Accepting Avestan and
Latin as characteristic representatives, we commonly
term the eastern group *Satem Languages*, the western,
Centum Languages. — In later, historical times, a similar process can be observed in most centum languages
too — compare the change from Lat. *centum* to French
cent = [sã], but purely Germanic languages are practically exempt from such sound transitions.

On the other hand, the centum languages, in their
earlier periods, rather accentuate the labializing tendency
of the labio-velars: the labial element develops, under
certain circumstances, into an independent sound, and

sometimes the velar element is lost altogether. Compare Latin *quod* (Sanscrit *ka–*), Eng. *what* = [hwɔt], Ger. *was*. — Here, too, the Romance tongues gradually fall in line with the satem languages, as is shown in the transition from Lat. *quod* to French *que* = [kə].

Philology expresses the divergent tendencies of the palato-velars in the eastern and western groups of the Indo-European languages by the statement that the velars and labio-velars fall together in the eastern, the palatals and velars in the western group, so that, as a matter of fact, each of the two branches possesses two, not three kinds of these sounds:

Indo-European:	k̂	k	q
Satem Group:	ʃ, s	k	
Centum Group:	k		qu

Osthoff calls the three kinds of palato-velar tenues the *hekatón-k*, *karpós-k*, and *póteros-k*, referring to the Greek words meaning 'one hundred,' 'fruit,' 'which,' which contain those three sounds (IE. *k̂m̥tóm*, *k̥r̥pós*, *q̊óteros*).

Examples. Only one instance — represented by several languages — is given for each consonant; no instances are given for the spirants, liquids and nasals, because their changes in the individual languages are not sufficiently characteristic for the purposes of this book. Where a sound does not exactly correspond to the IE. sound in question, because it was changed thru a phonetic law of the respective language, the word is given in parenthesis.

IE. **p, t, k̂, k, q.**
" *pətér, Lat. *pater*, Gk. *patér*, Sc. *pitár–*, 'father.'
" *treies, Lat. *trēs*, Gk. *treis*, Sc. *trayas*, 'three.'

IE. *k̂m̥tóm, Lat. *centum*, Gk. *–katón*, Sc. (*ʃatam*), 'hundred.'

" *leuk–, Lat. *lux*, Gk. *leukós*, Sc. *rōkas*, 'light,' 'white.'

" *qo–, Lat. *quod* 'what,' Gk. (*pou* 'where'), Sc. (*kas* 'who').

IE. bh, dh, ĝh, gh, gh.

" *bher–, Lat. (*fero*), Gk. (*phero*), Sc. *bharāmi*, 'bear.'

" *dhūmós, Lat. (*fūmus*), Gk. (*thymós*), Sc. *dhūmas*, 'vapor,' 'spirit.'

" *ĝheim–, Lat. (*hiems*), Gk. (*kheimṓn*), Sl. (*zima*), 'winter.'

" *ghostis, Lat. (*hostis*), Sl. (*gostъ*), 'enemy,' 'guest.'

" *ghermos, Lat. (*formus*), Gk. (*thermós*), Sc. *gharmas*, 'warm.'

IE. b, d, ĝ, g, g.

" *(s)lāb–, Lat. *lābor*, 'glide,' Sl. *slabъ*, 'weak.'

" *dwō(u), Lat. *duō*, Gk. *duō*, Sc. *dvā*, 'two.'

" *ĝenu–, Lat. *genu*, Gk. *gonu*, Avest. (*zanva*), 'knee.'

" *jugóm, Lat. *iugum*, Gk. *zugón*, Sc. *yugam*, 'yoke.'

" *gm̥–, gem–, Lat. (*venio*), Gk. (*baino*), Sc. (*gam–*), 'come,' 'walk.'

17. The Indo-European Vowels. In accented syllables, Indo-European possessed chiefly the vowels *e* and *o*, long and short. The vowel *a*, *ā* was comparatively rare. *i* and *u* (*ī*, *ū*) did not occur in accented syllables, but appeared in unaccented position as the representatives of diphthongs (*ei, oi, eu, ou*) that had lost their first elements thru the lack of stress (compare **18**).

All accented vowels could be combined with 'diphthongal glides,' i.e., high vowels, liquids, or nasals standing in the same syllable; theoretically, this means the possibility of the following diphthongs (aside from combinations with the vowel *a*):

ei, eu, el, er, em, en; ēi, ēu, ēl, ēr, ēm, ēn;
oi, ou, ol, or, om, on; ōi, ōu, ōl, ōr, ōm, ōn.
ēi, ēu, ōi, ōu, etc., are called *long diphthongs.*

NOTE. For the phonetic explanation of the fact that comparative philology treats such combinations as *el, ol, er, or,* in words like *helfen, geholfen, werfen, geworfen,* etc., as diphthongs, see **I, 54,** end.

In unaccented syllables, there occurred, in addition to *i* and *u*, the slurred vowel ə. In comparative philology, this is designated by its Hebrew name 'shva.' This, too, could occur as the first element of diphthongs: əi, əu, əl, ər, əm, ən.

Examples. — A. In accented syllables:

IE. ĕ: Lat. *ferō*, Gk. *phérō*, Sc. *(bharāmi)*, OHG. *beran*, 'bear.'
" ē: " *sēmen*, 'seed.'
" ŏ: " *octō*, Gk. *óktō*, Sc. *(aṣtāu)*, 'eight.'
" ō: " *bōs*, Gk. *bous*, 'cattle,' OHG. *kuo* < **kō*.
" ă: " *aqua*, 'water,' Goth. *aƕa*.
" ā: " *frāter*, Gk. *phrā́tōr*, Sc. *bhrā́tar–*, 'brother.'

B. In unaccented syllables:

IE. i: Lat. *piscis*, Ger. *Fisch*.
" ī: " *inclīno*, 'lean,' Gk. *klī́nē*, 'bed.'
" u: " *iugum*, Gk. *zugón*, Sc. *yugám*, 'yoke.'
" ū: " *mūs*, Gk. *mūs*, Sc. *mūṣ*, 'mouse,' OHG. *mūs*.
" ə: " *(pater)*, Gk. *(patér)*, Sc. *(pitár–)*, 'father.'

Instances for diphthongs are given on page 107 f.

18. Vowel Gradation (Ablaut). In very early Indo-European times certain vowels, especially the two chief vowels of accented syllables, *e* and *o*, were interchangeable to a certain degree. Both are mid vowels, but *e* is a front vowel, *o* a back vowel (**I, 39**). The pronunciation of a front vowel represents a somewhat greater articulating energy of the tongue, than that of a back vowel, just as a dental represents greater energy than a velar; besides — and this is probably the factor of greater importance, — front vowels are, for psychological reasons, generally pronounced with a greater tension of the vocal chords than back vowels, so that they constitute a more intense articulation in two respects. In a wider sense of the word 'accent,' it could be said that syllables with a stronger accent should have front vowels, those with a weaker accent, back vowels. — As a matter of fact, we find this to be true in Indo-European to a considerable extent, altho we cannot reconstruct such an early stage of the language that the vowel distribution would seem to be carried thru consistently. In general, we can say that the vowel *e* (at least, in the roots of words) still stands out rather clearly as denoting a stronger present interest of the speaker (being used especially in the present tense of verbs), while *o* indicates comparative indifference and is, therefore, preeminently used in verbal nouns (words that express conditions, qualities, etc.). Compare the following Greek words (the conditions are especially clear in Greek):

légō 'I speak,' *lógos* 'word'; *démō* 'I build,' *dómos* 'house'; *leípō* 'I leave,' *loipós* 'left over'; *spéudō* 'I hasten,' *spoudé* 'haste'; *arégō* 'I help,' *arōgós* 'helper'; *Hérē* 'goddess of seasons,' *hórā* 'season.'

This interchange between *e* and *o* (apparently also between *a* and *o*) is called *qualitative vowel gradation* (*qualitativer Ablaut, Abtönung*).

NOTE. Indo-European is by no means the only group of languages that possesses *Abtönung*. In Semitic languages, conditions are similar as far as the psychological and phonetic principle is concerned;

e.g., in Arabic, the vowel *i* in the middle of a verbal root denotes temporary, the vowel *u* permanent condition: *sakira* 'he is drunk,' *hasuna* 'he is handsome.'

Not only the quality, but also the quantity of vowels was variable, just as it is variable to-day in the forms of the English and German article (see Note, page 108): Most roots have short vowels in what might be called their 'normal forms' (e.g., the common infinitive forms of most verbs), but with some roots the long vowel is normal. Both short vowel roots and long vowel roots may be subject to shortening when unstressed; in this case, a short vowel is dropt entirely (in the case of a diphthong, the diphthongal glide remains), and a long vowel becomes 'shva.' — Under conditions of special stress, a short vowel may be lengthened. — Accepting the vowel of the 'normal form' of a root as its 'normal grade,' its shortened form is called 'reduced grade' (also 'zero grade,' in the case of the complete disappearance of a short vowel), and its lengthened form is called the 'lengthened grade' — in German: *Normalstufe* — *Schwundstufe, Nullstufe* — *Dehnstufe.* — This vowel interchange is called *quantitative vowel gradation* (*quantitativer Ablaut, Abstufung*).

Examples:

Normal grade	Reduced grade	Lengthened grade

A. Short vowel roots:

e|o, ei|oi, eu|ou, el|ol, etc.	i, u, l̥, etc.	ē|ō, ēi|ōi, etc.
Lat. *tegō,* 'I cover'		
toga, 'dress'		*tēgula,* 'tile'
Gk. *kléptŏ̄,* 'I steal'		
klopós, 'thief'		*klōps,* 'thief'
Gk. *léipein,* 'to be leaving'	*lipeīn,* 'to leave'	
loipós, 'left over'		

Gk. *phéugein*, 'to be fleeing'   *phugeîn*, 'to flee'
Sc. *vártati*,[1] 'he is turning'   *vrtāná–*, 'turned'

B. Long vowel roots:

ē|ō, (ā), ēi|ōi, ēl|ōl, etc.   ə, əi, əl, etc.   *No lengthened grade*
Gk. *(dí)dōmi*, 'I give'   Gk. *dotós*, ⎱ fr. IE.*dətós*, 'given'
Lat. *dōnum*, 'gift'   Lat. *datus*, ⎰
Gk. *(tí)thēmi*, 'I put'   *thetós*, fr. IE. *dhətós*
   (past part.)

Lat. *frāter*, 'brother'   *pater*, 'father,' fr. IE. *pətḗr*

NOTE. The interchange between front and back vowels (i.e., high-pitch and low-pitch vowels) corresponds to different degrees of interest on the part of the speaker, while the gradation of vowel quantity expresses different degrees of appeal to the person spoken to; in modern times, a characteristic example of the latter is found in the pronunciation of the German article, varying from zero to lengthened grade and expressing shades of emphasis from an indifferent element of grammatical form to a strong demonstrative: *Stell die Blumen aufn Tisch — auf dn Tisch — auf dən Tisch — auf den Tisch — auf dēn Tisch.*

From this point of view, as an expression of mental attitude, *Abtönung* and *Abstufung* might also be termed *subjective* and *objective*, or *internal* and *external* vowel gradation.

The exact function of the different vowel grades in IE. times cannot be determined, but the following are some of the chief categories: the *e*-grade appears primarily in the most common type of the present tense: Lat. *tegō* 'I cover,' Gk. *légō* 'I speak'; the *o*-grade, in many verbal nouns: Lat. *toga* 'dress,' Gk. *lógos* 'word'; the reduced grade, in certain types of the present tense, and in certain past tenses: Gk. *(é)lipon* 'I left,' *lipeîn* 'to leave,' 'to go away'; the lengthened grade, in certain verbal nouns and preterit types: Lat. *tēgula* 'tile,' *tēxi* 'I covered,' *lēgi* 'I (have) read.'

As to the occurrence of vowel gradation in suffixes (endings), see 53, 58.

The standard work on 'Ablaut' is: Hirt, *Der indogermanische Ablaut*, Strassburg 1901.

---

[1] for IE.*werteti*.

19. Indo-European Accent. The development of vowel gradation in its qualitative aspect, being dependent not on stress, but on pitch, and certain other phenomena seem to indicate that in an exceedingly early period IE. accent was rather of a musical than of a dynamic character (I, 56, 57), i.e., that the element of pitch predominated over the element of stress. But it is likely that even before the separation into individual languages the stress accent had gained the ascendency.

At all events, it is certain that IE. accent was 'free,' i.e., either the root or the suffix (or prefix) or an ending of a word could be stressed. Sanscrit, Greek, and several of the Slavic languages have preserved this original condition to a considerable extent. Compare: Gk. *patḗr*, 'father' (nominative sing.) — *patrós* (gen. sing.) — *páter* (vocative). — In consequence of the variations in stress, the root vowel (as also suffix vowels) may appear in different forms of quantitative gradation; compare Sc. *vártati*, 'he is turning' — *vṛtāná–*, 'turned.' In this function, vowel gradation is an especially important factor in the development of the typical verb forms, particularly among the Germanic languages. See **45, 46.**

The standard work on IE. accent is: Hirt, *Der indogermanische Akzent*, Strassburg 1895.

20. Indo-European Quantity. Aside from the self-evident difference between short and long syllables, i.e., generally speaking, between syllables with short vowels and syllables with long vowels, Indo-European also possessed syllables of a quantity which we might term 'over-long,' and which, in addition to their extreme quantity, had a peculiar accent quality ('double-pitch accent'). With reference to their relative duration in time units, we speak of syllables of one, two or three 'mores' or time units. Greek, Lithuanian, and, to a certain extent, Vedic Sanscrit retain these distinctions quite clearly; Greek uses the circumflex accent (˜) for three-more syllables: *patḗr*, nom. sing., *patrõn*, gen. pl.

Second Cycle

The Germanic Period

WILMANNS, *Deutsche Grammatik*, 1897 ff.

STREITBERG, *Urgermanische Grammatik*, 1901.

LOEWE, *Germanische Sprachwissenschaft*, ², 1911.

DIETER, *Laut- und Formenlehre der altgermanischen Dialekte*, 1900.

HENRY, *Comparative Grammar of English and German*, 1894.

WRIGHT, *Historical German Grammar*, 1908.

21. The Germanic Language is that language or group of languages that was spoken by those Indo-Europeans who remained longest in the West Baltic Basin (see **1, 2, 3**), at a time when the Slavic tribes had been formed in the east, and the Celtic tribes were forming in the west and south. In linguistic science, the Germanic language as spoken by the Germanic people before their final breaking up into tribes, is termed 'Pre-Germanic,' in translation of the German term *urgermanisch*. While not entirely correct logically, this term deserves the preference, for the sake of convenience, over the more accurate, but cumbersome translation 'Primitive Germanic.'

It is impossible to determine the dates of the 'Germanic period' with anything like chronological accuracy, but we are probably not far from the truth if we claim for it the last six or ten centuries of the Pre-Christian era. This would mean that the separation between Germanic and Celtic took place somewhere between 600 and 1000 B.C., while the formation of clearly distinct Germanic tribes began during the last centuries B.C.

Phonologically, the Pre-Germanic language is characterized by the predominance of a remarkably uniform tendency towards the strengthening of articulation in every respect. We find fairly distinct traces of the same tendency prevailing in Indo-European times and gradually disappearing, thru race mixture, when Indo-Europeans settled among non-Indo-European peoples. However, it was only during that indefinite period that we call the 'Germanic time,' and only among the Germanic people, that these tendencies were followed consistently and completely. In principle, every sound of the IE. sound system (with the exception of the liquids and nasals) went thru such a change as outlined in **13**; at the completion of this cycle, we are at the end of the Germanic period; this demarcation, however, must not be interpreted too rigidly, but allowance should be made for a certain amount of overlapping. The complete change that the consonants, vowels, accent and quantity of the language had undergone, points in the direction of a greater concentration on the psychological contents of the language (the meanings of words and sentences), and a relative weakening of the mere form elements.

22. The Germanic Consonant Shift. In 1822, Jakob Grimm made the discovery that a systematic comparison of the most important Germanic consonants, with those of other Indo-European languages, disclosed a remarkably regular process of sound transition which he called *Lautverschiebung;* in English, this process is frequently termed *Grimm's Law.* As far as the Germanic period is concerned, it consisted in the fact that each IE. stop followed the physiological direction indicated in **13**, **1a** and **2**.

(1) The **strong** stops became aspirated, and finally changed to voiceless spirants: p, t, k[1] >f, þ, x.

(2) The **middle** stops, being voiced, but pronounced

---

[1] Where there are no special reasons to the contrary, the signs k, gh, g will be used for all three series of IE. 'gutturals.' — Cf. **15**, Note.

with an over-normal force of breath, changed in the same way: the muscle tension, being slight as is always the case with voiced sounds, was overcome by the increased expiration, and **bh, dh, gh** became ƀ, ð, γ (see Note).

(3) The **weak** stops became voiceless in accordance with **13, 2**: b, d, g > p, t, k.

NOTES. (a) Step (1) and (2) may have occurred at the same or nearly the same time; step (3) was considerably later; the whole process, in every case, probably began with words of strong emphasis and gradually extended over all words containing the respective sounds; words that were habitually unaccented seem to have been affected late; this explains the fact that in the oldest stages of Germanic languages (Runic Norse and Gothic) a few words are found that do not exhibit change (3): Gothic *du* 'to' and *dis-* = Ger. *zer-* should be *tu, **tis-* (compare Eng. *to*, Lat. *dis-*), but retained the original sounds on account of their unemphatic character. Compare the treatment of final *t* in Middle Franconian, **33, 1**.

(b) Germanic *f* was originally bilabial (**I, 17**), but became labiodental in consequence of an inclination towards a sharper, more distinct pronunciation.

(c) Germanic χ in initial position became *h*, by reason of the relative inertness of the back of the tongue. This change took place during the first century A.D.

(d) ƀ is the usual philological sign for the voiced bilabial spirant [v] (**I, 17**); for the voiced velar spirant [γ], compare **I, 34**.

Examples. (1) p, t, k > f, Þ, χ.

Lat. *pecu* 'cattle,' Eng. *fee*, Ger. *Vieh*.
"   *tres* 'three,' Eng. *three*, Goth. *þreis*.
"   *cornu* 'horn,' Eng. *horn*, Ger. *Horn*.
"   *sequor* 'follow,' Ger. *sehen* (but: *Gesicht*) 'follow with the eyes.'

(2) bh, dh, gh > ƀ, ð, γ (later b, d, g, see **29**).

Lat. *ferō*, Sc. *bhárāmi* 'carry,' Eng. *bear*.

Lat. *medius*, Sc. *mádhyas* 'middle,' Eng. *mid*, Goth. *midjis*.
Gk. *steíchō* 'step,' Ger. *steigen*, Goth. *steigan* (=[stiiɣan]).

(3) b, d, g>p, t, k.

Lith. *balà* 'swamp': Eng. *pool*.
Lat. *decem* 'ten': Goth. *taíhun*, Eng. *ten*.
" *ager*, Gk. *agrós* 'acre': Goth. *akrs*.

NOTE. Lat. *f* comes from IE. *bh* or *dh*, medial *d* from IE. *dh*, Gk. *ch* from IE. *gh*.

The student should collect a complete list of all instances of the Germanic consonant changes occurring in the Gothic specimen text on page 198, and in the corresponding passage of the English gospel translation.

Whenever *p, t, k* were preceded by a voiceless spirant (either old, i.e., directly preserved from IE., or new, i.e., developt in the Germanic consonant shift), they remained unchanged because the preceding spirant consumed a comparatively large force of expiration: Lat. *stella* 'star,' from **sterula*: Goth. *staírnō*, Lat. *octō* 'eight': Ger. *acht*, *rectus* 'right': *recht*.

The Labio-Velars. *q, gh, g*, in principle, became Gc. χ*w*, γ*w*, *kw*, but these sound combinations show a gradually increasing tendency to give up either the velar, or the labial element; in general, before back vowels, which are habitually labialized, the labial element [w] is lost by being merged with the following vowel, while it is retained before front vowels. Compare: Lat. *quod*: Goth. *ƕa*, Eng. *what*, Ger. *was* — Lat. *sequor*: Goth. *saíƕan*, Ger. *sehen, Gesicht;* Gk. *omphē* 'voice,' from IE. **soŋ̇ghá*: Goth. *siggwan* 'sing,' Ger. *singen* — Gk. *thermós* 'warm,' from IE. **ghermós*, Ger. *warm;* Lat. *veniō* 'come,' from IE. **gṃjō:* (Goth. *quiman*), Ger. *kommen* — Lat. *vīvus* 'alive,' from IE. **geigos:* Goth. *qius*, Eng. *quick*, Ger. *Queck–*.

Analogy and other conditions have brought about so many complications in the treatment of these sounds that a detailed discussion would go far beyond the limits of this book.

23. Verner's Law (Grammatical Change). The great number of Germanic voiced spirants that had arisen from

the transition of IE. *bh, dh, gh* into ƀ, ð, γ received a further increase thru a peculiar consequence of the strong stress accent of later Indo-European times: When a voiceless spirant in Germanic (*f, þ, χ, s*) followed a syllable without the IE. stress accent, the contrast in the transition from the unaccented to the (relatively) accented syllable caused a narrowing of the glottis and tension of the vocal chords, so that the spirant became voiced — provided that it was surrounded by voiced sounds. Consequently, IE. *p, t, k, s* are represented in Germanic by voiceless *f, þ, χ, s* only when the preceding syllable had the IE. accent, or when they were in initial position, but by ƀ, ð, γ, *z* when they were *not* immediately preceded by the IE. accent. (Sievers: *Die stimmlosen Spiranten bleiben stimmlos im Nachlaut der indogermanisch betonten Silbe.*) — Theoretical IE. groups like *ápa, áta, áka* became Germanic *afa, aþa, aχa,* but *apá, atá, aká* changed to *aƀa, aða, aγa,* and *ása* remained unchanged, while *asá* changed to *aza.* Compare the analogous treatment of Engl. *éxit — exámine, éxercise — exért,* etc. — Germanic *z* later became *r;* this change is called *rhotacism* (from *rho,* the Greek name of the letter *r*).

This law was first discovered by *Eduard Sievers,* but the Danish philologist *Karl Verner* was the first to publish it, and for that reason it is commonly called *Verner's Law.* — In as far as these interchanges between voiceless and voiced spirants frequently mark distinctions between different grammatical forms of the same root (especially in the case of the verb, see **47**), it is also called *Grammatical Change (Grammatischer Wechsel).*

Examples.

(*a*) IE. *p* > Gc. ƀ: Gk. *heptá* 'seven': Goth. *siƀun,* Eng. *seven.*

Interchange *f* : *b* : IE. root **terp–*: Goth. *þarf* 'I want' — *þarba* 'want,' noun.

(*b*) IE. *t* > Gc. *ð*: Gk. *patḗr* 'father': Goth. *faðar* (but Gk. *phrā́tōr* 'brother': Goth. *brōþar*).

Interchange *þ* : *d*: IE. root **leit–* (with varying accent, see **47**) — OS. Inf. *līthan*, Pret. sing. *lēth*, but Pret. pl. *lidun* (compare NHG. *leiden — litten*).

(*c*) IE. *k* > Gc. *γ*: Gk. *dákru* 'tear': Goth. *tagr* (but OHG. *zahar*, NHG. *Zähre*, with different accent).

Interchange *χ* : *g*: IE. root **deuk–* (Lat. *dūcō* 'lead') — NHG. *ziehen — sie zogen*.

(*d*) IE. *s* > Gc. *z* (Ger. *r*): Lat. *auris* 'ear' < *ausis*: Goth. *ausō* for **auzō*, Ger. *Ohr*.

Interchange *s* : *z* (*r*): IE. root **wes–* 'be' — Eng. *was — were*.

24. Other Consonant Changes are comparatively rare. Aside from a number of more or less perspicuous assimilations, the following are the most important:

(*a*) **The Germanic Consonant Gemination** (i.e., doubling, or lengthening): If any IE. stop was followed by *n*, and the next syllable had the IE. accent, this consonant group was assimilated in such a way that a long voiced stop resulted, which became voiceless at the same time with the other voiceless stops. Expressed in a formula, this means: *pn', bhn', bn'* > *bb* > pp; *tn', dhn', dn'* > *dd* > tt; *kn', ghn', gn'* > *gg* > kk: IE. **lugnós* 'pliable': Ger. *Locke*. — Many NHG. double forms, such as *schneiden — schnitzen, stoßen — stutzen, schnauben — schnupfen, Knauf — Knopf, ziehen — zucken*, etc., are due to this process (the first form of each pair coming from a form without *n*, the second, from one with *n*).

(*b*) IE. *ŋ* followed by *k* disappeared in Germanic, after the latter had become *χ*: Gc. *ŋχ* > –*χ*, but the preceding vowel was lengthened ('compensatory lengthening,' *Ersatzdehnung*): Lat. *vinco* 'vanquish': Goth. *weihan* (pronounce [wiːχan]) 'fight'; this gave rise to some important parallel forms in verbs when certain forms of the stem ended in a voiced, others, by assimilation or on account of the accent (Verner's Law), in a voiceless consonant, e.g., Lat. *tongēre* 'know': Goth. inf. *þaŋkjan* 'think' (Germanic root **þaŋk–*), pret.

þāχta (Gc. root **þaŋχ–*, on account of the same assimilation that we see in Lat. *rectus*, from *regō* — Ger. *recht*); this process is reflected in such NHG. forms as *denken* — *dachte*, *dünken* — *däuchte* (Goth. *þuŋkjan* — *þūχta*), *bringen* — *brachte* (Goth. *briggan* — *brāχta*); or, thru accent variations, in *fāhen* — *fing*, *seihen* — *sinken*.

(c) *sr* in initial and medial position became **str** (*t* being inserted as a protection against assimilation): Sc. *usrá–* 'dawn': OE. *ēastron*, Ger. *Ostern* 'spring time, Easter'; Sc. *sru–* 'flow': Ger. *Strom;* Lat. *soror* 'sister,' from IE. **swesr–*: Ger. *Schwester* (Goth. stem *swistr–*).

25. The Germanic Vowel Shift. — Compare **13**, 6*a*. — The difference between long and short vowels is not merely one of time, but also of intensity: long vowels, by their very duration, demand greater energy of articulation than short vowels. The character of quantitative vowel gradation and the coincidence of the differences between long and short and narrow and wide vowels (**I, 40**) in German and other languages illustrate this fact. On this account, in keeping with the general tendency of the language in favor of sharp contrasts, IE. long and short vowels develop in opposite directions in Germanic: The contrast between them was intensified by *increasing* the articulation of long vowels, and *decreasing* the articulation of short vowels. This was done in accordance with the principles stated in **13**, 6: Long vowels develop in the direction ē̆ — ǣ — ā — ō (thereby becoming lower in pitch), short vowels in the direction ŭ — ŏ — ă. Expressed in linguistic formulas, this development means: IE. ē̆ > Gc. ǣ, IE. *ā* > Gc. *ō*; (IE. *ŭ* > Gc. *ŏ*), IE. *ŏ* > Gc. *ă*; IE. ǝ became *a* in Germanic, as in most other IE. languages (*i* in Sanscrit).

NOTE. Strictly speaking, these changes affect only accented syllables; unaccented syllables follow, in part, different principles, as will be seen in **29**.

Examples.

ē̆ > ǣ (Goth. *ē*, OHG. *ā*):

Lat. *sēmen:* Gc. **sǣ-*, Goth. *-sēps*, Ger. *Sáme.*

Lat. *rēri* 'think': Gc. **rǣ-*, Ger. *rāten.*

Lat. *ēdimus, vēnimus* 'we ate, we came': Gc. **ǣt-*, **qǣm-*, Ger. *wir āßen, kāmen.*

ā > ō:

Lat. *māter* 'mother': OS. *mōdor.*

Lat. *fāgus* 'beech': ON. *bōk.*

Lat. *frāter* 'brother': Goth. *brōþar.*

ŏ > ă:

Lat. *octō* 'eight': Ger. *acht.*

Lat. *nox* 'night': Ger. *Nacht.*

Lat. *hostis* 'enemy': Ger. *Gast.*

ə > ă:

IE. *pətér, Lat. *pater*, Sc. *pitár-*: Goth. *faðar*, (Ger. *Väter*).

The long vowels *ō, ī, ū* and, in part at least, the short vowels *ĕ, ă, ĭ, ŭ* (see below) remained unchanged in Pre-Germanic times. Instances have been given in **17**.

The first elements of diphthongs changed in the same way as simple vowels; therefore, IE. *oi, ai* and *əi* fell together in Germanic, all three of them being represented by *ai*: Lat. (old form) *oinos* 'one': Goth. *ains*, Ger. *ein;* Lat. *aes* = *ais 'bronze': Goth. *aiz;* Lat. *caedō* < *kəidō 'cut': Goth. *haitan* 'distinguish, call.' — The diphthong *ei* had to become *ii* = *ī*, on account of the change *e > i* indicated below: Gk. *steíchō* 'step': Gc. *stīγan 'climb.'

NOTE. 'Long diphthongs' (**17**) had three time units (**20**), namely, a long vowel and a glide; according to **27**, they were shortened — reduced to two units — and thus fell together with the common diphthongs, from which they can no longer be distinguisht in Germanic: *ōi — āi, ōu — āu, ēu, ōl — āl, ēl,* etc. > Gc. *ai, au, eu, al, el,* etc. IE. *ēi,* however, became close *ē*. Instances in **46**, Note.

The Syllabic Nasals and Liquids. Where, thru reduction in vowel gradation, the diphthongal glides had become 'syllabic' (I, 54 end, II, 17), they were treated differently in different Indo-European languages. Thus, in Latin, the vowel *e* generally developt in front of *n*, *m*, the vowel *o* in front of *l*, *r*; in Greek, *n* and *m* became *a* (as also in Sanscrit), while with *l* and *r*, *a* was inserted; in Sanscrit, *l* and *r* remained syllabic consonants. We can say, therefore, that the 'zero grades' of the IE. diphthongs *em*, *en*, *er*, *el* became *em*, *en*, *or*, *ol* in Latin, *a*, *a*, *al* (*la*), *ar* (*ra*) in Greek, *a*, *a*, *ṛ* (for *ḷ*), *ṛ* in Sanscrit. In Germanic, the vowel *u* developt under such conditions: IE. *m̥*, *n̥*, *l̥*, *r̥* > Gc. *um*, *un*, *ul*, *ur*:

IE. **km̥tóm*, Lat. *centum*, Gk. *hekatón*, Sc. *Ṣatám*, Goth. *hunds* 'hundred.'

IE. **mn̥tós* 'thought,' Lat. *commentus* 'contrived,' Gk. *autó-matos* 'of one's own accord,' Sc. *matás* 'thought,' Goth. *gamunds* 'memory.'

IE. **wl̥qós* 'wulf,' Sc. *vṛ́kas*, Goth. *wulfs*.

IE. **tr̥nó-*, Sc. *tṛnám* 'blade of grass,' Goth. *þaúrnus* (for *þurnus) 'thorn.'

Conditional Changes. IE. *u* (including the *u* that developt in Germanic before *m*, *n*, *l*, *r*, see above) became *o* in Germanic — fully in keeping with the tendency of decreased articulation of short vowels, — but only if it was followed by some vowel other than *i* or *u*: Gk. *zugón*: Ger. *Joch*, Sc. *vṛ́kas*: Ger. *Wolf*. — Apparently, IE. *i* became *e* under the same conditions, but this is not entirely certain.

IE. *e* became *i* in Germanic: (*a*) if the following syllable contained *i* or *j*: Lat. *medius* 'middle': OHG. *mitti*; compare **30**. Likewise, the diphthong *ei* became *ii* = *ī*; see above, Gk. *steíchō*, Goth. *steigan*, OHG. *stīgan*; (*b*) if it was followed by nasal+consonant: Lat. *ventus*: Ger. *Wind*. Both of these changes occur very late; Tacitus still has *Segimundus*, *Fenni* for later *Sigimundus*, *Finni*; some of the oldest loan words from Latin exhibit this change because they were adopted before it took place: Lat. *census*: Ger. *Zins*. (*c*) in unaccented position; see **53**.

26. The Germanic Accent Shift. The free accent of the Indo-European parent language was regulated in Germanic according to logical principles: In simple words the root syllable was stressed, i.e., the accent became confined to that element of the word that conveyed the meaning, instead of the grammatical form. — In compound nouns, the prefix retained the accent — a principle inherited from the parent language — but compound verbs stressed the root; this is still apparent in NHG. *Antwort — entgehen* (*antworten* is derived from *Antwort*), *Urteil — erteilen, Vorsorge — versorgen.*

Final Syllables. In consequence of the strong Germanic stress accent on the stem syllable, the mere form elements of words, especially the grammatical terminations, were greatly weakened and, eventually, even lost. Of the complicated rules concerning this weakening of final syllables, the following are the most important:

(*a*) Vowels in final syllables are, in general, shortened by one '*mora*' (**20**); therefore, short vowels disappear, common long vowels become short, and over-long vowels remain long. Compare Gk. *chórtos* 'garden,' *patḗr*, Sc. (Vedic) *dēvās* 'gods': Goth. *gards* 'house,' *fadar, dagōs* 'days' (but Lat. *pecu, mare* < **mari:* OHG. *fihu, meri*).

(*b*) Of final consonants, *r* is preserved everywhere, *s* in Gothic (and Norse); all other final consonants are dropt in all Germanic dialects. Compare Gk. *patḗr, chórtos*, Lat. *verbum* 'word' with Goth. *fadar, gards* (*dags*), *waúrd* 'word' and OHG. *fater, tag, wort.*

27. The Standardization of Quantity. Aside from the weakening of final syllables, the distribution of quantity remains the same as in Indo-European; however, the difference between long and overlong vowels disappears, all vowels being simply long or short. Compare **20**.

28. Table of the Most Important Germanic Sound Changes.

	IE.	Gc.	Instances	Par.
Strong Stops:	'p, 't, 'k	f, þ, χ (h, hw)	fee, three, horn, what	22 [1]
Middle Stops:	p', t', k' ⎫ bh, dh, gh ⎭	ƀ, ð, γ (b, d, g; w)	seven, hundred, Ger. zogen, Au[1]	23
			bear, mid, Ger. steigen, warm	22 [2]
Weak Stops:	b, d, g	p, t, k (qu)	pool, ten, acre, quick	22 [3]
	's	s	was	23
	s'	z (r)	were	23
Long Vowels:	ā, ō	ō	mother, cow	25
	ē	æ (ā)	Ger. Same	25
Short Vowels:	ă, ŏ, ə	a	Ger. Acker, acht, Eng. father	25
Diphthongs:	ai, oi, əi ⎫ āi, ōi ⎭ ai		Goth. ais, ains, hai-tan (inf.), haihait (pret.)	25
Syllabic Cons.:	m̥, n̥, l̥, r̥	um, un, ul, ur (om, on, ol, or)	hundred, Goth. ga-munds, wulfs	25

To make this table as practical as possible, only the most important sounds have been included, chiefly those that exhibit characteristic changes.

The Intermediate Period

29. **The Germanic Voiced Spirants.** The changes described in the preceding paragraphs were 'Germanic,' i.e., they took place before the final formation of Germanic dialects — in general, before the beginning of the Christian era. During the first centuries A.D., another change took place which affected all Germanic languages to a certain extent, but was carried thru entirely only in a small part of them. This is the transition of the Germanic voiced spirants ƀ, ð, γ into the corresponding stops b, d, g.

---

[1] Derivative from Gc. *aχwa 'water' — Gc. form *aγwja < IE. *aqjá.

Increase of muscle tension, as explained in **13, 4**, was the physiological cause; the last step of the Germanic consonant shift had consisted in the change of *b*, *d*, *g* to the corresponding voiceless lenes, *ḅ*, *ḍ*, *ǵ*, and then, thru simultaneous increase of expiration and muscle tension, to the voiceless stops *p*, *t*, *k*. The phonetic habits expressed in this latter transition led to the change of ƀ, ð, γ to *b*, *d*, *g*. In its beginnings, this process can be said to be generally Germanic; its continuation belongs to the phonology of the separate dialects. In initial position, in gemination, and after consonants,[1] the voiced spirants became stops everywhere, tho, perhaps, not at the same time: we have stops in Goth. *baíran*, *lamb*, *daúr*, *haldan*, *guma*, *baúrg*, but spirants in *giban*, *fadar*, and probably in *biugan* (*b*, *d*, *g* = ƀ, ð, γ).

In *West-Germanic*, the transition was a gradual one, taking place in direct proportion to the agility of the articulating organs: the tip of the tongue is the most active of these, and dentals, therefore, are the first to change; the lips are next in activity, while the back of tongue is relatively inert, and we find, accordingly, that the labials change next, the velars last. This chronological order is apparent, as explained in § **5**, from the geographical distribution of the dialects: in the north, the change has taken comparatively little effect, in the south it is general.

The following changes took place in West-Germanic during this intermediate period:

(*a*) Germanic ð became **d** in all positions: OE. *fæder* 'father' had *d*, not ð (the change from *d* to ð in Eng. *father* took place during the sixteenth century).

(*b*) Initial ƀ became **b** everywhere, compare Goth. *baíran*, Eng. *bear*.

[1] Strictly 'Pre-Germanic', only after nasals.

Medial and final ƀ remained a spirant (generally voiceless when final: *f*) thruout the North and in Middle Franconian, but became a stop south of Middle Franconian: Eng. *give, gave*, MF. *geven, gaf;* Eng. *wife — wives*, etc.

(*c*) Initial **γ** remained a spirant as far south as MF. (including Northern MF.), but became a stop south of it, so that its treatment is essentially the same as that of medial ƀ: Eng. *yard, yield*, Ger. *Garten, gelten* (stops in English words like *garden, give*, are generally ascribed to Scandinavian influence).

Medial **γ** remained a spirant in all dialects except Upper German: Eng. *lay, lie*, North Ger. [laːɣən, liːjən] where Upper German pronounces stops (**I, 32**).

Final **γ** remained a spirant (generally voiceless) everywhere except in Alemannian and Swiss; only in these dialects, therefore, the pronunciations [taːk, ziːk], as required by the stage standard, are indigenous.

Compare the sketch maps and the table attacht to page 131.

NOTE. It should be kept in mind, however, that the boundaries are in reality considerably more complicated than indicated in these simple outlines; they do not coincide in every case with the dialect boundaries that have been suggested for the purposes of this book, but they are accurate enough to give an adequate picture of the general directions of development.

The most noteworthy exception is the fact that the dialects of Schleswig-Holstein, Mecklenburg and Pommern show initial *g*, Mecklenburg-Schwerin also medial *g*; ethnological reasons could easily be given.

Compare Behaghel, *Geschichte der deutschen Sprache*, p. 212 ff., 235 f.

30. The West-Germanic Consonant Lengthening. During the West-Germanic period every consonant (except *r*) was lengthened (doubled) when it was followed by *j*, and certain consonants were also lengthened before *l*, *r*, *w*, *n*, *m* (see Streitberg, *Urgermanische Grammatik*, 113): Goth. *sibja*, *bidjan*, *halja*, *akrs*, Lat. *cuprum* — Ger. *Sippe* (OE. *sibb*), *bitten* (OE. *biddan*), *Hölle*, *Kupfer* (Eng. *copper*). — It seems, however, that not all of the numerous cases of consonant doubling that we find in German can be explained either thru the West-Germanic or the Germanic consonant lenghtening; it is very probable that a spontaneous lengthening (not caused by any surrounding sounds) took place in OHG. in forms of special emphasis, like *plagen* — *placken* — a strengthening which would be entirely compatible with the principles of the consonant shift. — Compare 56, Note 2.

Third Cycle

The German Period

BEHAGHEL, *Geschichte der deutschen Sprache*, ³, 1911.
WILMANNS, *Deutsche Grammatik*, 1897 ff.
WRIGHT, *Historical German Grammar*, 1908.
LICHTENBERGER, *Grammaire historique de la langue allemande*, 1898.
PIQUET, *Précis de phonétique historique de l'allemand*, 1907.
SÜTTERLIN, *Die deutsche Sprache der Gegenwart*, ³, 1911.
BRENNER, *Grundzüge der geschichtlichen Grammatik der deutschen Sprache*, 1896.
CURME, *A Grammar of the German Language*, 1905.
SCHULZ, *Abriss der deutschen Grammatik*, 1914.

31. The German Language presents two clearly distinct linguistic phenomena: on the one hand, a multiplicity of dialects that has arisen thru ethnic disintegration in connection with the historical and geographical series of Germanic colonizations and invasions of Western and Southern Germany; on the other hand, the New High German standard language, formed as an unintentional compromise between the principal dialects — an artificial, unorganic structure at first glance, but, on deeper thought, revealed as a growth of wonderful historical significance. It is equally wrong to extol the dialects at the cost of the literary standard, considering them the real, genuine continuation of the language, as to underrate their importance by thinking them less 'correct' or 'refined' than *Schriftdeutsch* or *Hochdeutsch*. Both are of equal value, as expressions of the historical and cultural development of the German nation.

The previous chapters have made it appear obvious that the northern dialects, in their main characteristics, exhibit an older, the southern dialects, a relatively younger form of the language. But another factor seems to enter into consideration. In varying proportions, which we are no longer able to estimate even approximately, the Germanic immigrants had mingled with an older (chiefly Celtic) population. Celtic influence on the formation of the German vocabulary is indubitable.[1] Words like *Reich* (OHG. *rīhhi*), borrowed from a Celtic word denoting 'rule' (Lat. root *rĕg-*) and appearing in names like *Dietrich*, *Friedrich*, or *Amt* (from Lat.-Celt. *ambactus*), point to a close political contact between Germans and Celts; among the geographical names, very many are of Celtic origin, e.g., the masculine names of German rivers (*Rhein*, *Main*, *Neckar*, *Lech*, *Inn*, *Eisack*, *Regen*), occurring in that part of Germany that had been Celtic. In the east and southeast, Slavic influx is seen in such words as East Prussian *Schmant*, Austrian *Schmetten* for 'cream,' geographical names in *-a*, *-ow*, *-z* (*-tz*), *-tzsch*, *-in*, etc.: *Jena*, *Bützow*, *Graz*, *Liegnitz*, *Eutritzsch*, *Berlin*. Also the grammatical structure of the language along the boundaries shows many traces of foreign influence. (See Be-

[1] Compare, e.g., Much, *Deutsche Stammeskunde* (Leipzig, Göschen, 1900), p. 41 ff,

haghel, p. 29 f.). Under these circumstances it would be strange indeed if no foreign elements existed in the phonology of the German language, especially when we remember that the literary standard took its impetus primarily from colonial soil.

It is difficult to prove in detail just where the Celtic or Slavic influences are to be sought. There is one fact, however, that greatly alleviates the difficulty of the task, namely, the fact that the Germanic phonetic tendencies happen to be diametrically opposite to both the Celtic and the Slavic tendencies, the former going in the direction of strengthened, both of the latter, in the direction of weakened articulation. It is extremely unlikely that a language, at the same time and under like circumstances, should exhibit contrary tendencies within itself; therefore, wherever we find evidences of weakening tendencies in the Germanic dialects or in the German standard language, there is at least a considerable probability of foreign influence. — At any rate, there can be no doubt that it is of pedagogical and systematic value for the beginner to have a clear conception of the consistency or inconsistency of a given phonetic change in its relation to the general phonetic character of the language.

The striking uniformity of the sound development during the Germanic period — and this uniformity is real, not merely a theoretical construction — is set off all the more clearly by the complicated picture that the following centuries represent. But this complicity finds its exact counterpart in contemporaneous German history. The *nation* had lost its unity as much as the *language*. The centrifugal political tendencies came to a standstill when the greater part of the old Indo-Germanic and Germanic home, the land of the 'people themselves,' the *Suevi-Semnones*, had been recovered and, in the hands of an

Alemannian dynasty, the Hohenzollern, had become the nucleus of a new national unity of the German people. And at the same time the language seems to have been rejuvenated, completing the work of its reconstruction, and returning, as it were, to the very same phonetic tendencies that had been dormant for centuries. Thus, the reunited German nation has recovered its unity of language.

* * *

It cannot be the intention of an elementary introduction like the present book to point out every nook and corner of this linguistic labyrinth. More accurate details can be found easily enough in such excellent standard works as Behaghel and Wilmanns, which even the beginner ought to consult frequently. The following paragraphs are merely a rough sketch of the general directions in which the language moved, in no way adapted to supplant books like those mentioned, but rather serving as a guide making them more accessible to students without any linguistic training.

32. The High German Consonant Shift. At the end of the Germanic and the Intermediate periods — the latter partly overlapping the former — German possesses the voiceless stops *p, t, k* and, within the limits stated in **29**, the voiced stops *b, d, g*, in place of which certain dialects had retained voiced spirants. If the tendencies of the Germanic consonant shift had continued unchanged, the result would obviously have been: Gc. *p, t, k* > Ger. *f, þ, χ* and Gc. *b, d, g* > Ger. *p, t, k*. But (*a*) these changes took place only in a part of the German territory, namely, in the High German dialects; for this reason we speak of a **High German** or Second **Consonant Shift** (in contrast to the First or Germanic Sound Shift). (*b*) The phonetic direction was deflected in certain instances, so that the results slightly differed from those of the first consonant shift. (c) In some cases weakening tendencies set in that counteracted changes which actually had taken place.

The historical order and, therefore, the geographical spread of the second consonant shift appears from two phonetic considerations: first, according to **29**, the order must be supposed to have been: dentals, labials, velars; second, the expiration being stronger after vowels than initially or after consonants, stops after vowels can be assumed to have been strengthened earlier than those in other positions. From this appears: (a) that dentals were 'shifted' in the greatest, velars, in the smallest part of the territory, (b) that post-vocalic stops were shifted more generally than others; for the sake of convenience, we use the signs p^1, t^1, k^1 for the position after vowels, and p^2, t^2, k^2 for initial position and position after consonants (including 'gemination,' for which compare **30**).

Details and Examples.

(Since English has practically retained the West-Germanic consonants — y in *day*, w in *sorrow* representing Germanic γ, — the instances are chiefly taken from English.)

In its extreme form, the High German Consonant Shift leads to the following results:

1. $t^1 > ₃₃$, i.e., a strong voiceless dental spirant, expressed by *zz* or *z* in OHG. and MHG. manuscripts. Probably, this was originally a slit-spirant (þ), but in the course of time (during the MHG. period) it became a rill-spirant, at first with a flat rill, which gradually became sharper, and at last in most dialects fell together with IE. *s*. In the beginning, ₃ was articulated farther front (strictly dental) than *s* (alveolar), but most dialects have aban-

doned this distinction too. — The doubling of the sign ʒ, occurring for the most part medially after short vowels, merely indicates the fortis pronunciation, distinguishing the new spirants from the old (Germanic) ones, which had become lenes.

Instances: Eng. *eat* — Ger. *essen* (OHG. *ezzan*), *let* — *lassen, water* — *Wasser, it that what* — *es das was.*

NOTE. The fact that rill formation is absolutely not in keeping with the general habits of Germanic articulation, but is a very common phenomenon in the Romance languages that originated on Celtic soil, especially French, leads to the suspicion that the transition from a theoretical *þþ* to ʒʒ and then to *ss* was due to Celtic influence.

2. $p^1 >$ **ff** (f) (at first bilabial, later labio-dental): Eng. *open* — Ger. *offen, hope* — *hoffen, sleep* — *schlafen, up* — *auf.*

3. $k^1 >$ **xx** (χ), i.e., Ger. *ch*; this was not subject to the transition to *h*, as Germanic χ had been (22, Note *c*), but remained a strong spirant, which, thru assimilation to the preceding vowel, divided into an *ich-* and an *ach-* sound in all dialects with the exception of Alemannian and Southern Bavarian, where the original *ach*-sound was retained in all positions.

Instances: Eng. *book* — Ger. *Buch, wake—wachen, seek* — *suchen.*

4. $t^2 >$ **ts** (spelled *z*), at first, probably, something like *tþ*. As mentioned above, the figure [2] refers to initial position, position after consonants, and to the West-Germanic geminates (*pp, tt, kk*) that had been formed according to 30.

Instances: *two* — *zwei, tongue* — *Zunge, heart* — *Herz, sit* = Goth. *sitjan* — *sitzen, whet* = Goth. *hwatjan* — *wetzen* (WGc. *sittjan, *hwattjan*).

5. $p^2 >$ **pf** (originally bilabial affricate, [pF]): *plow* —

Pflug, pound — Pfund, carp — Karpfen, but *sharp — scharf* (see below), Goth. *skapjan* — WGc. **skappjan, schöpfen.*

6. k²>kχ, an affricate consisting of *k* and the *ach*-sound, at present occurring in Southern Swiss only: Standard Ger. *kalt, Kuh, Werk, trinken, Acker, wecken* = Swiss [kχalt, kχuː, vɛrkχ, triŋkχən, ʔakχər, vɛkχən] (Goth. *akrs, wakjan,* WGc. **akkr, *wakkjan*).

7. d>d̦>t (voiceless fortis, but unaspirated; see below): *do — tun, door — Tür, wade — waten.*

8. b->b̦>p (unaspirated fortis, occurring only in a few words of South German origin): Eng. *bolster* — Ger. *Polster;* but *bear — gebären.*

9. -ƀ->b>b̦(>p): *love — Liebe, give — geben, wives — Weiber;* see below.

10. γ->g>ǧ(>k): *yard — Garten, yield — gelten, yellow — gelb* (as to Eng. *g* in words like *garden, give* — probably due to Scandinavian influence, see **29** *c*).

11. -γ->g>ǧ: *eye — Auge, days — Tage; Jäger, Lager.*

These changes are carried thru to the following extent:

Steps **1, 2, 3, 4** took place in the whole High German territory; however, Middle Franconian retains a few characteristic exceptions: *dat, it, wat* and, in part, the corresponding neuter adjective endings (*großet*), for standard German *das, es, was,* (*großes*), remained unchanged on account of their habitual unaccented position, similar to Goth. *du, dis–* (**22**, Note *a*); the same is true with the preposition *up = auf.* Step **5** extended over Upper German and East Franconian; in Middle Franconian this change did not take place at all, and in Rhenish Franconian only after *l* and *r; lp, rp* changed at first to *lpf, rpf,* but later to *rf, lf;* accordingly, we find in Upper German and East Franconian *Pfennig, Pfund, Pfalz,* but in Rhenish and Middle Franconian (and, of course, Low German) *Penni(n)g, Pund, Palz* (the motto of the Rhenish Palatinate is: Fröhlich **P**alz, Gott erhalt's!); the older form *rpf* is preserved in the word *Karpfen,* but elsewhere we find *f: scharf, Harfe, helfen:* Eng. *sharp, harp, help.*

NOTE. Many scholars accept the change from p^2 to pf as criterion between Upper German and Middle German, and accordingly class East Franconian with the former instead of the latter; for the present time, this is quite justified, but the arrangement followed in our book takes the historical development more closely into account.

Step **6** appeared only in Alemannian and Bavarian in early OHG. times, but in general the affricate was soon replaced by the aspirated voiceless stop from which it had come (retrogressive development); at present, $k\chi$ is found only in the southern dialects of Switzerland, while χ is pronounced in the Tyrol and in other Swiss dialects ([χalt, χuː]).

Step **7**. General West-Germanic d (from $\eth$, § **29**) became voiceless everywhere in High German territory; in Upper German and East Franconian, this voiceless lenis originally became an unaspirated fortis, but at present, only High Alemannian and most of Bavarian proper (not Austrian) have retained the fortis pronunciation, while East Franconian, Lower Alemannian, and Austrian reintroduced the lenis. Accordingly, words like *tun*, *Tür* are pronounced with lenis, [d̦], in Franconian and Austrian, with fortis (unaspirated) in most of Alemannian and Bavarian. — After nasals, the lenis pronunciation set in especially early and is recognized in standard German forms like *Länder*, *Winde* (compare Eng. *land*, *wind*), but after other consonants in general t is accepted: *Worte:* Eng. *words*. (See **35**.) — In gemination, tenuis appears in all HG. dialects: Goth. *bidjan*, OE. *biddan*, Ger. *bitten*.

Steps **8, 9, 10, 11** are carried thru only in the Upper German dialects, as far as the fortis stage is concerned, but voiceless lenis occurs within the limits indicated in the attacht table. Fortis p is general in older Upper German, but in medial position it disappeared in Alemannian in the ninth, and in Bavarian in the eleventh century; in initial position it is found, by the side of b, to the end of the Middle Ages; it is sometimes supposed that this fluctuation is merely an orthographical one, both p and b merely being efforts to represent the voiceless lenis, but the consistently different treatment of initial and medial position, and of b and g, as well as the chronological development, make it much more likely that p represents a fortis which, in the course of time, was back-developt to a voiceless lenis. — Standard German has, in general, adopted the Upper (=East) Franconian form with b: Eng. *bear* — Ger. *gebären*, *bring* — *bringen*, *give* — *geben*. — *bb* was shifted to *pp* in Upper

Middle-Franconian	Rhenish-Franconian	East-Franconian	Alemannian	Bavarian	New High German Examples
ȝȝ	ȝȝ	ȝȝ	ȝȝ	ȝȝ	Wasser (M.F. dat)
ff	ff	ff	ff	ff	offen (M.F. up)
xx	xx	xx	xx	xx	machen
ts	ts	ts	ts	ts	zwei
—	lf, rf	pf	pf	pf	Pflug
—	—	—	(kχ)	(kχ)	kalt
d̥	d̥	d(t)	d(t)	(d̥)t	tun (Wind)
b̥	b̥	b̥	b̥(p)	b̥(p)	Berg (Passau)
v	b̥>v	b̥>v	b̥(p)	b̥>v	Weiber (Rippe)
—	g̊	g̊	g̊(k)	g̊(k)	geben
—	—	—	g̊(k)	g̊(k)	Auge (Rücken)
			k	(k)	Tag
d̥	d̥	d̥	d̥	d̥	der

PLATE II

1. The Germanic Voiced Spirants
(Intermediate Period)

ð>d, ƀ>b ▭
-ƀ->b, γ->g ▤
-γ->g ▥
-γ>k ▨

2. The H.G. Shift of
Voiceless Stops

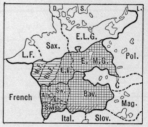

$p^1t^1k^1>$ff, ʒʒ, χχ }
$t^2>$ts
$p^2>$pf ▥
$k^2>$kχ ▨

3. The H.G. Shift of
Voiced Stops

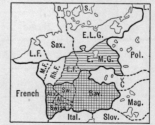

đ>t ▤

ƀ>p, g>k ▥

German, comp. Goth. *sibja*, **ribja*, OE. *sibb*, *ribb*, UG. *sippa*, *rippa*; NHG. has adopted the Upper German forms.

k from initial *g* is general in older Upper German, but is found rarely in medial position (UG. *kepan*, *ouca=ouka* 'eye'). NHG. does not accept it anywhere. — *gg* became *kk* in High German: OS. *hruggi* < **hrugja* — Ger. *Rücken;* Goth. *brugja* — Ger. *Brücke.*

NOTE. The dialects which had retained medial b — namely, those north of Rhenish Franconian — soon replaced it by labiodental *v*; of those that had changed it to *b*, only the greater part of Alemannian and Swabian kept it as ƀ, while RF., EF. and Bav. weakened it to bilabial *v*: [vaivə] for NHG. *Weiber.*

In the second consonant shift, as in the first, *p, t, k* after voiceless spirants were left unchanged; see **22.** Besides, initial *tr* was not affected: compare Eng. *tread, true* — Ger. *treten, treu.*

Final stops and spirants became voiceless in all dialects, chiefly towards the end of the OHG. period: *Weib* = [viːf] in the north, [vaip] in the south, *Rad* = [raːt], *Tag, Sieg* = [taːχ, ziːç] chiefly in the north, [taːk, siːk] in the south. The stage pronunciation has decided in favor of the voiceless stop everywhere with the exception of the suffix *–ig;* this exception is due to the fact that in this unaccented position the change from γ to *g* had taken place only in most of Alemannian and in Bavarian; present dialect pronunciation has [–ik] only in the Alemannian territory (with the exception of the utmost north), and the stage pronunciation has merely accepted the actual condition in arriving at its decision.

33. Diagrams of the High German Consonant Shift. In the attacht maps and table, the shaded areas indicate the territories in which the respective changes took place.

34. Other Consonant Changes. The High German Consonant Shift constitutes the chief bulk of all consonant changes of the German period; the most important additional consonant transitions are the following:

(1) *The Old Voiceless Spirants,* f, þ, χ, s (<IE. p, t, k, s), show a tendency to become voiced; since this is primarily due to a contraction of the vocal chords, it *may*, theoretically, be interpreted as consonant strengthening, thru increased muscle tension. But in the case of Gc. þ, the historical development makes it entirely clear that we have to deal with sound weakening: decreased expiration led to a corresponding decrease of the muscle tension of the tip of the tongue and to a slight contraction of the vocal chords (**13**, 3). This weakening started at the very beginning of the OHG. time in the Bavarian dialect and spread to the north; unaccented words and syllables were affected first, but soon the weakening was generalized. The voiced spirant ð, which was the temporary result, soon changed to *d*, exactly like Gc. ð during the Intermediate Period, and this was treated like *b*, *g*, i.e., it became voiceless everywhere in High German. Compare Eng. *thin*, *then*, *bathe* — Ger. *dünn*, *dann*, *baden*.

NOTE. This weakening can be explained in several ways; it seems most likely that, under conditions of a strong sentence stress, the unaccented words beginning with þ underwent this weakening first (just as the forms of the pronominal stem *the-* are pronounced with [ð] in English), and that these, on account of their great number (definite articles, words like *da, dann, denn, doch*, etc.), led to a generalization of the new voiced sound.

The other Germanic voiceless spirants became lenes, thru a lessening of the muscle tension; in the case of χ, this led to a transition into *h* (**22**, Note *c*) in the position before vowels; initially before consonants (*hn, hl, hr, hw*) χ disappeared as early as the ninth century: OHG. *hring, hlūt, hwaʒ* >NHG. *Ring, laut, was*. In final position and before consonants, it remained a real spirant, but even there it was often dropt thru analogy: *hoch, der höchste: höher; nach,* preposition, but adjective *nah,* with *h* instead of *ch, näher, der nächste; sehen, wir sahen: das Gesicht,* MHG. *er sach,* but NHG. *er sah.*

Initial f became *v* in Dutch and partly in MF., medially it became voiced in LG. and most of the MG. dialects: *Kewer, elewe* for *Käfer, elf.* — *s* shows a similar treatment: initially and medially it became a voiced lenis in the north, but a voiceless lenis in the south, cf. **I, 24;** initially before consonants it became ʃ in Middle and Upper German during the Middle High German period: LG. *Slange, smal, snell, Sreck, swak, Stein, springen* — HG. *Schlange, schmal,* etc.; in the case of *st-, sp-,* this development took place after a standard spelling had become fairly settled in the usage of the printers: the sound changed, but the spelling was retained. *sk* became ʃ, partly as early as the twelfth century: Lat. *scrībō,* NHG. *schreiben.* In some dialects, especially in Alemannian, the change *s* > ʃ was much more general (*du hascht, weischt = hast, weißt*).

NOTE. The phonetic cause of this transition from *s* to ʃ is not entirely clear; in the case of *sk* we have probably to deal with mutual assimilation, each consonant approaching the other in regard to the place of articulation. As to the other combinations, the undoubted fact that IE. *s* was articulated farther back than NHG. *s* < ʒ is not sufficient because it does not explain why this change took place before consonants only; it seems probable that the contrast between the sharp *s*-rill and the convex shape of the tongue in the pronunciation of other consonants brought about a sort of assimilation.

There is no doubt that the change of fortis to lenis (in part, voiced) which we find in the case of *þ, s, f, χ* (again, in the arrangement: dental, labial, velar) represents a weakening of articulation, but this need not be ascribed to any non-Germanic influence. The fact that the sound strengthening appearing in Verner's Law and this sound weakening partly lead to the same results, need not surprise us; weakened expiration frequently brings about the same effects as stronger muscle tension of the vocal chords.

(2) *Medial b and g* underwent a weakening, to a greater or smaller extent, in most southern dialects (least so in Alemannian): *b* between vowels became *v* (bilabial): *Weiḫer > Weiver*. — In a number of words, medial *b*, *g* were even dropt, especially in Bavarian: *du hāst < habest*, *gīst < gibest*, *Getreide < gitragidi*, *Meister < magister*, *Eidechse < agi-dechsa* ('*Schreck-Echse*'), *Maid < maget*, *verteidigen < ver-tage-dingen* (*beim 'Tage-Ding' = Gericht für einen sprechen*), *steil < stegil* (*steigen*), *Rübezahl < -zagel* (= Eng. *tail*), *Nelke = Nägelchen*, *Sense < saginsa* (related to *Sichel*), *Laie < laicus*, *kasteien < castigare*, *benedeien < benedicere*, etc.

(3) *The Nasals* show a slight tendency towards weakening, as in the Germanic period: final *-n* in unaccented syllables is dropt in many dialects (*geve = geben*); final *m* in unaccented syllables usually becomes *n*: MHG. *besem, bodem, vadem, buosem > NHG. Besen, Boden, Faden, Busen;* also OHG. *bim, tuom = NHG.* (*ich*) *bin,* (dial.) *tun.*

(4) *The Liquids*, in general, remain unchanged; final *r* after long vowels was dropt in OHG.: *dār, wār, ēr, hiar,* (= Eng. *there, where, ere, here*) > *dā, wā* (*wō*), *ē, hie*. This is reflected in modern forms like *darin: damit*, etc., in which *r* is retained if it stands before a vowel, thus beginning the next syllable, but is dropt when a consonant follows; in *eher, hier, r* is reintroduced from such combinations as *ēr͜als ich, hierin,* etc.

(5) *The Semi-Vowels, j, w*, may either emphasize their consonantic, or their vocalic character. *j* became *g* in a few words: *gähren Gischt* (Eng. *yeast*), *jäten* (by the side of *gäten*), *Gahr, gung*, in some MG. dialects, for *Jahr, jung;*

rj changed regularly to *rg* in OHG.: *scerjo* > *Scherge, ferjo* > *Ferge*.

w was originally consonantic *u*, i.e., a bilabial rill sound like Eng. *w*. That the back of the tongue was raised considerably is apparent from the fact that Romance languages have substituted *g* for Ger. *w* (thus reducing or omitting the lip-rounding, but increasing the elevation of the tongue): French *guerre:* Eng. *war*, Ital. *Guelfi, Ghibellini:* Ger. *Welfen, Weiblinge*. — During the MHG. time it changed to a slit-spirant, which became labio-dental in the north, but remained bilabial in the south. — Initial *w* before *l* and *r* was dropt very early (in prehistoric times) in Upper German, later in Middle German, and was retained in Low German; cf. Eng. *wring, wreak* — Ger. *ringen, rächen*. Words like *Wrack, Wrede* (name) are Low German. — Final *w* became a vowel (*u, o*) in OHG., which, since the ninth century, was gradually dropt: Eng. *yellow*, OHG. *gelo, gel* (but gen. *gelwes*), Eng. *clover, snow*, OHG. *klēo, klē* (gen. *klēwes*), *snēo, snē* (*snēwes*). — Medial *w* after *l, r* became *b* in NHG., thru the influence of those dialects in which medial *b* had become bilabial *w*, thus falling together with original *w*: OHG. *al-wāri* 'entirely true' — NHG. *albern* 'silly,' Eng. *swallow* — Ger. *Schwalbe*, MHG. *gerwen, farwe, narwe* — NHG. *gerben, Farbe, Narbe;* this produced paradigms like *gel — gelbes, fal — falbes, mel — melbes*, and later, a generalization of either of the two forms: *der Falbe, die Milbe — fahl, Mehl*.

35. Survey of the New High German Consonant System. The Germanic consonant shift had been the essential mark of the evolution of the Indo-Germanic to the Germanic language; in the same way, the High German consonant shift distinguishes High German from all other Germanic languages: Low German (including Dutch and English), Scandinavian, and extinct languages like Gothic, Burgundian, etc. (Langobardian, originally the language of Holstein and the adjacent territory, had participated in the most important features of the High German sound shift, because the Langobards had comparatively late severed their connections with the mainland).

Jakob Grimm, the originator of the term *Lautverschiebung*, explained the process underlying both consonant shifts in the following way (cf. especially *Geschichte der deutschen Sprache*, p. 276):

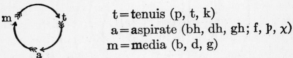

$$t = \text{tenuis (p, t, k)}$$
$$a = \text{aspirate (bh, dh, gh; f, þ, χ)}$$
$$m = \text{media (b, d, g)}$$

While at the present state of linguistic science this diagram can no longer be considered entirely correct, since it identifies the terms 'aspirate' and 'spirant,' it is a characteristic specimen of Grimm's ingenious intuition, for it shows as lucidly as possible the recurrence of the same tendency. — It should clearly be understood that the assumption of two separate sound shiftings is justified historically and methodically, since the first sound shifting affects all Germanic languages alike, and the second only a small part of them; but from a phonological point of view, the two sound shiftings are merely two phases of a uniform process, of which it is reasonable to suppose that it would have continued if Germanic tribes had remained in the old home, without any considerable mingling with non-Germanic elements.

A very slight alteration of Grimm's circle will make it acceptable even to pedantic strictness. In the following diagram, an 'inner' and 'outer' circle are assumed for Indo-Germanic and High German, while the middle circle stands for the Germanic period; words with dentals are chosen as instances in the diagram and the following table because their changes, being the earliest, are the most general and consistent ones; English examples are given for the Germanic period.

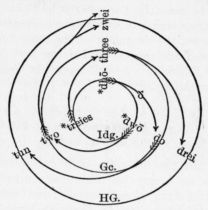

True to its historical source, the New High German standard language stands in general on the basis of the East Franconian consonant system, since its direct home, the East Middle German dialect, is primarily a continuation of East Franconian, but a number of factors have caused this East Middle German written form of the language to be interpreted in different sound values; this development is best characterized by Viëtor's statement that the NHG. language is composed of South German (Middle German) forms with North German sound values. That is, German *d*, e.g., is voiced in the north, voiceless in the south, but Standard German requires the northern pronunciation; Ger. *t* is the South German representative of North (Low) German *d* (Ger. *tun*, LG. *don*), and in its home it is pronounced voiceless, either as a lenis or as a fortis, but never aspirated; still, the 'standard' requires

this aspirated pronunciation which in North German occurs in those words which in South German have *z*, but
not *t* (*zehn*, LG. *ten*).   In the case of *p, b, g*,[1] *w* conditions
are similar, as a brief reference to the preceding paragraphs
(especially **32**) and a comparison with the phonetic part
will show.   In short, this standard of pronunciation de-
mands of all North Germans that they acquire a language
which really is not their own, but pronounce it with sounds
familiar to them; and of South and Middle Germans, that
they use a composite form of older historical stages of
their various dialects, and pronounce it to a great extent
with sounds that are strange and difficult for them: aspirated fortes (except *k*), all voiced stops, voiced *s*, labio-
dental *v* — these are nearly or entirely impossible for
South and Middle Germans without careful linguistic
training.

While, thus, the North German sound system is insisted
upon rather rigorously (a few exceptions have been mentioned in Part I), certain concessions in the form of words
have been made both to Upper and Low German.   A
few words have been accepted with UG. *p* instead of *b*,
due to the vacillation between lenis and fortis pronunciation:[2] *Panier* (but also *Banner*), *Pilz* (from Lat. *boletus*),
Polster (Eng. *bolster*), *Prügel* (related to *Brücke*), *prahlen*
(Eng. *brawl*), *Pracht* (rel. to Eng. *bright*), *prägen* (rel. to
brechen), etc.   Aside from such Upper German words,
NHG. initial *p* can occur only in foreign words, like *Paar*,
Palast (a later borrowing fr. Lat. *palatium;* the same word

---

[1] *k*– is practically the only stop that has the same value in Low
and High German — due to the 'retrogressive development' that
occurred in Upper German (*kχ > k*).

[2] On the other hand, the uncertainty on this point led to the substitution of *b* for *p* in *Birne* (Lat. *pirum*), *Bischof* (Gk. *epískopos* —
misinterpreted as a compound with *bi*–).

had been borrowed once before, at a much earlier date, and *p–* had been shifted to *pf–*: *Pfalz*); besides, it appears in names, like *Passau* (in Bavaria = *Castra Batava*), *Pöchlarn* = *Bechlarn*, in Nether Austria, etc. — In the case of *d > t*, the UG. and EF. form (*t*) has been adopted quite generally, NHG. *d* corresponding to Gc. *þ* (Eng. *th*), but we have a few LG. loan words with *d*, like *Damm*, *Deich* (HG. *Teich*), *dumm* (MHG. *tumb*), *Duft*, *Dampf* (Eng. *damp* — *pf* is, of course, HG.), and in words borrowed from foreign languages: *dauern* (Lat. *durare*), *dichten* (*dictare*), *Dom* (*domus*); these words were adopted after the process of sound shift had been completed, while many other Lat. words had been Germanized before that time; compare Lat. *tēgula*, Ger. *Ziegel*. — Some other instances of fluctuations in the selection of forms, like *gähren*, *fahl* — *Falbe*, have been quoted in **32, 33**.

The relation between the Germanic and the New High German consonant system is the following:

> High German *b, d, g; p, t, k* come primarily from:
> Germanic ƀ, *þ*, *γ*; [1] *d, k*.

This apparently inconsistent and artificial result, in which High German symbols are interpreted in Low German sound values, is in part to be explained by the fact that Northern Germany, which was soon to gain the political ascendency, had adopted the High German language as its literary standard, and implanted upon it its own habits of pronunciation; foreign languages, especially French and, on account of its musical importance, Italian, may have cooperated in creating the conviction that German *b, d, g* should be pronounced voiced; but the prime factor is probably to be sought in a striving for contrasts which were lacking in that state of partial development

[1] Upper German or foreign.

that is represented by East Franconian. This striving for contrasts is in perfect accordance with the general character of the Germanic and German language; in fact, as far as the general phonetic character of the language is concerned, we are quite nearly correct in saying that the High German language, in that form which is generally accepted as 'standard,' closely approaches that linguistic character which it would probably have if the consonant shift had continued without any interception, that is, if the second circle in Grimm's diagram had been completed. The Low German status being essentially identical with the Germanic consonant system, and being transplanted upon the incomplete and partly retrogressive High German consonantism, led practically to the same results that a completion of the second sound shift would have had. There is only one important element of difference between the Germanic and the New High German consonants, namely, the lack of the dental slit-spirant *þ*, or, rather, the substitution of the rill-spirant *s* for it; possibly, this is one of the traces of foreign admixtures to the ethnic evolution of the German nation.

36. The High German Vowel Shift. — Compare **13, 6a.** — During the OHG. and MHG. time the general direction of the Germanic vowel shift was continued: the articulation of Germanic *ō* was increased by a further elevation of the tongue; this led to a diphthongal vowel, intermediate between *u* and *o*, and spelled *uo* (partly, especially in Alemannian, *ua*); towards the end of the MHG. period, this development continued in Middle German, and long *ū* was the final result; the standard language, thru the medium of the Imperial Chancellery at Prague, accepted this Middle German form while South German dialects retained the old diphthong:

Goth. *brōþar*, OHG. *bruoder*, NHG. *Brüder;* OHG. *kuo*, NHG. *Kuh*.[1]

The treatment of Germanic *ē*, from IE. *ēi* (25, Note), runs on parallel lines: with this 'close' sound, the tongue articulation is the prime factor, while in the case of 'open' *ē* (IE. *ē*=[ɛɪ]) the tongue is nearly neutral, and the lip articulation prevails (Gc. *ǣ*>OHG. *ā*); for that reason, Germanic *ē* follows the same tendency as Germanic *ō*, viz., the tongue is elevated, and the result is, in OHG. and MHG., a diphthongal sound composed of *i* (or a very close *e*) and a middle vowel, written *ea, ia, ie;* in Middle German, long *i* resulted, and this pronunciation has become the standard, altho the MHG. spelling *ie* was retained: OHG. *heaz, hiaz*, MHG. *hiez*, NHG. *hieß* = [hiːs].

Germanic *ǣ* had become *ā* in West and North Germanic; standard German has preserved this sound, but many dialects, especially in the south, have changed it (thru increased articulation) to *ō* (usually open, but sometimes close): Bavarian [sɔɪt, dɔχt] = *Saat, gedacht;* in a number of High German words, this Bavarian (and Alemannian) form is adopted: *Argwohn* by the side of *Wahn, Odem* (: *Atem*), *wo* (: *warum*), *Mohn, Monat, Mond, ohne, Woge, sie woben, sie wogen* (MHG. *arcwān, ādem, wā, māhen, mānōt, māne, āne, wāc, wāben, wāgen*).

37. Monophthongization and Diphthongization. 'Monophthongization' is the change of a diphthong to a monophthong, i.e., a simple vowel, and 'diphthongization,' the change of a simple vowel to a diphthong. Strictly speaking, the High German change *ō*>*uo*>*ū* is diphthongization in its first, and monophthongization in its

---

[1] NOTE. The diphthong *üe*, arising from *uo* thru mutation (38*A*), was treated likewise: MHG. *brüeder*>NHG. *Brüder*.

second stage, but as long as the diphthong is only a transitory stage, this classification is not important.

(*a*) Real *monophthongization*, which is frequent in all languages of the IE. group, is found in OHG. under certain conditions (as to the Germanic changes *ēi* > *ē*, *ei* > *ī*, see **25** and Note): Germanic *ai*, *au* became *ei*, *ou* in very early OHG., thru an assimilation of the first to the second element (Goth. *ains*, *augo* — OHG. *ein*, *ouga*); but in final position, and before consonants whose articulation is unfavorable to the pronunciation of *i*, *u* (namely, *h*, *r*, *w* in the case of *ai*, *h* and all dentals in the case of *au*), mutual assimilation took place, so that *ē* < *ai*, *ō* < *au* resulted:

Goth. *áihts:* OHG. *ēht* 'possession,' Lat. *aes* (**ais*): OHG. *ēr* 'bronze,' Goth. *mais:* OHG. *mēr* 'more.'

Goth. *sáiwala:* OHG. *sēola* 'soul ' Goth. *wái:* OHG. *wē* 'woe!' —

Goth. *háuhs:* OHG. *hōh* 'high,' Goth. *áuso* (Lat. *auris*): OHG. *ōra* 'ear,' Lat. *caulis:* OHG. (borrowed) *kōl* 'cabbage.'

The diphthong *eu* was not subject to any such monophthongization, but on account of the peculiar treatment of Germanic *e* and *u* (**25**, end) it showed a twofold development: before *i*, *j* of the following syllable, it became *iu*, which in MHG. was pronounced *ū* and in NHG. became the diphthong *eu* (compare below); but before any other vowel, *e* remained, and *u* changed to *o*; the resulting *eo* became *io* (thru dissimilation) and later, in MHG., *ie*, which fell together with *ie* < *ē*. Thus, in NHG., Germanic *eu* (often in different forms of the same root) may appear either as *eu*, or as *ie* = [iː], e.g.:

OHG. *fliogan* — MHG., NHG. *fliegen;* 2nd sing. OHG. *fliugis*, early NHG. *fleugst;* the IE. stem **teuto*– leads to a Germanic **þeoða*– (Goth. *Thiudareiks* = **þeoða–rīks*,

NHG. *Dietrich* ('king of the people'), but the derived adjective Gc. **piuðiska–* becomes MHG. *diutsch,* NHG. *deutsch.* In the same way, *Licht* and *leuchten, siech* and *Seuche, kriechen* and *kreucht,* etc., belong to the same stems with suffixes that contained either *a* or *i* (*j*).

(*b*) *Diphthongization* proper appears in the transition from MHG. to NHG.: all long high vowels (*ī, ū, iu=ū̄*) became diphthongs, namely, *ei=ai, au, eu=äu.* This change in its results clearly presents a phonetic process diametrically opposite to the development of *ē* to *ī, ō* to *ū*: here the tongue is raised, there it is lowered. — Compare MHG. *bī, līht, mīn; brūn, hūs, tūsend; diutsch, hiuser, friunt:* NHG. *bei, leicht, mein; braun, Haus, tausend; deutsch, Häuser, Freund.*

NOTE 1. The MHG. **monophthongization** — *ie, uo, üe* (see **36**) >[iː, uː, yː] — originated in Middle German, possibly as early as 1200. The MHG. **diphthongization** — *ī, ū, iu>ei, au, eu* (*äu,* see **38**) started in the Austrian Alpine countries, around 1100. The Bohemian and Saxon Chancelleries, and thru them the standard language, adopted both of them; compare NHG. *lieb, gut, Güte; mein, Haus, Häuser.* Many dialects gradually fell in line with the standard language, partly thru 'spelling pronunciation' (imitation of the spelling in pronunciation), but Alemannian and Bavarian have retained the old diphthongs — [liəb, guət, gyətər] — while Southern Alemannian and Low German have preserved the old monophthongs: Al. [huːs, ʃviːtsərdyːtʃ].

NOTE 2. The following diagram illustrates the opposite phonetic character of the MHG. monophthongization and diphthongization (brackets connecting two vowels indicate diphthongs):

A, uo>ū, ie>ī   B, ū>ao, ī>ae

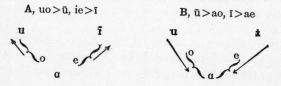

A is in perfect keeping with Germanic tendencies; it arose in the center of the German territory, occupied by the Germans many centuries ago. — **B**, representing a weakening of the articulation, is un-Germanic in character; as far as German is concerned, it originated in a country inhabited by a Slavo-Celtic population intermingling with a very recent German immigration; the same process, however, took place in the utmost northwest of the West-Germanic territory, namely, in Dutch and English (compare English *mine, house*) — again on essentially Celtic soil. This fact and the phonetic character of the foreign languages concerned (Celtic and Slovenian) make it extremely probable that the diphthongization is another instance of a foreign admixture in the development of the German language, caused by the articulating tendencies of the Slavo-Celtic population on colonial soil.[1]

NOTE 3. The following table represents the diphthongizing and monophthongizing tendencies combined in modern German.

Gc. *ai, au* > $\left\{ \begin{array}{ll} \text{Ger. } ei, au & - ein, \quad Auge \\ \text{``} \quad e, o & - Seele, Ohr \end{array} \right\}$ *37a.*

Gc. *ē, ō* > MHG. *ie, uo* > NHG. *ī, ū, (ū̄)* — *hier, Bruder* (*Brüder*) — **36 (38)**.

Gc. *ī, ū* > NHG. *ei, au, (eu, äu)* — *mein, Haus* (*Häuser*) — **37b (38)**.

38. Vowel Mutation (Umlaut).

The vowel changes described in **36, 37** were spontaneous (see **11**). But there also occurred in OHG. and early MHG. a number of conditional (assimilatory) vowel changes, called *mutation* or *Umlaut: Accented back vowels became front vowels under the influence of an i or j of the following unaccented syllable:*

A. Genuine (old) Mutation:

a>e: OHG. *faran* 'drive': *feris, ferit* 'you drive, he drives.'

OHG. *gast,* plural *gesti;* Goth. *branjan:* OHG. *brennen.*

NOTE. This mutation is sometimes prevented by certain intervening consonant combinations, especially in Upper German: *maht,* plur. *mahti,* Franc. *giweltig,* Upper German *giwaltig.*

The *e* resulting from this mutation was narrow, while old Ger-

---

[1] Cf. p. 124 and Note to p. 147.

manic *e* was wide; MHG. poets do not rhyme words like *fest* 'festival,' from Lat. *festum*, and *fest* 'firm,' from Gc. **fasti*. — Many modern dialects, especially in the Alemannian and Bavarian territory, are still making this distinction. See I, 43, Note.

u > ü: OHG. *turi*, MHG., NHG. *Tür*.

NOTE. This mutation, too, is prevented by certain consonant combinations, especially (in Upper German) by geminates and *l* + consonant; compare Upper German *–bruck* (*Innsbruck*), *drucken*, *Gulden* — Middle German *–brück* (*Saarbrücken*), *drücken*, *gülden* (*=golden*).

ā > ǣ: pret. subj. OHG. *nāmi*, MHG. *nǣme*, NGH. *nähme*.

ō > œ̄: OHG. *hōhir*, MHG. *hœher*, NHG. *höher*.

ū > iu = [yɪ]: plur. OHG. *krūtir*, MHG. *kriuter*, NHG. *Kräuter*.

uo > üe: pret. subj. OHG. *fuori*, MHG. *füere*, NHG. *führe*.

ou > öu: MHG. *boum* — *böume*, NHG. *Baum* — *Bäume*.

These mutations belong essentially to the OHG. period, altho OHG. spelling does not always take account of them. The change of *a* to *e* is much earlier than any other, occurring between 750 and 800.

B. Grammatical (analogical, secondary) Mutation: During the MHG. period, the process of mutation was greatly extended. It took place:

(*a*) in many words where consonant combinations had prevented the change from *a* to *e*: NHG. plur. *Mächte*.

(*b*) in forms that never contained *i* (*j*) in their endings: *Nächte* (OHG. *naht*, without ending), *Brüder* (OHG. *bruoder*), *Väter* (OHG. *fater*), *Häuser* (OHG. *hūs*). — As to *Hörner*, *völlig*, etc., see Note 2.

NOTE 1. The secondary mutation of *a* resulted in wide [ɛ], written *ä*; this was nearly or entirely the same sound as 'old' Germanic *e*, but differed distinctly from that *e* which had arisen from the old mutation of *a* (see above). Later spelling confused the original conditions very badly, so that it is neither a representation of the phonetic character, nor of the historical origin of *ä* and *e*; it was the intention of printers to use *ä* where other grammatical forms of the same word contained *a*: *Hände* for MHG. *hende,* but *behende; Gäste* for MHG. *geste,* but *brennen* for Goth. *branjan* (so-called 'Rückumlaut,' since, apparently, the mutation *brennen — brannte* goes in the opposite direction from *hand — hende*). While in this way *ä* displaced *e* in many cases where the latter was the result of old mutation and therefore narrow, it came to be used in place of Germanic (wide) *e* in a few words, e.g., *Käfer, jäten, gären, währen.* — To an extent, German dialects, especially in the south, have preserved the old phonetic values of *e*; compare Note to *A* and **I, 43,** Note.

NOTE 2. The change of short *o* to *ō* was necessarily analogical. Since Germanic *o* could arise from *u* only when this was *not* followed by *i* or *j* (**25** end), there could not be any phonetic mutation *o > ō,* but there had to result such parallel forms as OHG. *fora — furi =* NHG. *vor — für, Gold — gülden, Hof — hübsch* (*< hüvesch,* i.e., that which is customary at court), *Horn — hürnen, voll — füllen.* Thru this new, analogical mutation the process of the change of *ō to æ* and *u* to *ü* was imitated, and forms like *höfisch, hörnen, völlig* were establisht.

NOTE 3. The cause of mutation is not known definitely. Psychologically, it is explained as a tendency to anticipate in the accented vowel the articulation of the following unaccented vowel; physiologically, as an assimilation of the intervening consonant to the following front vowel ('palatalization'), and, then, of the accented vowel to the consonant. The first theory is possible, but insufficient, the second stands in sharp contrast to the general phonetic tendencies of the Germanic languages, which do not admit of any change of consonants under the influence of either following or preceding vowels (compare *Indogermanische Forschungen,* XXXIII, 377). The following seems to be the most probable theory: Chronologically, the process of mutation is in keeping with the order of the Germanic and German colonizing movements (**3, 4**): it is oldest in the north, most recent in the south. The Germanic consonant shift came to a standstill some time after the emigration of each tribe; mutation seems to have started in the new homes; within the German dialects it is fairly safe to say: the more elements of consonant shift, the less mutation is found in any given case (compare especially the limitations of the mutation in Upper German). While un-Germanic in its phonetic character, mutation is perfectly in agreement with the articulating habits of Celtic (Romance), Slavic, Finnish, etc., languages. Therefore, it is reasonable to assume that the palatalization of intervening consonants and, thru this, the mutation of the accented vowels, started among the Celts in the new homes of the Germanic colonists.[1] However, as soon as such forms as *gast — gesti* had become establisht, this new vowel exchange seemed equivalent to the old vowel exchange (Ablaut) in *gab — geben*, and was transferred to an ever increasing number of similar grammatical forms, regardless of whether their stem vowels had ever been followed by *i* or not. This explains the immense extent of 'analogy' in the case of vowel mutation: starting out as an un-Germanic phonetic process, it gradually became a thoroly Germanic psychological factor, a new kind of Ablaut, as it were. — Both ethnic and phonetic reasons make it probable that the conditional changes of Germanic *u* and *e*, mentioned in **25** end, should be classed with the general process of mutation.

39. Sporadic Vowel Changes. (1) *o* became *u* in old loan words from Latin, especially before nasal: L. *pondus* — OHG. *pfunt;* L. *monachus* — OHG. *munich*, MHG. *münech* (compare *München*); L. *monasterium* — OHG. *munistar*, MHG., NHG. *Münster;* L. *moneta* — OHG. *muniza*, NHG. *Münze*.

(2) *u>o* and *ü>ö* is very common in Middle German and the standard language, especially before *nn, mm: Nonne, begonnen, gewonnen, Sommer, fromm, geschwommen* had *u; König, Mönch, können*, etc., had *ü*. But compare *Brunnen, dünn, Trümmer, dumm, Kummer*, etc. — No rule can be given, nor has any satisfactory explanation been found.

(3) Rounding of *e* and *i* to *ö* and *ü* occurs in many words, especially such as are often used solemnly or reproachfully, or that belong to elevated style; the neighborhood of labials, *l*, and *sch* seems to favor the change. *e* has been replaced by *ö* in *Hölle, zwölf, Schöpfer, Geschöpf, schöpfen, Schöffe, stöhnen, Schnörkel, ergötzen, trödeln, nörgeln*, etc.; *ü* stands for older *i* in *Würde, flüstern, Rüffel, lügen, trügen*, and others.

---

[1] Cf. Wundt, *Elemente der Völkerpsychologie*, Leipzig 1913, p. 58: „Bei dem Kampf einer überlegenen mit einer weniger kultivierten Rasse bestimmt erstere Wortvorrat und Sprachform, letztere Lautcharakter."

(4) Unrounding is common in most dialects and has been transferred to the standard language in a few words of the colloquial language; e.g., *Schlingel, Bimstein, Kissen, Pilz* have *i* for older *ü*.

40. The German Accent Strengthening.

The transition from Indo-Germanic to Germanic is marked by the shifting of the accent to the logical center of the word, the 'stem syllable' (compare **26**) and a subsequent weakening of final syllables. In German, the accent remains, in general, stationary, but its contrasting force is increased by a further weakening of the unaccented syllables; during the transition from OHG. to MHG. the clear vowels in all inflectional and most other unstressed syllables become slurred *e* [ə]. E.g., OHG. nom. pl. *tagā, gesti, zungōn* became *tage, geste, zungen;* gen. pl. *tagō, gestō, zungōnō* became *tage, geste, zungen;* the infinitives *neman, habēn, salbōn* changed to *nemen, haben, salben.* Unaccented *e*, especially in 'third syllables' and in habitually unaccented words, frequently disappeared, as in OHG. nom. pl. *engele,* inf. *zwīfalōn,* dat. sing. *blindeme*>MHG. *engel, zwīfeln, blindem;* OHG. adverbs *ane, mite, obe* became *an, mit, ob.* — During the MHG. and NHG. periods this dropping of unaccented *e* is continued, especially in Upper German; compare MHG. *spæte, līhte, swære, gemüete, ochse, fürste, herre, grave*: NHG. *spät, leicht, schwer, Gemüt, Ochs(e), Fürst, Herr, Graf.*

41. The German Standardization of Quantity.

In MHG., accented syllables, whether open or closed (i.e., whether they ended in a vowel or a consonant), could be long or short.

(a) *stelen, sehen, nemen* — short and open;

(b) *stal, sah, nam; helfen, recht* — short and closed; the stem syllables of words like *offen, brechen, essen*, containing 'new' spirants (results of the High German sound shift), are to be classed as closed syllables, since, in MHG., these spirants were pronounced with both the preceding and the following syllables (*of-fen*);

(*c*) *stālen, sāhen, nāmen* — long and open;

(*d*) *brāchte, gienc, stuont* — long and closed.

Towards the end of the MHG. time, these four different kinds of syllables were in principle reduced to two, namely, long-open and short-closed: short vowels in open syllables were lengthened, long vowels in closed syllables, shortened. Thus we obtain:

(*a*) *stehlen, sehen, nehmen* and *stahlen, sahen, nahmen;*

(*b*) *helfen, recht, offen, brechen, essen,* and *brachte, ging, stand.*

Thru this standardization of quantity, the contrast between accented and unaccented syllables became still more marked; in its psychological aspect, this process may be said to be closely connected with the Germanic accent shift and the weakening of final syllables.

Monosyllabic forms with short vowels in closed syllables became long thru leveling with inflected forms of the same words, at least in Middle German and Upper German: *Tāg, Glās, gāb, nahm, sah* (North German *Tăg, Glăs,* etc.). — Isolated monosyllables (adverbs, prepositions, etc.) usually remained short: *weg, ab, mit,* but frequently, especially before *r,* their vowels were lengthened: *er, der, wer, mir, vor, für.* — To a great extent, the quantity of such words depends on sentence stress.

Vowels followed by *m* and *t* — sounds of relatively energetic articulation — often remained short, especially in words with unaccented suffixes like *-el* and *-er: kommen, nimmt, fromm, Hammer, Kummer, Sommer, Himmel, sammeln, tritt, Schritt, Gott, Kette, Sitte, Stadt, Vetter* (but *Vater*), *bitten, betteln;* in a few words, MHG. long vowels followed by *m* or *t* and the suffix *-er* were shortened: MHG. *jāmer, muoter* > *Jammer, Mutter.*

Vowels followed by *r* + consonant were lengthened in many dialects, especially in the north (the standard language is in favor of these long vowels): *Art, Bart, zart, Schwert, Herd, Pferd, Erde, werden;* but we have short vowels in *scharf, hart, Scherz, arg, Berg.*

42. Table of the Most Important German Sounds.

NHG.	MHG. Gc. (<IE.)	Examples	Paragraph
	VOWELS		
a = { a	a <a, o, ə	Acker, Gast,	25
ā	ā <aŋχ	dachte [Macht	24, 36, 41
ā = { ā	ǣ <ē	Same	25, 36
a⁻¹	a <a, o, ə	nahm, Vater	25, 41
ä = { e	a/i, j	Gäste	38A
ä	[a/i, j]	Mächte, Nächte	38B
ǟ = { ǣ	ā(ǣ)/i, j	nähme	25, 38A
e–	e	gebären	38 Note 1
e–	a/i, j	fährt, Väter	38AB
e = { e	e	helfen	——
e	a/i, j	Henne	38A and Note 1
ē = { ē	ai/h, r, w, –	mehr	37
e–	e	nehmen	41
e–	a/i, j	Meer	38A, 41
ǣ	ā(ǣ)/i, j	angenehm	38A
i = { i	i	Fisch	——
ü	u/i, j	Kissen	38A, 39
ie	ē <ēi	hing	25, 37, 41
ī = { ie	eu/a, ē <ēi	Diet(rich), hieß	25, 37
i–	i	Friede	——
o = { o	u/a	Joch	25
u	u	Sommer	39
ö = { ö	[u/i, j]	Hörner	38B
ü	u/i, j	können	38A, 39
e	e	zwölf	39
ō = { ō	au/h, dent., –	hoch	25
ā	ǣ <ē	Argwohn	25
ȫ = { œ	ō/i, j <au/i, j	hören	38A
ü–	u/i, j	König	38A, 41, 39
e–	e	schwören	38A, 39, 41
u = { u	u (<u, ų, etc.)	hundert	25
uo	ō	Mutter	25, 37, 41

¹ – after vowel indicates open syllable.

NHG.	MHG.	Gc. (<IE.)	Examples	Paragraph
ü = {	ü	u/i, j	kürzer	38A
	i	i	fünf	39
ū = {	uo	ō<ā, ō	Buch	25, 37
	u–	u	Zug	41
ǖ = {	üe	uo/i, j<ō/i, j	Brüder	25, 38A
	ü–	u/i, j	Züge	38AB, 41
	ie	eu/a	lügen	39
ei (ai) = {	ei	ai<ai, oi, əi	ein, Laib	25
	ī	ī	mein	37
au = {	ou	au<au, ou, əu	Baum	——
	ū	ū	Maus	37
eu (äu) = {	iu	eu/i, j	deutsch	37
	iu	ū/i, j	Häuser	37, 38A
	öu	au/i, j	Bäume	38A

CONSONANTS

b = {	b	ƀ<bh, p'	Liebe, sieben	22², 32⁸ ⁹, 23
	w	w	gelb	34⁵
p = p		ƀ<bh	Polster	32⁸
pp = pp		ƀj, etc.	Sippe	24a, 32
f(v),(ff) = {	f, v	f<p	für, Vieh	22¹
	f, ff	p¹<b	offen, schlafen	22³, 32²
pf = pf		p²	Pfund	32⁵
w = w		w, hw<q	Werk, was	34¹
d = {	d	ƀ<t	drei	22¹, 34¹
	t	ð	Wind	32
t = t		ð<dh, t'	tun, Vater	22², 32⁷, 23
s, ss = {	s	s	sechs	——
	ȝ, ȝȝ	t¹<d	das, Wasser	22³, 32¹
sch = sk, s–		sk, s–	schreiben, Schlange	34¹
z, tz = z, tz		t²<d	zwei, sitzen	32⁴, 22³, 24a
g = g		γ<gh, k'; j	Garten, zogen; gären	22², 32¹⁰ ¹¹ 34⁵
k, ck = k, ck		k², gj, etc.	kalt, Acker, Rücken	32⁶, 24a
ch = ch, h		χ<k; k¹	Gesicht, Buch	22¹, 32⁸
h = h, ch		χ<k	Horn, sehen	22¹, 24
r = r		r; z< s'	rot, Ohr	—, 23

B. THE DEVELOPMENT OF FORMS
(MORPHOLOGY)

43. Word Structure. The essential element of an IE. word is the 'root,' i.e., that part of the word that conveys its meaning, its logical contents. Thus, the IE. root *bher– embodies the idea of bearing or carrying (to bear, borne, bearable, bearer, etc.); the roots *oq– and *weid– contain the conception of seeing or perceiving (to see, seen, visible, eye, know, etc.).

The root is utilized for the expression of various grammatical categories — different aspects of the same idea. This is done, first, by vowel gradation (**18**): *bher–, *bhr–, *bhēr– indicate various forms or aspects of the action of carrying; they are the basis of genuine verb forms; *bhor– expresses the objective, concrete aspects of the same action (the carrier, the thing carried, the state of being carried, etc.), thus forming nouns or adjectives. Second, roots are classed as categories by the addition of sounds or syllables called '**formant elements**'; these are either **suffixes** or **prefixes**. Root and suffix together form the 'stem' of a word.

The logical relation of a stem to the other parts of the sentence is establisht chiefly by means of inflectional **endings** — speech elements which are added to the stem for syntactic purposes, but did not possess any independent meaning at any known period of the IE. language. Thus, in the form *bher–e–ti 'he is carrying,' we distinguish the root *bher–, the suffix –e–, and the ending –ti; in *bhor–o–s 'carrier' we find the suffix –o– and the nominative singular ending –s. The imperfect *e–bher–e–t(i)

152

'he carried' possesses a suffix –e– and an ending –t(i), but also a prefix e–, which expresses past time and is called the 'augment'; in *bhe–bhor–e 'he has carried,' the syllable bhe–, called 'reduplication,' refers to the action as completed, or, rather, as resulting in a state of being.

The Verb

44. Tense and Aspect. At a very early time of its history, the IE. language did not possess tenses in our sense of the word. Instead, the different forms of the IE. verb expressed different aspects of the action, signifying, especially, *continued* action, *momentary* action, and *completed* action (state attained). Among modern IE. languages, Slavic has best preserved these distinctions; in English, an approximate parallel exists in such forms as *he is (was) going — he went — he is gone.* Classic Greek distinguisht continued and momentary action and state attained consistently thru the use of forms like *leipein* 'to be leaving' — *lipein* 'to leave' = to be on the point of leaving — *leloipa* 'I have left.' (The form *lipein* is called 'aorist'; when used to express past tense, e.g., *e-lipon* 'I left,' it corresponds to the French passé défini.)

NOTE. In accordance with Greek grammar, the terms 'aoristic action, aoristic forms,' etc., are sometimes used instead of our term 'momentary aspect.' The expression 'perfective action' is often used with the same meaning; it will, in general, be avoided in this book so as not to cause confusion with the term 'perfect' in the sense of completed action.

45. The Germanic (Simple) Tenses. In the course of the development of the several IE. languages, the objective element of aspect gave way more and more to the subjective element of time. In oldest IE., the principal factor in the construction of verb forms had been the manner of action; in a later period, the question became paramount: Does the action take place *now* (i.e., at the time of the speaker's mentioning it), or at some other time? 'Tenses' gradually took the place of 'aspects.' Latin and Celtic have gone very far in this direction, and in Germanic the development is so nearly complete that we find hardly more than faint traces of the aspects (as, e.g., in NHG. *steigen*[1] — *besteigen*[2]). The forms of the aspects were turned over to the expression of relative time, i.e., to tenses. Vowel gradation, which had been the principal means of distinction between aspects, now became the chief characteristic of time contrasts.

With the most important types of IE. verbs, the vowel grades had been distributed as follows (compare **18**):

Continuous action: e-grade		Momentary action: (a) reduced grade (b) lengthened g.	Completed action: o-grade in sing., reduced g. in plur.
I. 'point out':	*déik–*	*dik–'*	*dedóik–, dedik–'*
II. 'lead':	*déuk–*	*duk–'*	*dedóuk–, deduk–'*
III. 'turn':	*wért–*	*wr̥t–'*	*wewórt–, wewr̥t–'*
IV. 'take':	*ném–*	*(nm̥–') ném–*	*nenóm–, nenm̥–'*
V. 'sit':	*séd–*	*(sd–') séd–*	*sesód–, sesd–'*

Usual Gc. development: present tense	'Non-present,' therefore preterit tense

This means: With most verbs, continuous action is the normal, usual aspect. Therefore, the form which used to express continuous action came to denote the normal, usual tense of the average verb. By sheer force of contrast (together with certain logical requirements), the remaining forms were used for 'non-present,' i.e., for a new past tense, commonly called the preterit. The form of the

---

[1] Continuous action.   [2] Completed action.

preterit is a combination of the forms of momentary and completed action; its meaning combines the functions of the Greek aorist and perfect tenses, Gothic *nam* meaning both 'I took' and 'I have taken.'

NOTE 1. The Latin development is similar in principle, tho different in method. The so-called Latin perfect, whose functions are very nearly identical with those of the Germanic preterit, likewise exhibits forms of momentary and of completed action, i.e., so-called aorist and perfect forms; e.g., *dīxi, dūxi, vēni, lēgi, sēdi* are aorists, but *cecidi, pepuli*, etc., are perfects proper; still, they do not differ in function in any way.

NOTE 2. THE VOWEL GRADES. Undoubtedly, the forms with reduced grade and those with lengthened grade had not always been identical in use; possibly, the lengthened grade had originally had 'iterative' meaning (denoting repeated action), but this is quite uncertain; in historical times, their functions are alike. — The *o*-grade of the perfect forms was weakened to the reduced grade in the plural on account of the difference in accent indicated in the table. — I–III are genuine diphthongal roots, with which lengthened grades do not occur; in their reduced grades, the diphthongal glide appears as a syllabic vowel (compare 18); class IV, in which the root ends in a liquid or nasal, stands intermediate between diphthongal and simple vowel roots; in OHG. *nāmun* 'they took' < IE. **nĕmņt*, it is treated like a simple vowel root, in the past participle *ginoman* < **-nṃonó*– like a diphthongal root.

NOTE 3. Aorist Presents. In a number of verbs that usually denoted momentary action, the present tense was formed from that type which generally expressed that aspect, namely, the reduced grade, corresponding to certain Greek aorists. The most important instance of such verbs — called 'aorist presents' — is the verb OHG. *koman* 'kommen' < IE. **gṃ*–. Other aorist presents are mentioned in 46, Note.

NOTE 4. In Gothic and Norse, the whole singular of the preterit was taken from the perfect system: Goth. *nam, namþ, nam* = IE. **(ne)nóma, *(ne)nómtha, *(ne)nóme;* in West-Germanic, the 2nd sing. is an aorist form: OHG. *zigi, zugi, wurti, nāmi, sāzi* = IE. **dikési, *dukési, *vṛtési, *nĕm(es), *sĕd(es).* — The root forms of the plurals of classes I–III may either be called perfect or aorist forms, since both show reduced grade in IE.; their Germanic endings are taken from the perfect system, but the disappearance of the re-duplication is due to the association with the aorist forms. — The plurals of the fourth and fifth classes, OHG. *nāmun, sāzun,* are pure aorists.

NOTE 5. Present philological tradition considers the Germanic preterit wholly a continuation of the IE. perfect. This view is chiefly due to the close resemblance between such Germanic preterit forms as **warþ — *wurðum* and Sanscrit perfects like *vavárta* 'I have turned' — *vavṛtimá* 'we have turned' (cf. p. 108), from IE. **we-wórt-a — *we-wṛt-əmés.* Vowel gradation and Verner's Law (Gc. *þ — ð*, **23, 47**) are perfectly in accordance with this view, but a number of reasons, principally the lack of reduplication and the peculiar vowel grades of the fourth, fifth, sixth, and seventh Ablaut series (**46**), make it more than doubtful. Besides, the development of the preterit ('perfect') in Latin and Celtic has important features in common with the general structure of the Germanic preterit (see Note 1), and points distinctly to a combination of perfect and aorist forms.

46. The Seven Classes of Strong Verbs. On the basis of this merging of types, there develop in Germanic the following seven classes of strong verbs:[1]

(For practical reasons, the past participle, which will be explained in 54, is included in this table.)

I, II, III = diphthongal classes (with i-, u-, and l-, r-, m-, n-diphthongs).

IV: semi-diphthongal class (the root ends in a liquid or a nasal, which may be treated as diphthongal element or as consonant).

V: simple vowel class.

VI, VII: long vowel roots and others; see Note on page 158.

[1] By the terms 'strong' and 'weak' verbs, Jakob Grimm, the originator of these terms, intended to express the fact that 'strong' verbs form their tenses thru an inherent ability to change their root vowels, while 'weak' verbs, lacking that ability, have to resort to the external means of suffixes. See 49.

GERMANIC

Pret.

Inf.	1st sing.	1st pl.	Past Part.
I. *tīχan[1]	*taiχ	*tiγum[7]	*tiγan–[7]
II. *teoχan[2]	*tauχ	*tuγum[7]	*toγan–[9]
III. *werþan	*warþ	*wurðum[7]	*worðan–[9]
*singan[3]	*sang	*sungum	*sungan–[15]
IV. *neman	*nam	*nǣmum[8]	*noman–[9]
V. *sitjan[4]	*sat	*sǣtum[8]	*setan–
VI. *faran	*fōr	*fōrum	*faran–
VII. *haitan[5]	*hēt[6]	*hētum[6]	*haitan– [5]

OLD HIGH GERMAN

Pret.

Inf.	1st sing.	1st pl.	Past Part.
I. zīhan 'zeihen'	zēh[10]	zigum	gizigan
II. ziohan 'ziehen'	zōh[11]	zugum	gizogan
III. werdan 'werden'	ward	wurtum	giwortan
singan 'singen'	sang	sungum	gisungan
IV. neman 'nehmen'	nam	nāmum[12]	ginoman
V. sitzan 'sitzen'	saz	sāzum[12]	gisezzan
VI. faran 'fahren'	fuor[14]	fuorum	gifaran
VII. heizan[13] 'heissen'	hiaz[14]	hiazum	giheizan

---

[1] Gc. ī < IE. ei, 25. [2] Gc. eu/a > eo, 25 end. [3] Gc. e/nasal +cons. > i, 25 end. [4] The present of some verbs is formed by means of a j-suffix. [5] Gc. ai < IE. əi, 25 and 46, Note. [6] Gc. ē < IE. ēi, 25 and Note. [7] Verner's Law, 23. [8] Gc. ǣ < IE. ē, 25. [9] Gc. u/a > o, 25. [10] OHG. ai/h, r, w > ē, 37. [11] OHG. au/h, dent. > ō, 37. [12] Gc. ǣ > OHG. ā, 36. [13] Gc. ai > OHG. ei, 37. [14] ō > uo, ē > ia, 36. [15] u > o did not take place before nasal combinations.

NOTE. The sixth and seventh classes are difficult to explain within the limits of this book. — The seventh class, and many verbs of the sixth class developt from long vowel roots (18*B*); most of them, however, are 'aorist presents' (45, Note 3), i.e., the reduced grade was used for the present tense, the normal grade, in West-Germanic and Norse, for the preterit. Gothic has made a different selection in the case of the seventh class by using a pure perfect paradigm for the preterit: Goth. *haihait* (pronounce *hehait*), *haihaitum* < IE. **kekṓida* — **kekəidəmés*. Inasmuch as it was formerly believed that this reduplicated form was also the basis of OHG. *hiaz* < Gc. **hēt*, this class is frequently called the reduplicating class. — In OHG. *rātan* 'counsel,' *hruofan* 'call' (NHG. *raten* — *riet*, *rufen* — *rief*) — both of which are clearly durative — and several other verbs, the normal grade was used for the present (OHG. *rātan* = Lat. *rēri*, past part. *rătus* < IE. roots **rē-: *rə-*), while the establisht type of *hiaz* was analogically transferred to the preterit. — The sixth class comes partly from a similar source (aorist presents: reduced type in the present, normal grade in the preterit), e.g., *skaban* — *skuob* = Lat. *scabo* — *scābi* < IE. **skəbh-* — **skābh-*, partly from 'causatives,' having the *o*-grade in the present and the lengthened *ō*-grade in the preterit, e.g., OHG. *faran* — *fuor* < IE. **por-* — **pōr-*. Analogical forces have combined these two different types into one class.

47. Grammatical Change (Verner's Law, 23).

In the common present type (*e*-grade) and the singular of the perfect (*o*-grade) the IE. accent was on the root. But in the plural of the IE. perfect, in the reduced grade aorist, and in the past participle (54), the suffix or the ending was stressed. Therefore, IE. *p*, *t*, *k* had to appear as Germanic *f*, *þ*, *χ* in the first two forms, but as *ƀ*, *ð*, *γ* in the last two; compare OHG. *zīhan*, *zēh* — *zigum*, *gizigan*; *ziohan*, *zōh* — *zugum*, *gizogan*. — In the fifth class, the accent must be supposed to have been stationary, but OHG. and other Germanic dialects have transferred the general principle of grammatical change to a very few verbs of this class too: OHG. *wesan*, *was* — *wārum*, (*giwesan*). In the sixth and seventh classes, analogical generalization has greatly obscured the original conditions.

Most NHG. verbs have leveled out the grammatical change. It is preserved, more or less, in *gedeihen — gediegen* (adjective), *schneiden — schnitt(en)*, *leiden — litt(en)*, *kiesen — kor(en)*, *war(en) — gewesen*, also in *frieren — Frost*, *verlieren — Verlust;* it has been abandoned in *meiden, leihen, frieren, verlieren, zeihen, sehen, lesen, genesen, schlagen*, and others.

48. New High German Vowel Leveling. In addition to the leveling of grammatical change mentioned above, the vowels of the German strong preterits (as to the present vowels, see **52**) have undergone considerable changes, partly thru the MHG. standardization of quantity (**41**), partly thru analogical transfer of forms.

Class I: The plural vowels were partly lengthened according to **41**, and were transferred to the singular: OHG. *sneit — snitum, zēh — zigum:* NHG. *schnitt — schnitten, zieh — ziehen.*

Class II: The singular had either *ou* or *ō* in OHG., according to **37** (e.g., *biogan* 'bend' — *boug*, but *ziohan* 'pull' — *zôh, kiosan* 'choose' — *kôs*). In NHG., *ō* was carried thru in both numbers, probably partly under the influence of the vowel of the participle, *o > ō:* OHG. *gizogan*, NHG. *gezōgen. — sott, schmolz, schoß*, etc., have short vowels according to **41**.

Class III: The singular vowel was transferred to the plural: NHG. *half — halfen, sang — sangen* (but compare the older form in *'Wie die Alten sungen, so zwitschern die Jungen'*; also *ward — wurden*).

Classes IV and V: The singular vowel was lengthened according to **41**, under the influence of the long plural vowel: NHG. *nahm, gab.*

In class VII, the vowel of OHG. *hiaz* (NHG. *hieß*) had spread far beyond its original sphere during West-Germanic times; see 46, Note.

49. Weak Verbs. It has been shown above that the type of the Germanic strong verbs dates back to Indo-European times, tho its conservative retention and the consistent utilization of the vowel grades for the formation of tenses are specifically Germanic.

But in addition to this inherited type, the Germanic languages have develolpt a new system of the formation of tenses, the so-called 'weak verbs' (see foot-note on page 156), i.e., verbs that form their preterit tense by means of the suffix Gc. *-ða*, NHG. *-te*. The origin of this suffix has been a matter of dispute for a long time, but there can hardly be any doubt that Brugmann (PBB 39, 84) has solved the problem. According to him, Germanic, like other IE. languages, possessed a type of verb that formed its stem by the addition of *-to-* to the root (e.g., Lat. *plecto*, Ger. *flechten*). After the principle of using the forms of the continuous and momentary (present and non-present)' aspect for the designation of time contrasts had been establisht, parallel forms with and without *-t-*suffixes were treated analogously. The more usual form without *-t-* assumed present meaning, the *-t-*form, preterit force. The number of such verbs was probably not very large to start with, but it was greatly increased by subjecting numerous derivatives to the new principle. Thus the following types of weak verbs develolpt:

(*a*) Verbs with *e/o* or *je/jo* presents, but without middle vowel in the preterit: OHG. *bringan — brāhta, denken* < **þaŋkjan — dāhta, zellen* (NHG. *zählen*) < **zaljan — zalta, decken* < **þakjan — dahta*.

(*b*) Verbs with *j*-suffix in both tenses. *j* stood before vowels (Gc. *laɣjan), *i* before consonants (Gc. *laɣida);

according to **30**, *j* caused doubling of the preceding consonant, but this was carried thru only after short vowels, and frequently it was leveled out, e.g., Gc. **staljan, *laɣjan, *hauzjan* > OHG. *stellen, leggen* (NHG. *legen*), *hōren* (undoubtedly with *ö*, altho the spelling does not indicate it). —

Rückumlaut. The middle vowel *i* was dropt in West-Germanic whenever the stem syllable was long: OHG. *nerita* (= NHG. *nährte*), (Goth. *nasida*), but *hōren=hören* — *hōrta*; thus, the *j*-verbs of class (*a*) and the long stem verbs of class (*b*) had mutation in the present, but not in the preterit. In OHG. and MHG. the number of such verbs — called *rückumlautend* by Jakob Grimm, see **38**, Note 1 — was considerable, but in NHG. most of the forms have been leveled. Rückumlaut still appears in *brennen* — *brannte, kennen* — *kannte, nennen* — *nannte, rennen* — *rannte*, and often in *senden* and *wenden*, but has been leveled out in MHG. *zellen* — *zalte, setzen* — *sazte, decken* — *dachte*, and many others. — Also in *hörte, löste*, etc., the mutated stem vowel had been transferred from the present to the preterit.

(*c*) Verbs with *ē*-suffix, like Lat. *habēre:* OHG. *habēn* — *habēta* — (*gihabēt*), *lebēn* — *lebēta* — (*gilebēt*).

(*d*) Verbs with *ō*-suffix (*ō* < IE. *ā*), like Lat. *amāre:* OHG. *betōn* — *betōta* — (*gibetōt*), *salbōn* — *salbōta* — (*gisalbōt*).

In MHG., the connecting vowels were weakened to *e* according to **40**, and in New High German they were dropt altogether, unless reasons of pronunciation prevented this: *lebte*, but *redete*. — In *hatte* (also in *hast, hat*), *b* was elided after the disappearance of the vowel, see **34, 2**.

50. Preterit-Presents. The Indo-European form for state attained ('perfect form') generally had reduplication, i.e., the initial consonant with the vowel *e* was prefixed to the root: Greek *leipō* 'I leave' — *leloipa* 'I have left.' Apparently, the reduplication imputed the past action resulting in the state attained: *leloipa* 'I am away because I have left,' *loipos* 'left over' (without reference to the action preceding).

Certain verbs specifically expressed state attained as such and, therefore, had unreduplicated perfect form; since they did not imply any allusion to preceding action, they became purely presentic in meaning, e.g., IE. **woida* 'I know,' from root **weid–* 'see, perceive' = Goth. *wait*, NHG. *weiß*.

Such verbs are called 'preterit-presents' because they resemble preterits in form, but are presents in meaning. They never had any reduplication, and their paradigms, in Germanic, are not combinations of perfect and aorist forms, as are other Germanic preterits, but they are 'perfects' pure and simple. — The most important preterit-presents preserved in NHG., are the following (arranged according to the classes of vowel gradation, **46**:

I. '**weiß**': Gc. **wait* — **witum* < IE. **wóida* — **wid–* (*əmés*)

III. '**darf**': Gc. **parf* — **þurƀum* < IE. **tórpa* — **tr̥p–'*
   '**kann**': Gc. **kann* — **kunnum* < IE. **góna* — **gn̥n–'*

IV. '**soll**': Gc. **skal* — *skulum* < IE. **skóla* — **skl̥–'*

VI. '**mag**': Gc. (**maɣ* — **muɣum*, for **mōɣ* — **mōɣum*): IE. **māgh–*??
   '**muß**': Gc. **mōt* — **mōtum* < IE. **mōd–*.

A great deal of leveling, from various sources, has taken place with these verbs; e.g., **maɣ*, undoubtedly a long vowel root, has followed the model of the short vowel roots **skal*, **kann*; NHG. '*soll*' introduced its *o* from the infinitive **skulan;* the disappearance of the *k* has not been satisfactorily explained. The mutated vowels in *dürfen, können, mögen, müssen* (plural and infinitive) came probably from the optatives of these verbs (**52**). The variations between *ü* and *ö* are to be explained according to **39**.

The preterit-presents developt a weak preterit of the type of *dachte, brachte* (**49**, Note): *durfte, konnte, mochte, mußte, sollte.* The stem vowels of these preterits were not selected according to any phonetic laws, but were the products of various analogies. — *u* in *wußte* (instead of MHG. *wiste, weste*) is probably due to the forms *mußte, durfte;* the velar and labial articulation of *w* may have contributed; see **39**.

NOTE. The verb *wollen* originally was not a preterit-present, but in NHG. it was leveled according to *sollen.* The MHG. infinitive was *wellen*, which is the same as NHG. *wählen* < **waljan.* *e* became *o* thru the influence of the surrounding *w* and *l* (**39**); the present singular *will* was an optative (**52**), Goth. *wiljau.*

51. Anomalous Tense Formation occurs with the following verbs:

'**Be**': The third singular *ist* comes from the normal grade of the root **es–*, the plural ind. and the subjunctive from the reduced grade **s–* of the same root; compare Latin *es–t — s–unt.* — *Bin* and *bist* belong to the root **bheu–* which appears in Lat. *fui* 'I was' and Greek *phuo* 'I grow.' — *war* and *gewesen* are derived from the root **wes–* 'be, dwell.'

'**Go**': *Gehen* (<OHG. *gēn, gān*) and *ging* come from different roots; *gehen* belongs to a root **ghē(i)–* (probably 'approach'), *ging*, to a root **ghoŋgh–* 'walk'. The vowel grade of *ging* is modeled after *hieß, fing*, etc.

'**Stand**': In appearance, NHG. *stehen — stand — gestanden* is very much like *gehen — ging — gegangen*, and undoubtedly the two verbs have influenced each other, but all forms of *stehen* come from the same root, IE. **sthā–* (Lat. *stăre*, Gk. *stē–*). The OHG. forms are *stēn* (*stān*) — *stuont — stuontum — gistantan; stēn* comes from the simple root (the explanation of the vowel is uncertain), the other forms have '*n*-infix' like many Latin verbs (*frango, pango, fundo,* etc.). The vowel of the preterit is IE. *ā* (normal grade of a long vowel root), while the participle has the reduced grade, IE. *ə*. The addition of IE. *–t–* in the preterit is the same formation as has been explained in the section on weak verbs, and is also found in Latin *statuere* 'put up.' NHG. has leveled the preterit vowel with the vowel of the participle (*stand — gestanden*), partly under the influence of forms like *fand, trank.*

'Do': OHG. *tuon — teta — tātum — gitān* comes from IE. **dhē–/dhō–* (long vowel root, Lat. *fē-ci*, Gk. *thē-*). The present tense has an irregular *ō*-grade, the past participle, *ē*-grade. The singular of the preterit, *teta*, is a reduplicated form, = IE. **dhe–dhōm;* the plural *tātum,* which has been leveled out into the singular in NHG., was formed as a compromise between this singular and such similar forms as *gābum, nāmum.* (The form *teta* is still found in popular poetry and in dialects, as '*tät*': '*Ich tät mich zu ihm setzen.*')

52. The Optative (=Subjunctive) states an action as merely possible, or subject to a condition. Its stem is formed by means of an *i*-suffix. This forms an *i*-diphthong in connection with the suffixal *–o–* of the Germanic present stems, but appears as *–ī–* with those 'aorist' stems which, according to **45**, are used in the formation of the Germanic preterit. Thus we find the following optative types:

A. IE. 3rd sing. **deik–o–i–t, *wert–o–i–t, *nem–o–i–t,* etc. >Gc. **tīχ–ai, *werþ–ai, *nem–ai*>OHG. *zīhe, werde, neme*>NHG. *zeihe, werde, nehme* (so-called present subjunctive; Gc. *ai* in endings is monophthongized in OHG. — **37**; — final *–t* is dropt in Germanic).

B. IE. 3rd sing. **dik-í-t*, **wrt-í-t*, **nēm-í-t* > Gc. **tiɣi*, *wurði*, **nǣmi* > OHG. *zige, wurti, nāmi* > NHG. *ziehe, würde, nähme* (so-called preterit subjunctive).

NOTE. There never existed any difference in tense between these two subjunctive (optative) types. Both were without any tense signification and remained so much longer than the corresponding indicatives. After compound tenses had been establisht (55), both forms were gradually limited in use to present (or future) time; OHG. *wāri* could stand for the present as well as the past, and even in MHG. such use occurs now and then, but in general, the restriction of all simple (uncompounded) optative forms to the present took place during the OHG. time.

The modern, as well as the old, distinction between the functions of the two forms is one of manner, not of tense. The old contrast between continuous and momentary action which, in the case of the indicative, had become a characteristic of tense, now signifies different degrees of uncertainty with the optative forms, the old forms of continuity denoting personal impression (indirect discourse, purpose, admonition, solemn wish), and the old forms of momentary action — the so-called preterit subjunctives — referring to statements contrary to fact (unreal conditional sentences, unreal concession, ordinary wish, now and then also possibility, etc.). On account of their distinctive forms, the 'preterit subjunctives' have been gradually encroaching upon the original sphere of the 'present subjunctives,' especially in indirect discourse; this, however, belongs to descriptive rather than to historical grammar.

53. The Personal Endings. The most important Indo-European endings were: *-mi* or *-ō, -si, -ti; -mes, -the, -nti*. In this form, the endings appear chiefly in the indicative of the present; elsewhere, certain conditions of the accent had brought about a weakening: *-m, -s, -t; -men, -te, -nt*. The full endings are called *primary* or *absolute*, the weakened, *secondary* or *conjunct* endings. — The singular of the perfect, which originally seems to have been a verbal noun, had the endings *-a, -tha, -e*.

Thru the reduction of final syllables, these endings

undergo considerable changes in Germanic, which lead to the following results:

Present Indicative:

1. IE. *nem–ō > OHG. nimu > NHG. nehme.

It is generally believed that in OHG. *u*, like *i*, caused a change of *e* to *i*; if so, the NHG. form is analogical.

IE. *–mi* is found in NHG. only in the form *bin* < *bim*. OHG. had also *tuom*, *gām*, *stām*, *habēm*, *salbōm*, etc.

2. IE. *nem–e–si > OHG. nimis > NHG. nimmst.

The addition of the (enclitic) pronoun of the second person was responsible for the modern ending *–st*: *nimistu* > *nimmst*.

Gc. *i* in the suffix caused mutation, according to **25** end and **38**A.

3. IE. *nem–e–ti > OHG. nimit > NHG. nimmt.
4. IE. *nem–o–mes > OHG. nemamēs > NHG. nehmen.

The OHG. form is not entirely explained.

5. IE. *nem–e–the > OHG. nemet, nemat > NHG. nehmt.

Analogy. The form should be identical with the 3rd sing.

6. IE. *nem–o–nti > OHG. nemant > NHG. nehmen.

–t was dropt by analogy with the 1st pl.; it is retained, as *–d*, in *sind*.

Preterit (perfect endings in perfect forms, conjunct endings in aorist forms):

1. IE. *ne–nom–a > OHG. nam > NHG. nahm.
2. IE. *nēm–(e)s > OHG. nāmi > NHG. nahmst.

The connecting vowel *–e–* of this aorist form really belonged to the verbs of the first three classes only, IE. *dik–e–s, *duk–e–s, *wrt–e–s, but was transferred to the long vowel aorists by analogy. The ending *–st* in NHG. was borrowed from the present.

The perfect ending IE. *–tha* is found in the preterit-presents, OHG. *darft, kannt, maht, muost, scalt*, since there had not been any aorist forms in these verbs.

3. IE. *ne–nom–e > OHG. nam > NHG. nahm.

4, 5, 6. OHG. *nāmum, nāmut, nāmun* > NHG. *nahmen, nahmt, nahmen.*

The IE. forms are uncertain — probably they were **nēm-men, *nēm-te, *nēm-ṇt.* The vowel of the ending of the Gc. second person is analogical.

Optative (conjunct endings):

A. OHG. *neme, nemēs, neme; nemēm, nemēt, nemēn* < IE. **nem–oi–m, *nem–oi–s,* etc.

B. OHG. *nāmi, nāmīs, nāmi; nāmīm, nāmīt, nāmīn* < IE. **nēm–ī–m, *nēm–ī–s,* etc.

In type *A,* mutation could not take place because IE. *oi* in unaccented syllables became OHG. *e;* in type *B,* mutation was necessary. — In NHG., type *A* has practically given up those forms that are not sufficiently distinct from the indicative, and the forms in actual use are:

—, *nähme*	—, *nähmen*
nehmest, nähmest	—, *nähmet*
nehme, nähme	—, *nähmen.*

Imperative:

The Germanic imperative is not an independent form; the singular goes back to the stem form of the verb, without ending, IE. **nem–e;* the plural forms are indicatives or subjunctives.

54. The Verbal Nouns. 1. The Germanic INFINITIVE was a noun of action (similar, in function, to the NHG. nouns in *–ung*) with the suffix *–no–,* added to the stem of the verb: OHG. *nem–a–n, zellen* < **zal–ja–n, habēn, salbōn.*

2. The PARTICIPLES were verbal adjectives with various IE. endings of which the following have been preserved in Germanic: *–nt–* (compare Lat. *amant–, legent–*) for the present participle (OHG. *nemanti, habēnti, salbōnti*), *–no–* for the past participle of strong verbs (OHG. *gi–noman*), and *–to–* for the past participle of weak verbs (OHG.

gizalt, gihabēt, gisalbōt).   The prefix *gi–* of the past participles denotes completion (see **57**) and is probably related
to Lat. *com–, co– (conficio* 'I complete').

Compare Wilmanns III, 1, § 9.

55. The Compound Tenses.   A. The PERFECT. Being
an adjective, the past participle could at all times be used
predicatively in sentences with the verb 'to be' ('to
seem,' 'to become,' etc.).   But facts of logic caused a
tense difference according to the aspect of the verb: With
'perfective' verbs (verbs of momentary action, especially
of result) such sentences refer to a preceding action and
are, therefore, 'perfect' as to tense; with durative verbs
(verbs of continuous action) they refer to the present:
'He is slain' indicates perfect, 'he is liked,' present. —
Past participles could also be used as objective comple-
ments in sentences with 'to have.'   The character of such
sentences is clearly apparent from the fact that in the older
language the participles take inflectional endings in agreement with the nominal object, e.g., OHG. *sia eigun mir
ginomanan* (acc. sing. masc., 'genommenen') *mīnan druhtin
liaban* 'sie haben mir meinen lieben Herrn genommen.'

Sentences of these two forms were by no means new
types in Germanic; they were matters of course.   Starting
from them, however, there was developt in the Germanic
languages, especially in German, a system of compound
tenses of such abundance as to be somewhat cumbersome.

First, the verb 'to be' with the past participle of intransitive perfective verbs, and the verb 'to have' with
the past participle of transitive verbs assumed the character of a specific tense of completed action: *ich bin gekommen* (= *ein Gekommener*), *ich habe ihn gefangen* (= *als
einen Gefangenen*).   In part, this is to be attributed to
the fusion of the old 'perfect' tense with the old aorist

which had deprived the language of a specific form for completed action. — Durative intransitive verbs were constructed like transitive verbs (*er hat geschlafen*), but gradually the principle of distinction for the use of *sein* and *haben* was shifted somewhat, so that the present distinction is one of result obtained (thru motion or change of condition) versus action as such: *er ist ins Wasser gefallen — er ist blaß geworden — er hat geturnt.* — The 'pluperfect' was developt simultaneously with the perfect.

NOTE 1. A few verbs, like *sein* and *bleiben* (in South German also *stehen, sitzen, liegen, hangen, schweben, stecken*, etc.) take *sein*, altho they do not express result. This was due to a newer tendency, which was carried thru incompletely, to lay stress on localized versus absolute action: *er ist vor der Tür gestanden*, but *er hat lange gestanden.* Compare Wilmanns II, 1, § 8; Sütterlin, § 268.

NOTE 2. In South German, the complete loss of final –*e* destroyed the difference between the 3rd sing. of the present and preterit of regular weak verbs: *er lebt — er lebt(e)*. This was the chief reason that the preterit (even of strong verbs) was given up altogether in South German (and largely in Middle German), the perfect form being used not only for completed action, but also as a historical tense: *ich bin gestern dort gewesen.* A new pluperfect was formed on this basis: *ich habe ihn gesehen gehabt, ich bin gegangen gewesen.*

NOTE 3. Certain strong verbs (e.g., *kommen, werden, treffen, lassen*) originally formed their past participles without the prefix *ge–*; apparently, this became the starting-point for the 'double infinitive' forms in the compound tenses of the modal auxiliaries and similar forms, which have developt since the 15th century: *ich habe ihn kommen lassen* led to constructions by analogy like *ich habe ihn kommen sehen, hören, ich habe kommen wollen, sollen, müssen*, etc. Undoubtedly, however, the close logical connection between the two verbs was a contributory cause, tending towards a parallelism of forms.

B. The FUTURE had no form of its own in Germanic (nor in Indo-European), aside from the fact that the present tense of 'perfective' verbs usually referred to future time; compare '*ich komme morgen.*' In OHG. *scal, willu, mag, muoz* frequently express future time due to their inherent meaning, and in most Germanic languages 'shall' has become the regular auxiliary of the future. — 'Werden' with the participle of the present could be used to denote transition into a state (compare: *er wurde leidend*). The reasons that caused the substitution of the infinitive for the participle in such phrases (towards the end of the MHG. time) are not fully understood. Mere phonetic weakening of the participle ending (*leidend* > *leiden*) undoubtedly contributed, the use of the infinitive in phrases like *er soll* (*will*) *kommen* may have been another factor of importance, and the development of the passive voice strengthened the preference for *werden* over those other auxiliaries. — The future perfect forms and the optatives (*er wird gekommen sein; er werde, würde, kommen, gekommen sein*) were developt in analogy with the existing compound forms.

C. The PASSIVE VOICE. Gothic possessed a specific form for the passive voice, just as other IE. languages, e.g., *bairada, bairanda* = Greek *phéretai, phérontai* 'er wird getragen, sie werden getragen.' Their lack of contrast to the active forms caused them to be replaced by compound forms in all Germanic languages. In OHG., the past participle with *wesan* 'to be' and *werdan* 'to become' existed side by side, in competition, but at the end of the OHG. time, the present conditions had become firmly established: *werden* + past participle, that originally had signified the transition into a state (*er wird geheilt* = *er wird gesund*) generally denoted the passive voice, while *sein* + past participle alone expressed condition as such (*er ist geheilt* = *er ist gesund; er ist geheilt worden* = *er ist gesund, weil man ihn geheilt hat*). — Only in optative and adhortative sentences, the use of *sein* still prevails: *Gott sei gelobt! Sei mir gegrüsst!*

For this whole chapter, compare Wilmanns III, §§ 73–93.

56. Verb Formation. *A.* SIMPLE VERBS. The following are the most important types of Germanic (and German) simple verbs:

(1) ROOT VERBS; the ending is added directly to the root, e.g., IE. **es–ti*, Ger. *ist;* IE. **dhō–ti*, OHG. *tuot*, NHG. *tut*. — The number of these verbs is small.

(2) *e/o*-VERBS, i.e., verbs that attach the ending to the stem by means of the connecting vowels *e* or *o* (qualitative gradation); this vowel is called the 'thematic vowel' and, therefore, these verbs and the *je/jo* verbs are frequently termed 'thematic,' the other classes, 'athematic' verbs. — Most strong verbs belong to the *e/o* class: IE. **nem–e–ti, *nem–o–nti*, 'er nimmt, sie nehmen.'

(3) *je/jo*-verbs are chiefly the first class of weak verbs (Goth. *nas–jan, nas–jis*, like Lat. *capio, capis*) and a few strong verbs, like Goth. *bidjan* = OHG. *bitten*, OHG. *liggen* < **ligjan, sitzen* < **sitjan*.

NOTE 1. Many weak verbs of this class are 'causatives,' i.e., verbs that express action (or condition) caused by some other action; the stem vowel of such verbs is IE. *–o–*: Goth. *satjan*, caus. to *sitjan*, = OHG. *setzen* = 'sitzen machen,' Goth. *nasjan* 'heal' = OHG. *nerien, nerren*, NHG. *nähren*, caus. to (Goth.) *ga–nisan* 'genesen,' etc.

NOTE 2. According to **30**, *j* caused doubling of the preceding consonant in West-Germanic; however, not all of the numerous West-Germanic and especially High German forms with double consonants can be traced to a *–j*-suffix; in some, Germanic doubling before an *–n*-suffix had taken place, but in many cases the doubling of the consonant was undoubtedly spontaneous, expressing intensity or frequent repetition of the action. It is not always possible to state the exact reason. Instances with single and double consonants are: *raufen rupfen, schnauben schnupfen, schneiden schnitzen, ziehen zucken, plagen placken, tauchen ducken, hängen henken gleißen, glitze(r)n, dringen drücken, schlingen schlucken*. — It will be observed that the majority of these 'intensives' or 'frequentatives' has the reduced grade of the stem vowel. — It is good practise for the beginner to explain the consonants of these verbs according to the principles of the second consonant shift.

(4) *ēi*-verbs (IE. *ēi* > Gc. *ē*): OHG. *habēn* (compare Lat. *habēre*), *sagēn, lebēn, folgēn, fragēn*. This suffix often derives verbs from adjectives, e.g., OHG. *fūlēn, rīfēn, altēn* 'faulen, reifen, altern.'

(5) *ā*-verbs (IE. *ā* > Gc. *ō*), compare Lat. *amāre;* these verbs are derivatives from nouns in *−ā*: OHG. *salbōn* (from *salba* 'salve'), *dionōn* 'serve,' *dankōn, machōn, rīchisōn* 'rule.'

Types 1–5 can, in principle at least, be traced to IE. verb types.

(6) Among younger (Germanic or German) derivatives the most important are those in **−ern** (*ackern, schlummern, hungern*, from the nouns *Acker, Schlummer, Hunger; folgern, plätschern*), **−eln** (*fesseln*, from the noun *Fessel, lächeln, spötteln, betteln, näseln*), **−sen, −schen** (*grinsen, grausen, herrschen, feilschen*), **−zen** (*ächzen, krächzen, auchzen*), **−nen** (*regnen, waffnen, rechnen, ordnen, öffnen*), **−gen** (*steinigen, peinigen, ängstigen*), **−chen** (*horchen, schnarchen*), **−ieren** (originally from foreign verbs, like *spazieren, promenieren*, but later also used for German derivatives — *halbieren, hausieren*, etc. — in such numbers that Jakob Grimm complains: ,,Von den Regierenden oben bis zu den buchstabierenden und linierenden Schülern hinab überziehen sie wie Schlingkraut den ebenen Boden unsrer Rede").

Compare Wilmanns II, 1, §§ 89–135.

B. COMPOUND VERBS. The difference between inseparable and separable prefixes in German is not due to any inherent distinguishing principle between the two kinds, but could rather be called a matter of chronology. Certain 'prefixes,' i.e., adverbial verb modifiers, had entered into verbal composition at a very early time, namely, before the Germanic accent shift; when the accent was shifted to the logical center of the word, they became unstressed, and subsequently underwent a similar weakening of sound as final syllables. In younger compounds, the prefix retained more or less the character of an independent word and received stress thru contrast (compare *aufgehen — untergehen*).

The details of the meaning and development of these prefixes belong either to descriptive grammar or to etymology; for the latter, students are referred to Kluge's *Etymologisches Wörterbuch* and to Paul's *Deutsches Wörterbuch.*

A few of the most important facts are:

ge−, the oldest of the inseparable prefixes, does not appear as an independent word anywhere in Germanic. It is probably akin to Lat. *co−*, and denotes completion or result, but with most verbs the original meaning has practically disappeared; compare *gefallen, gehören, gebären.* — *ge–* is the only Germanic prefix that is unaccented in nouns too: *Gesicht,* but *Beiwort, Antwort, Ausflug,* etc.

be– is identical with the preposition *bei,* related to Greek *am–phi* 'around,' and to the first element of *bei–de;* it denotes surrounding, covering, close contact: *besitzen, begraben, beschirmen, bespritzen.* — Compare the separable compounds *beigeben, beilegen,* etc.

ent–, related to Greek *anti* 'against' (originally 'on the other side, yonder'), denotes distance or separation: *entgehen, entrinnen, enthaupten.* There is no corresponding NHG. separable prefix or preposition. — In nouns, it appears in the form *ant–* (e.g., *Antwort*).

er– <OHG. *ur* (in NHG. *Urteil*) weakened form of *ūs* =NHG. *aus,* indicated removal, raising, completion: *ergießen, erbrechen, eröffnen, ersteigen, erwachsen, erhören, ertragen, erfüllen.* — Compare *ausgießen, aussteigen,* etc., and *erteilen* — *Urteil, urteilen* (see below).

ver– corresponds to two distinct Gothic prefixes, namely, *faur* 'in front of, in the interest of' (= NHG. *vor* and *für*) and *fra* 'away from': (a) *verdecken, verstopfen, versehen, versorgen, vertreten, versprechen;* (b) *vergießen, vertreiben, verachten, verfluchen, sich verschreiben, sich versprechen.* — Compare separable *vorsehen, vorsprechen.*

zer– = Lat. *dis–* 'asunder,' in *zerreißen, zerschlagen, zerspringen.*

miss–, related to the verb *missen,* perhaps also to *meiden,* indicates error or disapproval: *mißdeuten, mißverstehen, mißbilligen.* — Also **voll–** is generally inseparable: *vollenden.*

Spurious inseparable compounds. Many compound verbs are derived from compound nouns; grammatically, they are to be considered simple verbs, e.g., *antworten, urteilen* — past participle *geantwortet, geurteilt.*

The 'separable prefixes' are adverbs, adjectives or nouns, e.g., *aufstehen, hineingehen, heimkommen, durcheinanderreden, gutheißen, freikommen, achtgeben, haushalten, standhalten,* also, notwithstanding the orthographical separation, *zustande kommen, zugute tun, vonstatten gehen.* — Some of the adverbs no longer occur independently as such, but only as prepositions, e.g., (*ab*), *an, auf, bei, durch, hinter, mit, nach, ob, vor, wider, zu.* — The prefixes *durch, hinter, über, unter* were inseparable in OHG., but later a considerable number of separable compounds were formed; *um* and *wi(e)der* have been both separable and inseparable since OHG. times. In general, separable compounds with these prefixes have a concrete, literal, but inseparable compounds an abstract, metaphorical meaning (cf. *durch-bohren : durchboh'ren; über-gehen : überge'hen*), but there are many exceptions (e.g., *durch-nehmen, durch-setzen*).

The Noun

57. The Grammatical Categories of the Noun.
A. GENDER. The grammatical element of 'gender' was
not always connected with sex, nor are the two concepts
entirely identical in our times (compare *das Männchen*,
das Weib). The form that we may designate as the 'normal' form of an IE. noun is that which, in historical
times, generally appears as masculine gender; it did not
denote the male human being or animal exclusively, nor
did it originally refer to inanimate objects as 'male' thru a
process of metaphorical sexualization; taking as instances
the most common stem forms (in *−o−* and *−ā−*, see **59**),
IE. **ekwo–s* 'horse,' **wl̥qo–s* 'wolf' did not mean 'stallion,'
'he-wolf' (except by indirect implication, in contrast to
ā-forms), but merely signified an individual horse or wolf.
*ekwā, **wl̥qā* had either generic or collective force, i.e.,
they denoted the type 'horse, wolf,' or a group of horses or
wolves (*'Gestüte, Rudel'*). With reference to the female
as typical, the male as individual, these forms became
the starting-point for feminine gender; **ekwā*, **wl̥qā* came
to mean 'mare, she-wolf.' In their collective meaning,
these forms gave rise to the neuter plural, which has the
same ending as the fem. sing. (compare Lat. fem. sing.
mensa — neut. plur. *verba*). — Neither the generic use
of the *ā*-stems, nor the individualizing character of the
o-stems was necessarily restricted to the female or male
sex respectively; e.g., Lat. *scriba* 'scribe,' *agricola* 'farmer,'
Slav. *sluga* 'servant' (cp. Ger. *die Bedienung, die Kundschaft*) have so-called feminine forms, but denote male
(as well as female) beings of a general type.

The neuter singular was originally not distinct from
the masculine, except for the lack of the nominative form,
for which the accusative form was substituted: Lat.

verbum 'word' is both nom. and acc. This is due to the
fact that nouns of this type generally denote inanimate
objects that are not very likely to be used as active subjects of a sentence.—For similar development, cf. 61*A* (*a*).

Of these three categories — the individual, the generic,
and the objective-collective — the first two became iden-
tified with specific expressions for male and female sex, both
in nouns and pronouns, partly thru likeness of endings,
partly, however, thru the inherent relation between
the male and the individual on the one hand, the female
and the typical on the other hand. — Metaphorical sexualization (i.e., the comparison of inanimate objects either
with male or female beings) has but slightly contributed.

NOTE. Among the various IE. languages, there are considerable
differences in noun gender. It seems not unlikely that Germanic
(especially German) has clung more closely to the inherited distribution than other languages, for even in modern times certain
facts in German gender reflect the old conditions very perspicuously.
Thus, among animals, those that are hunted individually, or otherwise thought of rather singly than collectively, are apt to be masculine: *Bär, Wolf, Hund, Fuchs, Hase, Adler, Rabe, Schwan*, while
those that are generally felt as types are of feminine gender: *Maus,
Laus, Wanze* (but *Floh!*), *Fliege, Mücke, Schwalbe, Lerche*. Where
there are special names for the natural sexes, the type as such is of
neuter gender (*das Pferd, das Rind, das Huhn;* also their young:
das Fohlen, das Kalb, das Küchlein; but *der Hengst, der Stier, der
Hahn; die Stute, die Kuh, die Henne*). — The neuter singular as
belonging to a collective plural is apparent in *das Weib* (compare
the NHG. designation '*das Frauenzimmer*,' which was originally
the collective name for the women of the household) and, similarly,
in *Gott*, which was neuter in Gothic, while in OHG. the masculine
gender was used for the Christian God, the neuter, for pagan idols.

Many changes of gender in historical times point in the same
direction. Many animals, plants and objects that were masculine
in MHG. have become feminines in NHG. on account of their
collective (generic) character. Instances are *Ameise, Grille, Heu-
schrecke, Hornisse, Imme, Otter, Ratte, Schlange, Schnecke, Schnepfe;*

Binse, Blume, Dille, Distel, Hirse, Kresse, Rebe, Rose; Ähre, Gräte, Kohle, Locke, Scholle, Träne, Traube, Woge, Zähre; Wade, Schläfe, Niere. — An important formal element in this change of gender was the identity of the NHG. article of the feminine singular and the plural: the plural *die Locke* (which, in collective meaning, was, of course, much more frequent than *der Lock* 'the curl') could easily be understood as a feminine singular.

B. Number. There were three numbers in IE.: singular, plural, and dual. In modern Germanic languages the latter has become practically extinct, and the Germanic noun had lost it in prehistoric times; it appears, however, in the personal pronoun of the older Germanic dialects, e.g., Goth. *inqis* 'both of you' (dat. and acc.), preserved in modern Bavarian *enk*, which is used instead of standard German *euch*.

C. Case is the expression of the syntactic relation of a noun (pronoun or adjective) to some other part or parts of the sentence. Indo-European had eight cases: the nominative, genitive, dative, accusative, vocative, ablative, locative, and instrumental.

The nominative indicates the subject of a sentence, i.e., the center of the action expressed in the sentence. The accusative denotes the person or thing directly affected by the action, the genitive (chiefly) the person or thing only partly affected by it. The dative expresses interest for, or regard to, something or somebody. The locative points to the place where an action occurs, the ablative to its starting-point. The instrumental indicates the means thru which something is done. The vocative has no syntactic relation to the rest of the sentence, but is the form of address.

This multiplicity of cases was reduced in all IE. languages thru a process called *Syncretism*: one case — frequently a compromise between several forms — assumed the functions of several cases. In German the number of cases has thus been reduced to four; the nominative, genitive, and accusative have essentially retained the old functions, while our so-called dative (mostly with prepositions) combines the syntactical characteristics of the old dative, ablative, locative, and instrumental, all of which might be termed as adverbial cases; in form, the German dative is chiefly a locative. — Very largely the exact expression of old case functions has been taken over by prepositions. The genitive case seems to be slowly going out of use, the preposition *von* with dative chiefly taking its place.

58. Nominal Stems. Nouns, like verbs, consist of root, stem suffix, and ending; root and suffix form the stem. The noun suffixes are subject to vowel gradation, just as the verbal suffixes, compare IE. **nem–e–ti*: **nem–o–nti* and **dhogh–o–s* 'day,' nom.: **dhogh–e–so*, gen.

Among the IE. nominal stems, the following are of special importance for the Germanic languages:

NOTE. The nouns in heavy type, being typical representatives of their classes, will frequently be referred to in the following sections; their stem character will then be taken for granted.

A. VOWEL STEMS, i.e., nouns with vowel suffixes:

(1) **o**-stems = Germanic *a*-stems: Lat. *hortus < hort–o–s* 'garden' = Gothic *gards* 'house' < Gc. **garda–z*. IE. **dhogh–o–s* 'day' > Ger. **Tag.** — Note the genitive, Goth. *dagis < *dhogh–e–so;* see above.

jo-(Gc. *ja*-)stems: Goth. *hairdeis,* OHG. *hirti,* NGH. **Hirte** < IE. **kerdh–jo–s.*

(2) **ā**-stems = Gc. *ō*-stems: Lat. *mensa < mensā;* OHG. *geba,* NHG. **Gabe.**

(3) **i**-stems and **u**-stems; these suffixes are, strictly speaking, *i*- and *u*-diphthongs and can, therefore, appear (by gradation) as *ei, oi, i, eu, ou, u*: Lat. *hostis* 'enemy,'

manus 'hand'; Goth. *gasts* < *IE. *ghost–i–s*, NHG. **Gast;**
Goth. *sunus,* gen. *sunaus* (IE. **sun–u–s,* **sun–ou–so*),
NHG. **Sohn.**

B. CONSONANT STEMS; the consonants **r, n,** or **s,** to-
gether with vowels in gradation, are added to the root:
Lat. *pater* (gen. *patris,* with reduced grade of the suffix)
= Goth. *fadar,* Ger. **Vater;** Lat. *homō* (for *–ōn*), gen.
hominis (<*–en–es*) 'man'; *nomen,* gen. *nominis* 'name':
Goth. *guma, namō,* NHG. **Bote** 'messenger,' **Name;**
Goth. *tuggō* = NHG. **Zunge;** Lat. *genus* 'kin,' plur. *genera*
< **gen–es–ā:* Ger. *Lamm,* plur. *Lämmer* (*r* from *s* thru
Verner's Law).

C. ROOT STEMS, without any suffix (stem = root), e.g.,
Lat. *noc–s* = *nox* 'night,' Ger. **Nacht.**

o- and *jo*-stems are either masculine or feminine; *ā*-stems
are feminine; *i*-stems and *u*-stems, either masculine or
feminine (rarely neuter); *n*-stems belong to all three
genders; *r*-stems are names of relatives preeminently and
therefore masculine or feminine; *s*-stems (in Germanic)
are neuter.

59. The Case Endings of IE. nouns, as far as they are
of importance for the Germanic languages, are:

Singular	Plural
Nom. –**s** after short vowels and diphthongs and in root nouns; no ending after long vowels or consonantic suffixes (neuter: nom. = acc.)	–**es,** neuter –**ā**
Acc. –**m**	–**ms** > –**ns** (neuter: acc. = nom.)

Singular	Plural

Gen. **–so** after short vowels   **–ōm** (i.e., 'over-long'
    and diphthongs, **–s**   vowel, **20**)
    after *–ā*, **–es** after
    cons.

Dat. **–ai**   ⎫
Instr. **–mo**   ⎬ **–mis**
Loc. **–i** or no ending   ⎭ (Does not occur in Germanic)

The ablative and vocative are not important for Germanic grammar.

60. Weakening of Endings. Thru the weakening of final syllables (**26, 40**), the endings were subject to considerable changes. It cannot be the intention of an elementary introduction like this book to enter into the details of these complicated developments. In the following table only the clearest and most important origins of the NHG. terminations are indicated. The expression 'termination' is chosen arbitrarily in distinction from 'ending' to denote the inflectional elements of nouns from the point of view of New High German grammar, which does not always coincide with that of comparative grammar; e.g., *–en* of the 'weak declension' is a 'termination' in this sense of the word, but according to comparative grammar it is not an ending, but a stem suffix; on the other hand, the genitive termination *–s* is a real 'ending.'

The IE. 'terminations' (suffix+ending) are given in parentheses after each word.

The NHG. types of noun terminations are:

1. Nom. sing.: no termination.

    (*a*) *Tag* (–os), *Gast* (–is), *Sohn* (–us), *Bär* (–ō), *Vater* (—),
    Nacht (–s); *Hirte* (–jos), *Friede* (–us), *Sitte* (–us), *Gabe*
    (–ā), *Bote* (–ō), *Zunge* (–ōn), *Auge* (–ōn).

2. Acc. sing.: (a) no termination, (b) –en.

> (a) *Tag* (–om), *Gast* (–im), *Sohn* (–um), *Gabe* (–ām), *Vater* (–m̥), *Nacht* (–m̥).
> (b) *Wort* (–om), *Herz* (–ōn), (acc. neut.=nom.).
> (c) *Boten*, old form *Zungen* (ōn–m̥).

3. Gen. sing.: (a) –es (–s), (b) no termination, (c) –en (–n).

> (a) *Tages* (–e–so), *Gastes* (–oi–so), *Sohnes* (–ou–so).
> (b) *Gabe* (–ă̄–s).
> (c) *Boten*, *Herzen*(s) (–en–es), old form *Zungen* (–ōn–es).

4. Dat. sing.: (a) –e, (b) no termination, (c) –en (–n).

> (a) *Tage* (–o–i), *Gaste* (–oi–i), *Sohne* (–ou–i).
> (b) *Gabe* (–ā–i), *Vogel* (–o–i), *Vater* (–er–i), *Nacht* (–i).
> (c) *Boten*, *Herzen* (–en–i), old form *Zungen* (–ōn–i).

5. Nom. plur.: (a) –e, (b) no termination, (c) –en (–n), (d) –er.

> (a) *Tage* (–o–es), *Gäste* (–ei–es>Gc. –īz), *Söhne* (–eu–es> Gc. –īz), *Worte* (–ā).
> (b) *Vögel* < *Vogele* (–o–es), *Väter* (–er–es).
> (c) *Boten*, *Zungen* (–ōn–es), *Herzen* (–ōn–ā).
> (d) *Lämmer* (–es–ā).

6. Acc. plur.:=nom. plur.; as far as NHG. is concerned, the termination (IE. –o–ns, –i–ns, etc.) is dropt or retained under the same conditions as IE. –o–es, –ei–es, –eu–es.

> *Tage* (–o–ns), *Gäste* (–i–ns), *Väter* (–n̥s).

7. Gen. plur.:=nom. plur., the ending being treated like that of the nom. and acc.

8. Dat. plur. ends in –en (–n) with all nouns.

> *Tagen* (–o–mis), *Gästen* (–i–mis), *Söhnen* (–u–mis), *Gaben* (–ā–mis), *Zungen* (–ōn–mis), etc.

61. Transfer of Forms. The principles of noun declension underwent a similar shifting of the view-point as the principles of conjugation. Here, tense was substituted for manner of action; there, the stem classes — originally tantamount to differences of the way of designation — were gradually replaced by sharp contrasts between other categories, namely, (*a*) between the genders, (*b*) between the numbers, (*c*) between animate beings and things. While the process of establishing these contrasts has not yet been completed in NHG., and perhaps never will be, it is clearly marked in unmistakable directions of development. — The principal means by which these changes were effected consist in a generalization of vowel mutation beyond its phonetic sphere (**38***B*), and in a considerable extension of the *n*- (and *s*-)stems.

The final appearance of the NHG. declensional system, as brought about in this way, is represented by the recognition of a 'strong,' 'weak,' and 'mixed' declension; mutation, either actual or potential, characterizes the first, extension of the *n*-stems the second, and incomplete transfer of forms the third of these groups.

NOTE. In Latin and Greek there are clear traces of a similar process in its beginning, but in modern Romance languages and in English we find a tendency to eliminate rather than to intensify declensional contrasts. English, e.g., expresses nearly all plurals by one and the same ending, mutation having been given up almost entirely (exceptions: *mice, lice, geese, feet, teeth, men*); French hardly expresses the plural at all, except by the form of the article and by spelling.

A. THE CONSOLIDATION OF GENDERS. It is not very much of an exaggeration to say that NHG. possesses two or three declensional systems to correspond to the two or three genders (depending on whether one prefers to consider the neuter a special gender or a subdivision of the masculine). Their consolidation proceeded in the following way: Different genders tend towards different declensional classes; masculines are apt to enter (or remain in) the *o*- and *i*-classes, feminines, the *n*-class, neuters, the *o*- and *s*-classes. In general, we are almost certain to find that feminines that belong to the *i*-class now (by virtue of vowel mutation), e.g., *Kraft — Kräfte*, or masculines that are 'weak' in NHG., have always belonged to these classes; but that *n*-feminines, or *o*- or *i*-masculines as often as not have come from some other declension.

(*a*) About fifty MASCULINES of the *n*-declension have entered the *o*-class; this was done by leveling out the *–n* of the oblique cases into the nominative and adding *–s* to the genitive sing.; thus, *der Brunn(e)*, *des Brunnen* became *der Brunnen*, *des Brunnens*.

Some of the most important nouns of this group are *Balken, Bissen, Bogen, Braten* (compare *Wildpret = Wildbraten*), *Brunnen* (compare *Schönbrunn*), *Daumen* (: *Daumschrauben*), *Flecken* (: *Fleckseife*), *Galgen, Garten, Kasten, Knochen, Kuchen, Laden, Magen, Rahmen, Riemen, Tropfen* (: *der Tropf*); see list in Wright, Historical German Grammar, § 383. — *Garten* and *Graben* always, *Kasten, Kragen, Magen, Laden* frequently mutate their vowel. — As the forms in parentheses show, compounds often have preserved the older forms; as to *Tropfen* : *Tropf*, see below, *C*.
With some nouns, the old and the new (leveled) forms exist side by side, which means that the transition is not completed: *Funke, Gedanke, Glaube, Haufe, Name, Same, Wille, Fels, Friede* (*u*-stem) have nominatives in *–e* and *–en*, but new genitives. — The *n*-NEUTERS *Herz, Auge, Ohr* tend in the same direction; *Herz* is inflected like *Fels*, while the singular of *Auge* and *Ohr* has entered the *o*-class altogether, without leveling the *–n* ('Mixed Declension').

(*b*) Among the *ā*- and *n*-FEMININES, there took place a sort of interchange of forms (following principle *B*, see below). The MHG. declension of an *ā*-feminine like *gebe* 'Gabe' was: sing. **gebe**, *gebe, gebe, gebe;* plur. *gebe, geben, geben, gebe;* the *n*-feminine *Zunge* had in MHG. the forms: sing. **zunge**, *zungen, zungen, zungen;* plur. *zungen, zungen,*

zungen, zungen. A combination of these two paradigms yielded a new declensional type in NHG., in which the *ā*-feminines took *n*-plurals, while the *n*-feminines dropt their singular endings, thus giving up all differences between the types *Gabe* and *Zunge.* — The nouns in *-in,* *-ung, -heit, -keit, -schaft* (old *ā*- or *jā*-stems) form a large proportion of this new class. — Many feminine, but no masculine, *i*-stems followed the same model, e.g., *Arbeit, Last, Tat.* Also one root-feminine, *Burg* (old plural *Burg*), has entered the new 'weak declension.'

The *-n* of the oblique cases of *n*-feminines is preserved in a number of old phrases (*auf Erden, unsrer Lieben Frauen*) and in many compounds, like *Ammenmärchen, Tulpenzwiebel, Kirchenmaus, Sonnenstrahl, Wochentag,* etc.

The old plural of some *i*-nouns is preserved in singular meaning, e.g., *die Fährte* (old plural of *Fahrt*), *Blüte* (MHG. sing. *bluot*), *Ente, Leiche, Mähne, Stätte, Stute, Tür*(e); new *n*-plurals were formed to these secondary singulars.

(c) NEUTERS, originally, belonged chiefly to the *o-* (*jo-*)class and many of them have remained there, e.g., the *o*-stems *Bein, Brot, Ding, Haar, Jahr, Pfund, Recht, Roß, Schaf, Tier, Messer, Feuer, Mädchen;* the *jo*-stems *Kreuz, Netz, Gedicht, Gesetz, Gebirge, Gemüse, Getreide,* etc. — But in ever increasing numbers, neuters, especially those of one syllable, adopted a plural type, which originally had been very rare in Germanic, viz., the forms of the old *s*-stems, cp. Lat. *genera,* plur. of *genus* (with *r* for *s*). From hardly half a dozen in Germanic, their number has risen to more than a hundred in NHG., e.g., *Bad* (but *Baden,* name of a city, originally dat. plur.), *Blatt, Faß, Feld, Grab, Gras, Huhn, Gesicht, Kalb, Kleid, Lamm, Land, Nest, Schwert, Weib, Wort,* and the neuters (and masculines) in *-tum.*

About eight masculines joined this new neuter declension for reasons of analogy: *Mann, Geist, Wurm* (and perhaps *Gott*, which, however, was an old neuter) followed such names of human beings or animals as *Kind, Weib, Kalb, Lamm, Huhn; Leib*, perhaps, followed *Weib*, while differentiation form *Laib Brot* may have contributed; *Rand* followed *Band* and *Land, Wald* (old *u*-stem) followed *Feld* (cp. *Unterwalden*). — See B (a).

B. The Contrast of Numbers had partly disappeared thru the weakening of final syllables; root nouns (like *Mann, Nacht, Burg*), *o*-neuters, and masculines and neuters in *–el, –er, –en* had lost their plural endings altogether. With some masculine and neuter nouns, the identity of forms has been retained, the difference of the singular and plural articles offering sufficient contrast, e.g., with *jo*-stems like *Lehrer, Schüler, Meister, Gebirge, Gemüse*, *o*-stems like *Messer, Himmel, Esel, Wesen, Mädchen, Vöglein;* also after numerals old endingless plurals are preserved: *zehn Pfund, tausend Mann*. But in an overwhelming majority of cases, regardless of gender, identity of the singular and plural forms has been remedied in the following ways:

(*a*) By the addition of an ending:

–e was added to some *o*-neuters, especially monosyllabic ones, like *Wort, Brot, Roß*, etc. (see above); the OHG. and MHG. plural forms had been *wort, ros*, etc.

–er was added to the rest of the monosyllabic *o*-neuters and to some masculines (see above).

Sometimes both forms exist in competition; in such cases, the *–e* plural usually belongs to the elevated, the *–er* plural to the colloquial language, e.g., *Lande — Länder, Bande — Bänder, Gewande — Gewänder, Dinge — Dinger, Schilde — Schilder, Reste — Rester;* also *Bröter, Rösser, Jöcher, Beiner* occur colloquially.

–en was used extensively to establish sharp contrasts of number in the new weak declension; see above, *A* (*b*).

With masculines, it was rarely resorted to; OHG. *hirti*, plur. *hirte*, *hirta*, a *jo*-stem, became *Hirt(e)* — *Hirten*, with subsequent transition of the singular into the *n*-declension. Similarly, MHG. *rücke*, *weizze* (cp. *Rückhalt*, *Weißbier = Weizbier*) have added *-n* in the plural and then leveled it into the singular, so that the article remained the only distinguishing element between the numbers. — With the *o*-stems *Bauer*, *Nachbar*, *Staat*, *Zins*, the transition has not been completed ('mixed declension'). — With *Heide* and *Rabe*, the transition to *n*-stems is only apparent; see below. — Also a few neuters have added *-n* in the plural, namely, the *jo*-stems *Ende*, *Bett(e)*, *Hemd(e)*.

(*b*) By mutation:

The *r*-stems *Vater*, *Mutter*, *Bruder*, *Tochter* mutated their vowels, while *Schwester* (where mutation could not take place) added *-n*.

Many masculine *o*-stems mutated: *Baum*, *Frosch*, *Fuchs*, *Hof* (cp. *Zatzighofen*, name of a town), *Koch*, *Lohn*, *Stuhl*, *Wolf*; *Acker*, *Hammer*; *Faden*, *Wagen*; *Mantel*, *Schnabel*, *Vogel*, and many others.

In dialects, especially in South German, where the ending *-e* is dropt, their number is much greater: *Hünd'*, *Ärm'*, *Täg'*, etc.

(*c*) By mutation and ending:

The root stems *Nacht* and *Brust*.

The neuter nouns that added *-er* to the plural, see above.

The root nouns *Kuh*, *Gans*, *Laus*, *Magd*, *Nuß*, *Zahn*, *Fuß*, and others had become *i*-stems in prehistoric times.

C. ANIMATE VERSUS INANIMATE. This element of contrast which in Slavic languages, for instance, is of considerable importance is much less noticeable in Germanic than the former two. Aside from a few isolated cases (e.g., the transition of OHG. *fridu* to the modified *-n*-class: *der Friede*, *des Friedens*, while OHG. *sunu* remained in its class: *der Sohn*, *die Söhne*), there is only one group worth mentioning, namely, the masculines of the n-class; even here, however, the deciding factor was rather an element of form than of meaning: Masculine n-stems, when animate, have generally retained their type of declension: *der Knabe, des Knaben, die Knaben;* those that denoted things, have gone into the o-class in consequence of the leveling of the n into the nominative: *der Brunne–n;* see above.   More than to anything else, this was probably due to the fact that with things the nominative is much rarer than the accusative (objective) case — cp. **58,** concerning the IE. neuter — and was therefore replaced by the latter.

Many n-stems denoting living beings have dropt the –e of the nominative, especially those ending in –r, and those that were frequently used as titles, e.g., *Bär, Narr, Tor, Herr, Fürst, Graf, Prinz.* — A few n-stems, however, have passed over into the 'strong' declension, e.g., *Herzog* (cp. *Herzogenbusch*), *Schwan* (cp. *Schwanengesang*), *Hahn* (: *Hahnenfeder*), *Schelm, Gemahl, Junker, Aar, Adler,* and others; the reason for this is not entirely clear. — The o-stem *Held* has become weak.

The n-stems *Lump* and *Tropf* show the interesting peculiarity of following the type *Brunnen* in their literal meaning ('rag,' 'drop'), but when used metaphorically for human beings ('scoundrel,' 'good-for-nothing'), *Lump* retains its original n-declension (cp., however, Goethe's '*Nur Lumpe sind bescheiden*'), while *Tropf* (plur. *Tröpfe*) follows the i-stems.

Heide and *Christ* were originally o-stems ending in –en (MHG. *der heiden, der kristen*), but have dropt the –n in the nom. sing. in analogy with *Jude, Laie, Pfaffe,* etc., thus going over into the n-declension.

62. Noun Formation. *A.* Simple Nouns.   (1) Primary Nouns. — The parts of the body, the nearest relatives, native plants and animals, and the most common objects, ideas, and institutions of primitive life are generally designated by independent nouns that have little, if any, connection with other primary (underived) parts of speech.   Instances are: *Leib, Arm, Bein, Haupt, Hand,*

Fuß, Finger, Zehe, Mund, Zahn, Ohr, Auge. — Vater, Mutter, Bruder, Schwester, Sohn, Tochter, Weib. — Hund, Wolf, Bär, Storch, Adler, Biene, Baum, Wald, Feld, Eiche, Buche. — Haus, Stein, Holz, Balken, Beil, Dorf, Land, Meer, Kampf, Friede. — Tod, Kraft, Lust, Sitte, Ehe, Adel.

(2) Derived Nouns. By far the greater number of nouns is derived, (a) from verbs, in various ways and with various vowel grades, e.g., *fliegen: Flug, Fliege, Flügel; biegen: Bug, Bügel, Bucht; binden: Band, Bund, Binde, Bündel; graben: Grab, Grube, Gruft.*

(b) From adjectives, chiefly abstracts in *–e: Güte, Größe, Röte, Stärke.*

B. NOMINAL PREFIXES. The most important nominal prefixes are the accented forms of the verbal prefixes mentioned in 57, e.g., *Beifall, Beispiel; Antwort, Antlitz; Urteil, Ursache; Vorsicht, Vorsorge; Fürsorge; Mißgunst, Mißklang.*

ge– is always unaccented; with nouns, it has generally collective meaning, cp. *Gebirge, Gebüsch, Gehölz, Geschwister. — Be–, ent– (emp–), er–, ver–, zer–* are not genuine noun prefixes, but are found in many nouns that are derived from compound verbs containing these prefixes, e.g., *Bedarf, Empfang, Erwerb, Verdruß, Zerfall.*

The only nominal prefix that does not occur with verbs in any form is *un–: Unehre, Unglück.*

C. NOMINAL SUFFIXES.

Nouns of action are formed by

–er (OHG. *–āri,* perhaps from Lat. *–arius*), to denote the agent: *Bäcker, Lehrer, Schneider,* etc. — These nouns are generally formed from verbs.

–ei (of French origin), to denote the action itself or the place of the action: *Schmeichelei, Bäckerei, Fischerei.*

Feminines are derived from masculine nouns by

–in (plural *–innen,* an old *–jā-*stem): *Königin, Gattin, Fürstin, Wölfin.*

Descent (also youth, contempt, etc.) is denoted by

–ing, –ung, –ling: Karoling, Nibelung, Sprößling, Säugling, Frühling, Jüngling, Feigling, Frechling.

The diminutive suffixes are

–lein (High German) and *–chen* (of Low German origin): *Fräulein, Vöglein, Mädchen, Veilchen.*

Place, condition, circumstances are expressed by

–nis (plur. *–nisse*): *Wildnis, Gefängnis, Finsternis, Betrübnis.*
–icht: *Dickicht, Röhricht.*
–sal, –sel: *Mühsal, Schicksal, Rätsel.*
–tum: *Königtum, Heiligtum, Irrtum, Reichtum, Volkstum.*

Persons and matters are expressed collectively by

–schaft (related to *schaffen*): *Dienerschaft, Kundschaft, Feindschaft, Wissenschaft, Landschaft, Nachbarschaft.*

Abstracts are formed by

–heit (related to Gothic *haidus* 'manner'): *Dummheit, Krankheit, Hoheit;* with the adjective suffix *–ig*, it took the form –keit, which subsequently was transferred to nouns without *–ig: Einigkeit, Fähigkeit, Tapferkeit, Aufmerksamkeit.*

–ung (abstract nouns of action): *Achtung, Hoffnung, Sendung.*

D. NOUN COMPOSITION proper consists of the combination of a noun, as second element, with another noun, an adjective, a verb, or an adverb, as first element, e.g., *Hausvater, Süßwasser, Schreibtisch, Heimweg.* This is essentially a chapter of descriptive grammar. From the point of view of historical grammar it should be noted that many nouns as first elements of compounds have retained their old genitive forms, e.g., *Frauenkirche, Freudenbotschaft, Schwanengesang* (many such compounds have been mentioned in the preceding chapter), and that the genitive *–s* of masculines and neuters has been extended to many feminines, e.g., *Liebesbrief, Hoffnungsschimmer, Freiheitsfreund.*

The Pronoun

63. The Personal Pronoun exhibits exceedingly archaic forms, some of which are difficult to explain. — The first person is characterized by the labial element *m–*, the second, by the dental element *t–* in the singular and the velar element *–u–* (vocalic or consonantic) in the plural, the third (the so-called reflexive) by the sibilant *s–*.

In the accusative singular, *mich, dich, sich,* the final consonant of the nom. sing. *ich* was added to the stems **me–*, **te–*, **se–* (with Germanic *i* for *e* in unaccented position). — The ending *–r* of the datives *mir* and *dir*, from IE. *–s*, was probably transferred from the plural *uns*. — The genitives *mein, dein, sein* (*-er* was added in NHG. in imitation of the plural forms *unser, euer*) are adjectives, formed by means of the suffix *-īn-* (cp. OHG. *gold — guldīn* 'golden,' **38**B; **70**). — The nominative *ich* is really a demonstrative pronoun; *du* is an emphatic form of address of the *t*-element.

The plural form *uns* is the root element *m-* with the plural sign *-s: m̥s > n̥s > uns;* in *euch*, the *ch*-sound of *ich, mich, dich, sich* is added to the *u*-element in the normal grade: **eu- >* Gc. **iu(k) >* NHG. *euch.* — *ir* is formed in imitation of *wir*, and this latter (from **wei-* and the plural sign *-s*) is an isolated form without any clear etymological connection.

The usual pronoun of the third person, *er, sie, es*, is a demonstrative coming from two different roots: **e-* (partly weakened to *i-*) forms the masculine and neuter singular and the genitive and dative cases of the feminine singular and the plurals, the remaining forms come from a root **so- (*sjo-)*. The endings are, in principle, the same as those of *der*, which see below.

64. The Demonstrative Pronouns.

(*a*) **der**, IE. **to-* (and **tjo-*), Greek *to*, Lat. (*is-*)*te*, is by far the most important demonstrative pronoun of the IE. languages. Its declension, which is typical for most pronouns, is very similar to that of the nouns, but in Germanic its endings were much less subject to weakening than the nominal endings. — The endings of noun and pronoun correspond as follows:

SINGULAR

Nom. **der** contains the *s*-ending of the nominative of the noun;
   die is an accusative form (IE. **tjā-m*, like *-ām* of the fem. noun) which was substituted in NHG. for the MHG. nom. *diu < *tjā*.

Nom. **das** ends in IE. *–d* (cp. Lat. *id, quod*), which does not occur with nouns.

Gen. **des, der, des** have the usual *s*-element of the genitive under varying accent conditions (Verner's Law!). The dat. fem. **der** has the same *s*-element, tho followed by a different vowel originally.

Dat. **dem** has an instrumental ending (Goth. *þamma* <IE. **tosmē*), not occurring with the noun, but related to the ending of the dat. plur.

Acc. **den** is IE. **te–m;* the ending *–m* is weakened to *–n* in the pronoun, while it disappears in the noun.

die, das, see above.

PLURAL

Nom. **die** is the NHG. result of several older forms (OHG. *dē, deo, diu,* for IE. **toi, *tjās, *tjā*).

Gen. **der** (OHG. *dero*) shows the same *s*-element as the gen. sing., originally with the usual genitive ending *–ōm.*

Dat. **den** has the usual dat. (instr.) ending *–mis.*

Acc. **die** = nom., in part originally identical, in part thru transfer of forms.

er has the same endings; the neuter genitive was *es*, while the neuter nom. had been *eʒ* in OHG. and MHG. (**32**, 1); the old genitive form still occurs in phrases like *ich bin es satt, bin es müde.*

When used as pronouns proper, some of the forms of *der* were lengthened by the addiditon of *–en* to the dative plural and later also to the dat. sing. fem. and the gen. sing.: *denen, deren, dessen;* this was added, first, to the dat. plur. *den* by analogy with *Tagen,* etc. (the old dat. plur. *in* was lengthened to *ihnen* in the same way). — The absolute gen. plur. *derer* may have taken its *–er* from *unser, euer,* or it may originally be a gen. pl. of *dieser* (OHG. *desero* and *derero*).

Early in Germanic times (the process started in Gothic), unemphatic *der* was used as definite article, exactly as in Greek.

(*b*) **dieser** is a compound of two demonstrative stems, namely, the stem of *der* and a stem **so–*, which, in a modified form, also appears in the fem. and plur. pronoun *sie.*

(*c*) **jener**, too, is a compound, consisting of the stem form of an unemphatic demonstrative pronoun IE. **jo–/je–,* and another demonstrative stem, *–no–*, expressing contrast or distance.

(*d*) **solch** (MHG. *so-lich*) is an adjective derived from the demonstrative adverb *so* and the suffix *–lich* (**69**), = 'so geartet, so beschaffen.'

65. The Interrogative Pronoun came from the IE. stem **qo–* (cp. dat. *quod*) and was declined like *der:* OHG. *hwer* > NHG. *wer — wes, wem, wen;* OHG. *hwaz* > NHG. *was — wes, (wem), was.* The gen. *wes* added *–en* (*wessen*) in conformity with *dessen.*

In the same way as *so-lich* > *solch*, an interrogative adjective *we-lich* > *welch* was derived from the interrogative stem.

66. The Relative Pronoun. (1) **der.** The IE. relative stem **jo/je* has disappeared, as a pronoun, in the Germanic languages, but Gothic uses a locative form of this stem, **jei* > Goth. *ei* (pronounce *ī*) as a relative particle which usually is added to the demonstrative pronoun *þa–*, corresponding to German *der;* this construction is exactly the same as modern Bavarian '*der Mann, wo . . .*,' or '*der Mann, der wo . . .*,' instead of '*der Mann, der . . .*' In OHG., the particle *–ī* disappeared (as in English 'the man I saw'), and the remaining demonstrative was felt to be a part of the relative clause. Thus *der* (with the lengthened forms of the gen. and dat.) obtained the function of a relative pronoun. — In OHG. and MHG., and in elevated, archaic language also in NHG., the demonstrative adverb *so* occurs as a relative particle like Gothic *ei: das Gesetz, so gebietet „du sollst nicht töten.“*

(2) The interrogative pronouns **wer, was,** and **welch–** began to be used as relatives during the OHG. period.

Apparently, this development started from the generalizing use of *wer, was, welch–*, in the sense of *whoever, whatever, whichever*.

The Adjective

67. Strong and Weak Declension. Adjectives originally are nouns denoting qualities, and were, in IE., declined like other nouns. Gradually, however, the Germanic languages develompt a double system of adjective inflection, in which every adjective could follow either the *o-* (*jo-*), or the *n*-declension. — An indication of similar conditions is found in Latin, where many adjectives, when used as *o*-stems, had descriptive function, while they were determining adjectives when used as *n*-stems, cp. *vir rufus* 'a red-haired man': *Rūfō* 'Rotkopf,' a proper name. The same contrast between temporary designation and permanent appellation seems to have existed in a prehistoric period of the Germanic languages (names like OHG. *Brūno* 'der Braune,' *Kuono* 'der Kühne' — *n*-stems that belong to the adjectives *brūn, kuoni* — point to this), but in early historical times the distinction had become one between a generic (indefinite) use of 'strong' adjectives and an individualizing (definite) use of weak (*n*-)adjectives, as in NHG. *gute Menschen* — *die guten Menschen*.

Gradually, the logical basis of these two declensions was given up or, rather, expressed in the preceding pronominal adjective (especially the article), and the choice between the two declensions became one of mechanical syntax: Whenever a pronominal adjective preceded, the non-distinctive *n*-endings were chosen; when this was not the case, 'strong' forms were used, i.e., originally forms of the *o*-declension, which, however, were more and more replaced by the more distinctive pronominal endings, i.e., the endings of *der;* in this way, both declensional systems became equally distinct; in modern German, the characteristic endings of *der* either precede the adjective (*der gute Mann, dieser gute Mann*, etc.), or they form its inflection (*harter Stahl, festes Holz*, etc.).

Note 1. The nominative case, where clearness did not demand any characteristic endings, was the last to adopt pronominal endings; the endless forms were used for the nom. masc. and the nom. and acc. neut. thruout the MHG. time and even later; in certain phrases — *Jung Siegfried, Röslein rot* — they occur to this day, and with the possessive adjectives and the indefinite article they have never been given up.

Note 2. The feminine singular of the weak adjective has retained the old *n*-forms, with the exception of the accusative, which followed the nominative. Cp. MHG. *zunge — zungen — zungen — zungen:* NHG. *die gute Frau — der guten Frau — der guten Frau — die gute Frau.*

Note 3. The designations 'strong' and 'weak' were chosen in analogy with the nominal declensions.

68. Comparison. (1) The COMPARATIVE DEGREE had in IE. the suffix *-is-* (OHG. *-ir-*), from which NHG. *-er*, with vowel mutation, has develop: *lang — länger, hoch — höher, kurz — kürzer.* — Under certain conditions, *-ōr-* was used in OHG. instead of *-ir-*; such comparatives did not mutate their vowels, and thus a comparative type with unmutated stem vowel develop, which, in NHG., spread somewhat beyond its original sphere, e.g., *falsch — falscher, zahm — zahmer, stolz — stolzer.*

(2) The SUPERLATIVE DEGREE added *-to-* to the comparative, so that OHG. *-isto-, -ōsto-* resulted: *längst-, höchst-, kürzest-; falschest-, zahmest-, stolzest-.*

69. Adjective Formation. *A.* SUFFIXES.
Material is denoted by the suffix
-en, Gc. *-īn*, which requires mutation, e.g., *Horn — hürnen,*

Gold — gülden (38*B*). This suffix was usually added to noun forms in *-er* (originally neuter plurals in *-er*), but the combination *-ern* soon spread also to other forms, so that adjectives like *gläsern, hölzern, steinern, stählern* resulted.

General character, appearance, etc., is denoted by the suffixes
–**isch**, e.g., OHG. *diutisk* 'deutsch,' literally 'völkisch,' *englisch, höfisch, städtisch, tierisch;*

–**ig** and –**icht**: *steinig (steinicht), neblig (neblicht), prächtig, gütig, gnädig;*

–**lich** (from Gc. **līka–* 'shape,' contained in Eng. *like,* Ger. *g(e)leich*): *glücklich, heimlich, kränklich, schriftlich.*

The idea of possession or ability is contained in the suffixes
–**bar** (related to OHG. *beran* 'bear,' = 'bearing,' like Lat. *-fer* in *Lucifer* 'Light-bearer'): *schiffbar, ehrbar, strafbar, offenbar;*

–**sam**, akin to Eng. 'same' and '–some' (*toothsome*): *gehorsam, furchtsam, wirksam.*

Privation is denoted by
–**los**, identical with the adjective *los* 'free': *herzlos, leblos, furcht-los.*

B. Compound Adjectives may contain nouns, adjectives, verbs, or adverbs as first elements: *geistreich, dunkelbraun, tragfähig, wohl-edel.*

Note on Adverbs and Prepositions

Adverbs were formed from adjectives by means of an IE. termination *-õ*, e.g., OHG. *gilīhhō* 'gleich.' Probably, this was an old instrumental, denoting manner of action. Weakened to *-e*, this ending still prevails in MHG. (*swaere* 'schwer,' *harte* 'hart'), but in NHG. it has practically disappeared, and the endingless adjective is used adverbially.

Old case forms of pronouns are preserved in such prepositional adverbs as *da(r), wo (war–), hier, dort, dann*, etc. Many adverbs are derived from nouns and verbs, e.g., *flugs, eilends*, etc. — For details, consult etymological dictionaries and Wilmanns II, 637 ff.

Prepositions cannot always be distinguisht from adverbs; in many NHG. prepositions the adverbial origin is still clearly to be recognized, e.g., *längs, kraft, vermöge, während, wegen*, etc. Others, like *an, in, auf, aus, bei, mit*, etc., can be traced back to IE. times in their present function, without establishing any connection with other parts of speech.

The Numerals

70. The Numerals are noun stems most of which have been indeclinable since early IE. times. Efforts to etymologize them have frequently been made, but with little reliable result.

Eins (**oinos*=Lat. *unus*) is an *o*-stem, declined at present like a strong adjective, preserving the old endingless forms of the nom. masc. and the nom. and acc. neuter (**67**, Note 1). It has entered into the function of the indefinite article.

Zwei is an old dual; it had three genders in OHG. and MHG. (*zwēne — zwā — zwei*), which are still in use in some NHG. dialects. — *Zwei* and *drei* had a declension similar to that of adjectives in OHG. and MHG. times; the forms *zweier, dreier, zweien, dreien* still occur.

The numbers **elf** and **zwölf** (Goth. *ain-lif, twa-lif*) apparently meant ('ten and) one left', ('ten and) two left', and seem to point to a period of competition between a decimal and a duodecimal system of counting in prehistoric Germanic times.

The suffix **–zig** of the tens is a parallel form of *zehn*, changed according to Verner's Law (*zehn*<IE. **dékm̥*, cp. Lat. *decem*, *–zig*<IE. **dekém*, or some similar form). In OHG., *–zig* (*–zug*) is also used with 100, for which the usual word is *zehanzug*. — The word **hundert** is a compound of Gc. *hund*<IE. **km̥tóm*, and a Gc. noun **raðʒ–* 'measure, number,' related to Lat. *ratio*.

Tausend is a compound of IE. **tūs–* 'strong'>Gc. *þūs–*, and Gc. *hund;* Gc. **þūshund*, OHG. *dusund*='das starke Hundert, Überhundert.'

NHG. *t* for Gc. *þ* is irregular, cf. **32**; it is probably due to the frequent use of the word after voiceless sounds, as in *sechs tausend*.

The ORDINAL NUMBERS are superlative forms; in the ordinals from 4th to 19th, however, the suffix *–to–* was not added to the comparative suffix *–is–* (**68**), but directly to the stem: *vier–te — zwan–zig–s–te*. — *Erst–* has nothing to do with *eins*, but is the superlative degree of the adjective OHG. *ēr*=NHG. *eher* (now felt as a comparative, on account of its apparent ending), OHG. *ēristo* originally meaning 'the earliest.'

SPECIMEN TEXTS

These texts have been selected from the following sources:

Wulfila's Gothic translation of the Gospels (see page 75); the OHG. version of Tatian's Gospel Harmony (p. 87); the Hildebrandslied (p. 86); Walther von der Vogelweide (p. 88); Luther (p. 90); Ernst's Proben deutscher Mundarten (Leipzig 1914).

Notes on Spelling

Gothic. The Gothic alphabet, invented by Wulfila, was an adaptation from the Greek alphabet, with the approximate phonetic values of the Greek pronunciation of the fourth century. The following peculiarities are of importance for the pronunciation of Gothic texts:

VOWELS. Quantity is not distinguisht in spelling, but etymological reasons make it certain that *e* and *o* were always long, *i* always, *u* and *a* usually short. *ei* stands for [iː], *ai* and *au* either for the corresponding diphthongs, or (chiefly when followed by *h* or *r*) for [ɛ] and [ɔ] respectively.

CONSONANTS. *b* and *d*, probably also *g*, denote stops initially and after consonants, but spirants elsewhere; in final position, [b] an [ð] are replaced by the voiceless spirants *f* and *þ*, e.g., *giban — gaf*, *bidjan — baþ*. *ƕ* stands for [χw], *q* for [kw]; *g* followed by *g* or *k* denotes the velar nasal, e.g., *briggan* = [briŋgan].

Old High German spelling varied greatly according to dialects as well as with individual scribes, who endeavored to express their pronunciation phonetically with the insufficient means of the Latin alphabet. — Quantity is generally not indicated. The mutation of *a* is renderd by *e* (38*A*) while the mutation of *u* and *o* and all long vowels does not find expression. — Germanic *þ* was in transition to [ð, d] during OHG. times, and is, accordingly, rendered either by *th*, *dh*, or *d*. [χ] is expressed by *h*, *hh*, *ch*. *z* (*zz*) stands both for [ts] and for later *ss* (*s*), the voiceless spirant resulting from *t*[1] (32[1]).

Middle High German spelling shows a considerable tendency towards standardization; modern text editions of MHG. manu-

scripts have carried this standardization still farther, but even in
MHG. times the spelling was fairly phonetic, much more so than in
NHG. times; e.g., the voiceless final stops are expressed by *p, t, c*
(*gap, hant, tac*). The use of *z* is the same as in OHG. *iu* stands for
[y:]. Umlaut begins to be expressed more and more consistently,
by writing *e* after or above vowels; the latter usage has become the
origin of the NHG. Umlaut-sign above *a, o, u.*

New High German spelling was in a bad confusion at the beginning of the sixteenth century. Lack of a cultural center, arbitrariness
of printers and the red tape of the chancelleries were in a great
measure responsible for this. The two specimen texts from Luther
show the great progress made during his time towards the standardization of spelling. Since the sixteenth century, German spelling
has undergone but unessential changes, e.g., in the use of capitals,
which was regulated in the present way during the seventeenth century. — Interesting specimens of German script and print forms and
of German spelling are given in Hempl's *German Orthography and
Phonology*, pages 1–28.

I. The Lord's Prayer

Gothic

swa nu bidjaiþ jus:
atta unsar þu in hi-
minam, weihnai na-
mo þein. qimai þiu-
dinassus þeins. wair-
þai wilja þeins, swe
in himina jah ana air-
þai. hlaif unsarana
þana sinteinan gif
uns himma daga. Jah
aflet uns patei sku-
lans sijaima, swaswe
jah weis afletam þaim
skulam unsaraim.
jah ni briggais uns
in fraistubnjai, ak
lausei uns af þamma
ubilin.

Old High German

thanne ir betot,
thanne quedet sus:
fater unser thu thar
bist in himile, si ge-
heilagot thin namo,
queme thin rihhi, si
thin willo so her in
himile ist, so si her in
erdu, unsar brot ta-
galihhaz gib uns hiu-
tu, inti furlaz uns
unsara sculdi so uuir
furlazemes unseren
sculdigon, inti ni gi-
leitest unsih in cos-
tunga, uzouh arlosi
unsih fon ubile.

Early New High
German (1521)

Darum sult ir also
beten: Vater, der du
bist yn dem hymel,
geheiliget werdt dein
nahm. Tzu kum dein
reich. Dein will ge-
schehe als ym hymel
und yn der erden.
Unszer teglich broet
gib uns heute. Unnd
verlas uns unser schul-
de, als wir verlasen
unsernn schuldigern.
Und fure uns nit yn
versuchung. Sundern
erlosze uns von dem
ubel.

NOTES

G. **bidjaiþ**: 2 pl. imp. of *bidjan*, st. v. V, *jo*-pres.: *bidjan — baþ — bēdum — bidans*. 53, 45, 46, 56[2].=NHG. *bitten*, 30. OHG. betōn, NHG. beten, w. v. III, der. from OHG. *beta* 'Bitte'; 49, 56[5].— [IE. **bheidh-*, **bhedh-*: Gk. *peitho* 'persuade,' Lat. *fīdo* 'trust'; 22[2].]

G. **jus**, OHG. **ir** < **eu-s*, 63.

G. **atta**, synonym of *fadar;* diminutive is *Attila*, Ger. *Etzel*, 38*A*, 32[4]. OHG. fater, NHG. Vater: *r*-noun, 58*B*. — [**pətḗr*, Gk. *patér*, L. *pater*, 22[1], 23, 25, 26, 40.]

G. **unsar**, *unsarana, unsaraim*, OHG. unser, *unsar, unsaren:* 63, 67.

G. **þu**, OHG. thu, NHG. du: 63, 22[1], 34[1].

G. **himinam**, OHG. himile, NHG. hymel (Himmel): masc. *n*-stem, 38*A*; etymology uncertain.

G. **weihnai**: 3 sg. opt. of weak verb in *-nan* (like G. *fullnan* 'voll werden').

OHG. **giheilagōt**, NHG. geheiliget: past part. of w. v. III, der. from adj. *heilag* (cp. Goth. *hails*, Ger. *heil*, 56[6]).

G. **namo**, OHG. namo, NHG. nahm (Name): *n*-stem, neut. in Goth., masc. in Ger. —[L. *nomen*.]

G. **þein**, OHG. thīn, NHG. dein: 63.

G. **qimai**: 3 sg. opt. pres. of *qiman* =OHG. queman (opt. *queme*, 37) and *koman* (45, Note 3), st. v. IV: *qiman — a — ē — u; koman — a — ā — gikoman*. 53, 40, 46. — [IE. **gem-*, **gm̥-*: Gk. *baino*, L. *venio* < **gm̥-jō*.]

G. **þiudinassus:** der. from *þiuda* 'people'; *-nassus* =Ger. *-nis*, 62 C. — [**teutó-*, e.g., in the Celtic name *Teutones*, page 74.]

OHG. **rīhhi**, NHG. reich: *jo*-stem, neut., Gc. **rīkja-*; a Celtic loan word, rel. to Lat. *rēg-s* =*rēx* 'king'; identical with adjective *reich*, originally =Lat. *rēgius* 'royal.' 22[3], 32[3], 37.

G. **wairþai**, NHG. werdt (werde): 3 sg. opt. pres. (53) of st. v. III: G. *wairþan — warþ — waurþum — waurþans* (Verner's Law leveled out, 23), OHG. *werdan — ward — wurtum — giwortan*, 46. — [**wert-* 'turn, become,' Lat. *verto*, 22[1].]

G. **wilja**, OHG. willo, NHG. will(e): masc. *n*-stem, from root **wel-* (cp. *wählen* and *wollen*). 50, Note; 30.

G. **airþai**, OHG. erdu, NHG. erden: originally *ā*-stem, became an *n*-stem in MHG., 34[1], 59, 60.

G. **hlaif** (gen. *hlaibis*) =NHG. *Laib*, masc. *o*-stem, 34[1].

OHG. **brot**, NHG. broet (*oe* =long *o*) =Eng. *bread*, 37[7].

G. sin-teinan, acc. sing. masc. of adj. *sin-teins* 'perpetual, daily,' rel. to Lat. *senex* 'old,' *semper* 'always,' NHG. *Singrün* = *Immergrün*, *Sündflut*, for *Sinflut* 'great, general flood.'

OHG. taga-līhh, NHG. teglich, 69, 38*B*.

Goth. gif, Ger. gib, imper. of G. *giban* — *gaf* — *gēbum* — *gibans*, OHG. *geban* — *a* — *ā* — *gigeban*, st. v. V, 46.

G. himma daga, OHG. hiutu, NHG. heute: Goth. is the dat., Ger. the instrumental (<*hiu tagu*, cp. *hiu jāru*=NHG. *heuer*) of dem. *hi- <IE. *kjo- (preserved in *hier* and pronoun *her*=*er* in Tatian) and G. *dags*, OHG. *tag* 'day.'

G. -lēt(am), OHG. -lāz(emes), NHG. las(en): st. v. VII: G. *lētan* — *lailōt* — *lailōtum* — *lētans*, OHG. *lāzan* — *liez* — *liezum* — *gilāzum*, 46, Note. — [IE. *lēd-, *ləd-, Gk. *lēdein* 'be tired,' Lat. *lassus* < **ləd–tos* 'tired.']

G. skulans, -*am*, OHG. sculdi(gon), NHG. schulde, schuldigern: G. *n*-stem, OHG. *i*-stem (fem. pl.) and -*ig* adject., derivatives from Gc. *skal*, pret. pres., 58*B*, 50.

G. briggais, 2 sg. opt. pr. from *briggan* — *brāhta*, irreg. w. v., 49, Note.

G. weis, uns, Ger. wir, uns: 63.

OHG. gileitēst, 2 sg. subj. (opt.) pres., 63; w. v. I: *leitten, leiten*. — [Causative from Ger. *leiden*, literally 'go thru,' Gc. *laiðjan 'cause to go (thru'), 49, 56³.]

NHG. fure =*führe* (*u* for *ū* is only a matter of orthography), sg. imp. of *führen*, w. v. I. — [Caus. of *fahren*, Gc. *fōrjan.]

G. fraistubnjai, dat. sg. of -*tubni*, der. of *fraisan* 'tempt.'

OHG. costunga, der. from OHG. *kiosan* — *kōs* — *kurum* — *gi-koran* 'choose.' — [IE. *geus*-, Lat. *gustare*, Gk. *geu(s)omai* 'taste.']

NHG. Versuchung, der. from *suchen*, Goth. *sōkjan* = Lat. *sāgīre* 'hunt.'

G. lausei, OHG. -lōsi, NHG. -losze: sg. imp. of w. v. I, 37, 56³. — [Der. from adj. Goth. *laus*, Ger. *los* 'free,' rel. to *verlieren*, OHG. *virliosan*.]

G. ubilin, OHG. *ubile*, NHG. *ubel* = *Übel*: dat. sg. neut. of weak adj. in Goth., noun in Ger.

Þana, Þatei, Þaim, Þamma, NHG. der, dem: 63, 66.

II. The first lines of the 'Hildebrandslied'

Ik gihōrta ðat seggen || ðat sih urhēttun || ænon muotīn
Hiltibraht enti haðubrant || untar heriun twēm
sunufatarungo || iro saro rihtun
garutun se iro gūðhamun || gurtun sih iro suert ana
helidōs ubar (h)ringa || dō sie to dero hiltiu ritun.

Translation: Ich hörte das sagen, daß sich bedrängten als Einzel-
kämpfer Hildebrand und Hadubrand zwischen zwei Heeren — Sohn
und Vater. Sie richteten ihre Rüstungen, bereiteten ihre Kampf-
kleider, gürteten sich ihre Schwerter an, die Helden über die Ringe,
da sie zum Streite ritten.

The Hildebrandslied was probably written (dictated) by a Low
German who tried to render an older Low German version in East
Franconian; it contains a number of Old Low German (Old Saxon)
forms, e.g., *ik, ðat, ænon, twēm, tō, gūðhamun, seggen.*

III. Walther von der Vogelweide

Owê, war sint verswunden alliu mîniu jâr!
Ist mir mîn leben getroumet, oder ist ez wâr?
Daz ich ie wânde daz iht waere, was daz iht?
Dar nâh hân ich geslâfen und enweiz ez niht.
Nû bin ich erwachet, und ist mir unbekant,
daz mir hie vor was kündic als mîn ander hant.
Liut' unde lant, dâ ich von kinde bin erzogen,
die sint mir fremde worden, reht' als ez sî gelogen.
Mich grüezet maneger traege, der mich bekande ê wol.
diu werlt ist allenthalben ungenâden vol.
Die mîne gespilen wâren, die sint traege und alt;
bereitet ist das felt, verhouwen ist der walt;
wan daz daz wazzer fliuzet, als es wîlent floz.
Für wâr ih wânde mîn unglücke wurde grôz,
als ich gedenke an manegen wünneclîchen tac,
die mir sint enpfallen gar als in daz mer ein slac,
iemer mêre ouwê.

IV. From Luther's 𝕿𝖎𝖘𝖈𝖍𝖗𝖊𝖉𝖊𝖓, chapter 69

ich habe keine gewiſſe, ſonderliche, eigene ſprach im teutſchen, ſondern brauche der gemeinen teutſchen ſprach, daß mich beide Ober= und Niderländer verſtehen mögen. ich red nach der ſäch= ſiſchen cantzeley, welcher nachfolgen alle fürſten und könige im teutſch lande, alle reichſtätte, fürſtenhöfe ſchreiben nach der ſäch= ſiſchen und unſers fürſten cantzeley, darumb iſts auch die ge= meinſte teutſche ſprach. Kaiſer Maximilian und Churfürſt Friderich hertzog von Sachſen haben im römiſchen reiche die deutſchen ſprachen alſo in eine gewiſſe ſprach zuſammengezogen.

V. SPECIMENS FROM MODERN GERMAN DIALECTS

1. Dutch

Wilhelmus van Nassouwe
ben ik van duitschen bloet,
den vaterlant ghetrouwe
blijf ik tot in den doot;

een prince van Oraengien
ben ik vry onverveert,
den coninc van Hispaegnien
heb ik altijt gheeert.

2. Low Saxon

𝕻𝖑𝖆𝖙𝖙𝖉ü𝖙𝖘𝖈𝖍 𝕿𝖗ü

Faſt ſteiht de Saſſenſtamm,
faſter as Dik un Damm,
in Storm un Not.
Kem ſülfſt en Weltenbrand,
Kaiſer und Vaderland,
ſuch hürt unſ' Hart un Hand
bet in den Dod!

3. Middle Franconian

𝕯𝖆𝖘 𝕱𝖚𝖓𝖐𝖊𝖓𝖑𝖎𝖊𝖉 𝖛𝖔𝖓 𝕶ö𝖑𝖓
Der Mann:

Zau dich, Frau! Zau dich, Frau!
Gevv mer minge' Zabel her
onn ming Pihf onn Toback
onn min alt Gewehr!

Onn dann gohn mer üvver de Ring,
drinken do e got Glas Wing.
Komm' se dann, komme se dann,
marschiere wir heran.

Die Frau:
Ach leeve Mann, ach leeve Mann,
wann se schieße, dann loof dervan.

4. Rhenish Franconian

Ich kenn 'e Land am deitsche Rhei',
des glänzt vun Glück un Sunneschei,
do saa' ich: Gott erhalt's!
's hot Wei' genungk un Waaz un Korn
un eß en alle Arte vorn
un schreibt sich: Frehlich Palz.

5. East Middle German

(a) 's Leibz'ger I.

Daß mir'sch nich sprechen genn, das Ga,
trotz unsern Sprachscheniee,
bildt eich nur das nich ein etwa!
Denn sprechen gennen genn mersch ja, —
awwer 's macht uns zeviel Miehe.

(b) Mir in Sachsen

Redt ihr nur andersch anderwärts,
mir reden sächsch in Sachsen;
uns is der Schnawel gleichwie's Herz
ä bißchen weech gewachsen.

6. Bavarian

Wia d'Leut sei' soll'n

Kopf und Herz am rechten Fleck,
's Wort frisch von der Leba weg,
an hellen Blick, an guat'n Mag'n,
der aa was z'widas kann vatrag'n,
für d'Not und's Unglück offen Hand,
a Liab fürs freie Vaterland, —
und an Hamur frisch, g'sund und echt,
kurz „deutsch" bal d'Leut san, na' san's recht!

7. Swabian

Mueß i denn, mueß i denn zum Städtele 'naus,
un du, mei~ Schatz, bleibscht hier!
Wenn i komm, wenn i komm, wenn i wiederum komm,
kehr' i ei~, mei~ Schatz, bei dir.
Kann i glei net allweil bei dir sei~,
hani doch mei~ Freund an dir;
wenn i komm, wenn i komm, wenn i wiederum komm,
kehr' i ei~, mei~ Schatz, bei dir.

8. Alsatian (1852)

M'r g'höere hiet ze Frankreich wohl
un teile Not and Glüeck;
doch klingt uns d' Muedersprooch nit hohl,
si gilt noch großi Stüeck!

So lang noch unser Münster steht,
— und diß isch kerngesund —
au d' Muedersprooch nit untergeht,
denn viel gäng dnoh zu Grund!

9. Von den Alpen bis zur „Waterkant"
Innre Einkehr

1. Da gang' a in si und sprach: Wie vül' Toglina mainös
Vaada'n hab'm Brad im Überfluß, i aba vaderb vo Hunga.

(Salzburg)

2. Eiz is a=r=erst in si ganga=r=und hot g'sagt: Wei vil
Toglenâ hoben ba man Vodan Broud in Ibafluss, und i mouß
dou no dahungan.

(Amberg)

3. Hiz is öem a Löicht afganga und hat zu öem selba gsagt:
Wöi viel Tagwerka habn bei mein Vadan Bräud in Übafluß,
und i mäuß da no voa Hunga sterbn.

(Regensburg)

4. Jez is a=r=erſt in ſi ganga=r=und hot bei e͡am ſelm g'ſägt: Wie vill Täglehna häben bei mein'n Voda Brod g'nue, und i mueß do no' dahungan.

(München)

5. Dä goht ar t ſi und ſeit: Wie viel Taglüehner mi's Vaters heand z'iëſſet gnug, und ih hië gaär nünt.

(Vorarlberg)

6. Du chunts ihm über d's G'wüſſe, und er ſiet: Wie vil Tagwaner hat myn Alt, die hei z'eſſe mieh wan gnue, un i muß vor Hunger druf go.

(Berner Oberland)

7. Jez iſch er in ſich gange un hät g'ſait: Wi vil Talöner bi mi'm Vater hänn Brot im Überfluß, ich aber geh vor Hung'r zu grund.

(Straßburg)

8. Do ſchmöß heh ſich on ſoat: Bö vil Toalöhner hot min Voter, de Brot de Füll hohn, ohn ich verderb do Hongers.

(Fulda)

9. Hiz is ar zu ſi ſelbar kumma un hot gſogt: Bei mein Vottar kämm a loſt Daglühnar übarflüſſi brůt, un hiar ſtarb i Hungarſch.

(Würzburg)

10. Da gunk ä in ſ'ch un ſate: Wi veel Tagelüner hat nich mei Vat'r, de alle Bruds de Fülle han, un ich v'rdärbe hi ver Hung'r.

(Oberſachſen)

11. Da ſchlauk hei in ſik un ſprok: Wo vel Dagelöhner had min Vader, dei Brot dei Fülle hebbet, un ik vorkome vor Hunger.

(Braunſchweig)

12. Dou ſchloug hei in ſ'ick un ſiegte: Bu' ville Dageleiners ſett mi'n Vatter, dei genoch hatt, un ik verdïerbe in Hunger.

(Niederheſſen)

13. Da ſchlog he en ſeck un ſprack: Wie veel Daglöhners hed min Varr, de Fülle hevet, un ek verderbe in Hunger.

(Weſtfalen)

14. Da gink hei in seck sülben un seggte: Wo veele Tagelöhners mines Vaders hebbet Brat in Öberfluß, un ek verde'rbe vor Hunger.   (Hannover)

15. Do dacht' he torüch un sprök to sick sülfst: Wovêl Dachlöhners hett mien Vader, de Brod genog heppt, un ick verdarf hier vär Hunger.   (Hamburg)

16. Dar gink hei in sik un sprök: Wur veel Daglöners hett min Våder, de Brot de Meng hebbn, un ik verdarw in Hunger.
                    (Mecklenburg)

PLATE III

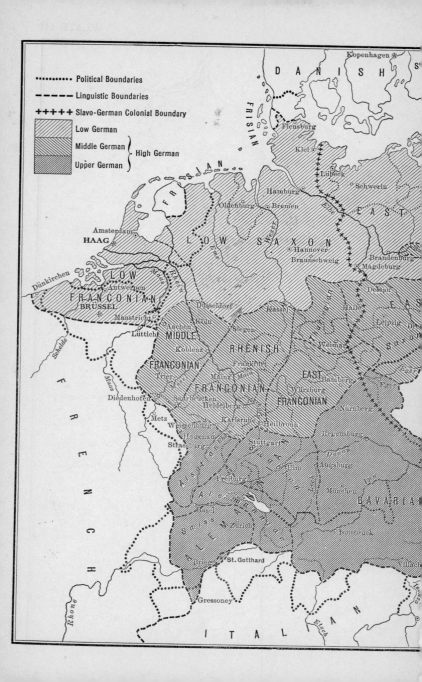

INDEX

The numbers refer to pages

ABBREVIATIONS

Eng. = English
Gc. = Germanic
Ger. = German
Gk. = Greek
Goth. = Gothic
HG. = High German
IE. = Indo-European
Lat. = Latin

LG. = Low German
MHG. = Middle High German
NHG. = New High German
OHG. = Old High German
OS. = Old Saxon
Sc. = Sanscrit
UG. = Upper German
WGc. = West Germanic